ALSO BY WARREN CHRISTOPHER

In the Stream of History:
Shaping Foreign Policy for a New Era

CHANCES OF A LIFETIME

◆

Warren Christopher

A LISA DREW BOOK

SCRIBNER

New York London Toronto Sydney Singapore

SCRIBNER
1230 Avenue of the Americas
New York, NY 10020

SCRIBNER and design are trademarks of Macmillan Library Reference USA, Inc., used under license by Simon & Schuster, the publisher of this work.

Manufactured in the United States of America

1 3 5 7 9 10 8 6 4 2

Library of Congress Cataloging-in-Publication Data

Christopher, Warren.
Chances of a lifetime / Warren Christopher.
p. cm.
"A Lisa Drew book."
Includes bibliographical references and index.
1. Christopher, Warren. 2. Statesmen—United States—Biography. 3. Cabinet officers—United States—Biography. 4. United States. Dept. of State—Biography. 5. United States—Foreign relations—1945–1989. 6. United States—Foreign relations—1989– . I. Title.
E840.8.C486 2001
327.73'0092—dc21   00-061186
ISBN 0-7432-1369-6

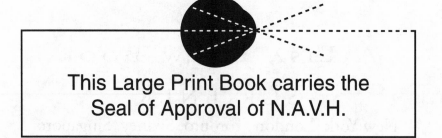

This Large Print Book carries the
Seal of Approval of N.A.V.H.

To my daughters, Lynn Collins
and Kristen Henderson,
and my sons, Scott and Thomas

Contents

CHANCES OF A LIFETIME

1

STARTING FROM SCRANTON

I HAD COMPLETELY FORGOTTEN FROM HOW FAR away you can see a storm coming in the Dakotas. After a rough landing in Rapid City, South Dakota, my wife, Marie, and I saw a line of dark clouds approaching from about twenty miles to the east. We made it to our rental car with about a minute to spare.

It was June 1998, and we were on a journey back to Scranton, North Dakota, the town of three hundred where I was born. I had been away for nearly sixty years.

The occasion was the ninetieth anniversary of Scranton's founding and Governor Ed Schafer's presentation to me of the Theodore Roosevelt Rough Rider Award. With it, the state honors North Dakotans who have done something prominent but

not notorious, people such as Lawrence Welk and Roger Maris. As a former secretary of state, I just made the "not notorious" cut.

I'd hesitated when I received the governor's invitation to attend the presentation. I'm embarrassed by awards and award ceremonies, and for more than a decade I've avoided them. But the Rough Rider was different. A return to my home would give me an opportunity to address a question I had long sidestepped: "How did you come to be who you are?"

Though I had not yet conceived the idea of this book, it seemed to me time to begin developing a better response to that question than the one I had used as my fallback for the preceding five decades: "I've been very lucky." While that answer was accurate, I had felt for some time it was not complete, and Scranton seemed the right place to begin filling in the blanks. Today, two years after my Rough Rider return to Scranton, it also seems like the right place to begin this book.

On October 27, 1925, the day I was born, Scranton was a classic small prairie town, located on the main line of the Milwaukee Railroad, which ran from Chicago to the Pacific. Situated in the southwestern corner of the state, it had been settled around 1900 by immigrants from Scandinavia and Germany. Though Norwegian, Swedish, and German may have been spoken within the confines of individual homes, the settlers and their descendants took great pride in learning English and speaking it in public places.

In 1913, at age twenty-five, my father moved to Scranton from Iowa with my mother to manage the local bank. Though his habits and public demeanor were those of a taciturn Norwegian Lutheran, he was respected and well liked. He was not, however, "one of the guys." While the guys held their weekly poker game above the firehouse, Dad was presiding over the school board. As the guys gathered at the Green Lantern Cafe to hoist a few, Dad was practicing the violin in our kitchen. A man of the community, he did not quite mirror the traits of the community. By his example, he made me feel it was all right to be just a little bit different from everyone else.

My father lived and played by a set of rules that combined common sense, ethics, and heart. I recall that a tipsy Scrantonian once came to our house asking to borrow $200 of the bank's money to buy a horse. Dad sent him away, telling me after he shut the door that he would never lend money to a man who had been drinking. He was less worried, I think, about whether the bank would get its money back than whether the borrower would use the money to buy something he didn't really need, such as more alcohol.

From my father I learned that you do not have to make a public display of compassion to be a compassionate person. During summer vacations and sometimes on Saturdays when I was ten and eleven, I rode along with Dad as he visited struggling farmers. This was in the depths of the Depression, and wheat crops, the backbone of the local economy, had suffered from drought, hail, rust, grasshoppers—and worst of all, low prices. Farmers were having difficulty making ends meet and, in many cases, simply surviving.

Behind the scenes, Dad fiercely resisted foreclosing on any of the bank's farm mortgages, but he could only do so much. As we drove along, he was usually silent, deep in thought as he pondered how to deliver the bad news he was carrying. Sometimes he described to me how the Depression had destroyed the plans of the families we were about to visit. The pain he felt was obvious. The human scenes I witnessed in the flat, dry North Dakota plains while at my father's side may account more than anything else for the tilt of my social and political concerns in the direction of the unfortunate.

The Depression years in Scranton taught me something else—the look and sound of dignity and stoicism in the face of adversity. The people of this town and its surrounding farms did not whimper or complain no matter how unfair life seemed to be. Their attitude was captured by one farmer who said, while surveying a crop that had been devastated by a hailstorm, "Well, at least it saves the cost of the harvest."

Dad's prolonged and intense battle with the Depression—for himself and for the people of his town—destroyed his health. On January 2, 1937, as he was walking home for lunch, he had a severe cerebral hemorrhage. The next day, the fast Milwaukee Road train made a special stop in Scranton, and he was taken to a hospital in Miles City, Montana, severely paralyzed on his right side and unable to read or speak. Although he lived for five more years, he suffered a series of even more debilitating strokes and was never again himself.

My father's early incapacitation and death put extraordinary burdens on my mother. Her grace and competence under this terrible pressure taught me another of the lessons that shaped my view of the world: when handed the baton, a woman can run as far, as fast, and as successfully as any man.

My mother was the daughter of a Methodist minister. Her own mother had died when she was fifteen, leaving Mom to help care for her five younger siblings in Iowa. She married Dad in 1910, when she was twenty, a few years before they moved to Scranton. Mother was more open and outgoing than Dad, and she was a popular figure in the town. Though she had five children of her own (I was the fourth), she somehow found the time to help young mothers who had trouble caring for their newborns.

During my 1998 return to my birthplace, I made a point of visiting the back porch of what had been our house, on the westernmost edge of town. Here, out of the vision of the rest of Scranton, my mother had displayed her most real self. The main line of the Milwaukee Road train passed less than half a mile from our back door. In the hard times of the early 1930s, hoboes on the move crowded onto open freight cars, sometimes hopping off close to our home. At least once a week, a world-weary man would knock on our back door with a plea for something to eat. My mother would ask him to wait on the back steps, then put aside whatever she was doing to make him a sandwich from the leftovers of our previous evening's meal. She would usually heat up some brown gravy to cover the meat, add mashed rutabaga or turnips on the side, and hand the plate out the door with a cup of black coffee. Typically, no more than a few minutes later the empty dish would be handed back to her, often with an offer to work in exchange for the modest supper. My mother inevitably declined these offers, consistent with her belief that our relatively good fortune was something to be shared, not bartered.

Apart from teaching me that I had parents worthy of emulation, my years in Scranton taught me something about dealing with people. I came to appreciate that while most people would rather talk than listen, listening was far more educational, even empowering. Only by listening carefully did one learn that one of the town merchants was a bootlegger; another had a mistress; one druggist dispensed condoms under the counter; a high school basketball star got drunk on weekends; and a pretty high school senior who went away to live with a relative was pregnant when she left. I also began to suspect something that in later life ripened into a conviction: the more listening you do, the more people will trust you. Silence, once associated with discretion, begets confidence as well as confidences. I learned that people also tend to read wisdom from silence—even when silence means only that you know nothing about what they are talking about.

In June 1939, my mother decided to take my father to California in the hope that the friendlier climate would help him mend. As we prepared to sell our home, I realized I would miss my school the most. Losing the fabric of relationships and rhythms familiar to me was going to be hard, and the prospect of developing a comparable set of friends and routines in California seemed impossibly remote. I saw my life being cut up into a jigsaw puzzle, and I despaired of being able to fit the pieces back together. In retrospect, this early encounter with personal upheaval, and the resulting realization that I could quickly adapt to unexpected changes, was one of the most liberating revelations of my childhood.

HOLLYWOOD, CALIFORNIA

In 1939, as one traveled farther from either coast toward America's center, the word *Hollywood* took on increasingly romantic, almost mythical, connotations. For those of us in Scranton, North Dakota, Hollywood was a place of glamour, sophistication, and wealth—the source of the thrilling entertainment that made Saturday movie night the high point of our week. When Mother told me that we were moving to Hollywood to be near my grandmother, I knew that my new home was going to be a great deal more of everything than Scranton.

Hollywood High School was a sprawling campus that accommodated twenty-three hundred sophomores, juniors, and seniors, about twelve times more students than were in all of Scranton's twelve grades. I entered Hollywood High's tenth grade at age thirteen, and there with me, just as I'd fantasized, were the children of movie stars. Girls looked like pictures out of a magazine, each positioning herself, by dress and posture, for discovery at the ice cream shop across the street, as Lana Turner had done. Boys wore letterman's sweaters and talked about beach parties, car races, and "making out." This was not exactly my kind of crowd, but I was determined to find my place. It didn't take me long to discover that the thread that tied me to these seemingly sophisticated teenagers was negotiating the common obstacle course of adolescence.

In contrast to the glamour of my school surroundings, these were hard times for the Christopher family. Dad's frustration grew as he realized he couldn't overcome the effects of the strokes on his walking, talking, and reading. Mother had to take a job as a salesclerk at Sears to help make ends meet, and I tried to do my part by delivering the *Hollywood Citizen News* and managing the complaint desk after delivery hours. After a year of bicycling up and down the Hollywood Hills, tossing papers to the right and left, I persuaded the editor to take me on as a copyboy in the newsroom during summer vacation. Before long, I was covering sports and local events—for ten cents an inch.

I found out right away that I liked gathering and reporting the news. The constant action and clatter of the city room were part of it. For a teenager whose motor never stopped running, the pace was exactly right. Beyond that, I liked a job that was defined by a regular cycle. The newspaper's day started with a jumbled mass of unorganized information, leads, and demands. Everyone knew that by deadline everything had to come together. This realm appealed both to my sense of orderliness and to my desire to be in the middle of what was going on in the world.

My afternoon jobs for the *Citizen News* kept me from trying out for the high-powered Hollywood High sports teams, but I was able to squeeze in interscholastic debating tournaments, which were held on the weekends. With war raging in Europe, the most debated topic was whether a military draft was needed. My debate partner and I became one of the top-ranked teams in the city, which ultimately led to my being offered a debate scholarship from the University of Redlands, a small liberal arts college sixty miles east of Los Angeles.

In March of my senior year, 1942, my father suffered his final stroke and died. Knowing I was graduating, the *Citizen News* offered me a full-time job at $25 a week, and I was tempted to stay. Though I really wanted to go on to college, I knew that my family and I couldn't possibly make up the difference between what I'd need and what Redlands had offered. I wrote to Redlands to explain my dilemma, and within a week, the university wrote back, announcing they had doubled my scholarship offer. I was on my way to college.

WORLD WAR II

I entered Redlands in September of 1942, nine months after Pearl Harbor. Knowing I was likely to be drafted into the army when I reached eighteen, I enlisted in the navy shortly after October 27, 1942, my seventeenth birthday. This path to military service held out the possibility that I could continue in school and become an officer. The navy made no promises, but told me to finish my freshman year at Redlands and await further orders. Those orders soon came, and I was told to stay right where I was: the navy would come to me in the form of a new officers training unit at Redlands.

The next six months were spent alternately studying and marching. In early 1944, the navy ordered me to leave Redlands and report to the University of Southern California's NROTC unit. At USC, I completed an accelerated undergraduate program, receiving both a degree in finance and my commission as a navy ensign in February 1945.

Following graduation from USC, I found myself assigned to the USS *Tomahawk,* a tanker-type ship converted to carry high-test gasoline for refueling aircraft carriers at sea. I joined the *Tomahawk* in Portland, Oregon, in April, and after taking on a full load of aviation fuel, we steamed for the South Pacific to refuel aircraft carriers in the combat zone.

At sea on August 8, 1945, word came that the United States had dropped bombs of unprecedented destructive power on Hiroshima. That night, this nineteen-year-old ensign tried to make sense of things in a note home to his mother: "One finds his mind in a turmoil, pondering how awful and how wonderful it is all at once. If it is as powerful as we understand, world peace ceases to be an aim and becomes a necessity for survival."

When the Japanese surrendered on August 14, 1945, the navy ordered my ship into Tokyo Bay as part of a carrier force. While we bobbed up and down in a typhoon that overtook the bay, General Douglas MacArthur, on the nearby USS *Missouri,* signed the peace treaty that officially ended the war. We saw nothing of the ceremony, and though MacArthur demanded neither fuel nor help from us during our stay, I suppose that our presence—along with the scores of other ships bouncing up and down in Tokyo Bay that day—was a useful part of the armada.

Before we sailed home from Japan, our captain got permission to take a group of us ashore. What I saw on that trip has stayed with me to this day. The American firebombing had demolished whole blocks of the city of Tokyo. Buildings in ruins outnumbered those left standing. Huge piles of rubble still smoldered, sending up acrid, white clouds. Large groups of frightened Japanese huddled together in the streets, drifting aimlessly, hungry and homeless.

When someone mentions war, these are the images that are called up for me. Not flags waving or bands playing, but rubble, hardship, and suffering. As I looked at the devastation, I was taken back to an argument I'd had with a roommate in the NROTC barracks at USC in 1944. He said he was worried the war might be over before he could join the fighting. I told him that was a selfish and unfeeling way to look at things. The argument hung in the air between us for days before dissipating, each of us still wed to his view. As I toured the ruins of Tokyo, I thought he might have changed his mind if he had been beside me.

With the war over, the *Tomahawk* returned to the United States, and by the end of 1945 I found myself on the USS *Fayette,* an attack transport, en route to

Mobile, Alabama, for its decommissioning. Mobile was the first Southern city in which I'd ever spent time. At first glance, I thought it was one of the most beautiful and charming places I'd ever seen. Shortly, however, my opinion changed. I found that Mobile in 1945 embraced and practiced racial discrimination with an appalling fervor.

I had never before witnessed categorical, unvarnished bias. The few black Americans I had known in high school and college were accepted with apparent (though possibly not genuine) equanimity. Mobile was different. Blacks were officially and absolutely banned nearly everywhere I went—from restaurants, hotels, movies, even clubs for servicemen. There were no apologies, explanations, or apparent embarrassment. If you were a local, this was the way it was supposed to be.

In July 1946, a Mobile family invited me to their bay-front home for a day of swimming and tennis. After our pleasant dinner, a white hired hand came to the door to report that some "niggers" were hanging around the perimeter of the estate. The man of the house rose, walked to his gun cabinet, took out a rifle, and strolled out the door with the hired hand, saying as he went that he'd "make damn sure they don't come back again."

My experiences in Mobile had an indelible impact on me. Before my visit, I had understood, on an intellectual, almost abstract level, that some white Americans disliked and refused to associate with black

Americans. After Mobile, I knew what discrimination looked like and how it felt to be in its presence. I also felt the powerlessness and anger of someone repelled by the majority's behavior but who, for the present, could do nothing but witness it in silence. I knew this experience, like the look and feel of war that I took away from my visit to Tokyo, would shape my views and actions for a long time.

En Route to a Career

The decision to go to law school sneaked up on me. I had begun to toy with the idea of a legal career while in college, thinking that my success in debating and my interest in writing pointed logically in that direction. I also liked the notion of being a professional, with the aura of security and responsibility that that status implied. Ultimately, however, it took a spur-of-the-moment visit to the Stanford University campus to crystallize these musings.

In the spring of 1945 I was on navy leave in San Francisco and decided I'd take a day trip down to Stanford, a place I'd heard people talk about but had never seen. Although my conscious purpose in taking the trip was a little vague, I knew as I took the short train ride to Palo Alto that I wanted to see Stanford's law school.

Once I'd found the law school, I walked into the dean's office, saw a white-haired lady at a desk, and asked whether I might talk to the dean about a career in law. She said she was the dean's secretary, that he wasn't in, and she asked whether she could help me. I told her I was thinking about applying to law school but didn't know whether I had the right credentials. She asked where I'd gone to school and how I'd done there. I told her. With a nonchalance and authority that would today put a dean of admissions into fits, she replied that she was sure Stanford would take me. This brief, reassuring moment was ultimately decisive. Soon after the navy released me from service in September 1946, I appeared for my first day of legal training at Stanford.

While my legal education at Stanford was typical and traditional, two elements had a special impact on my future. The year I started law school, Carl Spaeth, a Rhodes Scholar and Yale law graduate, resigned from his State Department position to become dean. He quickly decided that Stanford must have a law review to compete with the elite Eastern schools, and when the faculty chose me as the first president (editor in chief) of the review, I arranged to have regular lunches with Spaeth about the new enterprise. As we became acquainted, he sparked my interest in his former colleague Dean Acheson, who became secretary of state when President Truman won election in 1948. Spaeth described how Acheson combined private law practice with stints of public service, and he urged me to follow a similar course.

I got some early training in crisis management

when a leading article intended for the first issue of the law review turned out to be a "self-plagiarism" by a renowned professor from another law school. I thought about keeping it quiet—a private matter between us and the author—then realized that I had to fill the gap that withdrawing the article would create. I put out a call for help to the Stanford faculty and got it, courtesy of a crash writing effort by the law school's former dean Marion Kirkwood. The experience taught me an important lesson: when a crisis hits, don't keep it to yourself. Out of embarrassment or false heroics, people often try to handle things entirely on their own at such moments, forgetting that people usually welcome the chance to help save the day, and that the reason we build teams is to create a depth of talent that enhances and transcends individual ability.

Prior to 1949, Stanford Law School had never placed one of its students in a U.S. Supreme Court clerkship. With the advent of the law review, the faculty decided it was time to try, and that I would be a good guinea pig. With their help, I was selected to serve as law clerk to Justice William O. Douglas for the 1949–50 term of the Court.

I did not meet Justice Douglas until months after I'd arrived for work at the Court in September 1949. Just before the start of the term, he was seriously injured when a horse he was riding in the hills of Washington State stumbled and fell on him. The accident nearly killed him, and he spent the next six months in great pain and discomfort as his twenty-three broken ribs slowly healed. During his convalescence in the West, I prepared a memorandum on every petition for review filed in the Court and helped him, long distance, to draft sections of a book he was starting, *An Almanac of Liberty.* As draft after draft of my material returned from the West Coast in green-lined tatters, my anxiety grew over just what life would be like when he returned to work.

When Douglas finally appeared at the Court in March 1950, he set a furious pace, producing a significant opinion or dissent at least weekly for the remainder of the term. Oral arguments in two cases of great importance had been postponed until he was well enough to retake the bench. The decisions in those cases, which Douglas did not write but in which he voted with the majority, held that a graduate school could not constitutionally operate on a separate-but-equal basis. In the cloistered offices of various justices, I joined other clerks in intense debates over the exact language of the decisions, knowing that the words used would be of enormous importance in subsequent battles over whether other kinds of separate-but-equal educational facilities could survive constitutional scrutiny. When the opinions were released on June 5, 1950, I felt sure they would put America on the road toward eliminating this critical emblem of discrimination. Four years later, in *Brown v. Board of Education,* the Supreme Court, relying on the language of these opinions, struck down separate-but-equal education in primary and secondary schools.

Justice William O. Douglas, June 1950.

I've never worked closely with a person more brilliant than Douglas. After ten years on the Court, he
had established a reputation not only as a wizard on
corporate finance (he was head of the SEC when
appointed), but as a vigorous and eloquent defender
of First Amendment rights. From a law clerk's perspective—in fact, from any perspective—he was a
complex figure. He thought and wrote with awesome
speed—too fast, some said. Gregarious and affable
with peers, he was an entirely different person—distant and yet demanding—with his staff. At the end of
my year's clerkship, it took me several days to screw
up my courage to go into his office and ask his advice
about my future. He looked right through me, then
responded, "Get out into the stream of history and
swim as fast as you can."

I waited for more words but got only a penetrating stare and continued silence. When I realized that Douglas had nothing more to say to me, I backed out of the room, thanking him as I went. After reaching my desk, I plopped myself down to think about what to make of his Delphic remark.

After mulling it over for a while, I decided that with that single sentence Douglas had given me two messages. First, he'd told me that I had a chance to become a person of consequence, a judgment he had never even hinted at before. Given what I knew and thought of Douglas, it was the most empowering vote of confidence I could imagine. Second, Douglas had advised me to aim high—to risk my strength against a current that had the capacity to sweep me away. I realized then that if I ignored his advice, for the rest of my life I would feel that I had failed myself. What follows in this book describes what I hope Justice Douglas would regard as a respectable effort to heed his words.

———— ✦ ————

2

THREE TO GET READY

WHILE I WAS BOLSTERED BY JUSTICE DOU-glas's implication that I could survive in the stream, it was one thing to talk about it and another to plunge in. That baptism, as it were, consumed much of the next decade of my life. In that time, a combination of timing, friends, and luck gave me opportunities to test myself in each of the spheres that were to become key to my professional life: law, politics, and diplomacy.

AN UNEXPECTED APPOINTMENT

The law firm associate, like the untenured university teacher, operates in simultaneous states of increasing responsibility and unenlightened servitude. Although his (or her) skills, reputation, and rewards may grow, he is a salaried employee, nothing more, until someone says otherwise.

At O'Melveny & Myers, the Los Angeles firm that employed me in 1950 after my clerkship with Justice Douglas, the line between tenure and mere employment was clear. Partners lunched together. Associates were not invited. Partners knew the amount and distribution of the firm's income. Associates did not. And partners, not associates, were the lawyers who took the important calls for the firm.

On June 18, 1957, in my seventh year as an O'Melveny & Myers associate, something unusual happened. I was sitting in my small office sipping my morning coffee when my phone rang. I picked it up and a voice on the other end said, "Hello, Mr. Christopher, this is Chief Justice Warren."

My first instinct was to laugh. It was the kind of intraoffice gag that associates routinely played on one another. But I paused because the voice seemed familiar. In fact, I'd heard that distinctive voice utter public pronouncements when it belonged to someone I still identified in my mind as the governor of California. It was, without question, the voice of Earl Warren, now the chief justice of the U.S. Supreme Court.

My mind shifted instantly from the question of who was talking to why he was talking to me. "We've been thinking about you," said the voice of the chief justice. I was sophisticated enough to know that when the chief justice said "we," he could be referring to any number of persons from one to nine. Consequently, I didn't know whether this call was about a personal matter or some grander business.

The chief quickly clarified things. He said the Court wanted me to file a brief and to argue as a "friend of the Court" (in legalese, amicus curiae) in a case involving a poor black woman named Virginia Lambert. In 1955, Lambert had been found guilty of failing to register with the Los Angeles chief of police as a convicted felon. Lambert sought to overturn that conviction on the ground that the Los Angeles ordinance under which she had been convicted was unconstitutional.

The Court's request was unusual. The Supreme Court frequently appoints counsel to represent indigent defendants who do not have a lawyer and whose cases are yet to be heard by the Court. But this was not such a situation. Virginia Lambert had a lawyer, and her lawyer had already briefed and argued her case to the Court. The justices, however, were dissatisfied with the briefing and argument that had been presented, feeling that neither Lambert's lawyer nor the attorneys for the City of Los Angeles had fully addressed the issues. The chief justice told me that the Court wanted the case argued again and had asked the California attorney general to supplement the arguments of the Los Angeles city attorney, just as I was being asked to supplement those of Lambert's counsel.

Our conversation ended with Chief Justice Warren

telling me he needed an answer within two days. I put the phone down in semi-shock, wishing someone had been around to witness what I feared might have been a hallucination. Once I convinced myself that what I thought had just occurred had, in fact, occurred, the question uppermost in my mind was "Why me?" I had been in practice for all of seven years, was not yet a partner in the law firm, and was hardly a recognized expert in constitutional law. Then it dawned on me. This was a message, or a gift, from "my" justice— William O. Douglas. He knew it would be a feather in the cap of any young lawyer to be asked to argue before the Supreme Court, and he had most probably suggested my name to the chief. Apparently Douglas had decided he was not going to wait any longer for me to move into the stream on my own. He was going to give me a push.

The next step—taking the chief justice's request to the senior partners of O'Melveny & Myers—was, I thought, going to be a little tricky. First, I had never before argued in any appellate court, much less in the pinnacle of appellate courts. That fact alone would have caused the eyes of most law firm partners to narrow at the prospect of my taking on this assignment. The Supreme Court was reserved for the gods (and the occasional goddess) of the legal art. A seventh-year associate was not typically thought to rank among the deities.

The other issue that I thought might give pause to the firm's partners was the subject of the proposed assignment. A black, female convicted felon was challenging an ordinance of the City of Los Angeles and, by inference, the performance of Los Angeles police officers who had charged her. Would O'Melveny & Myers, a highly regarded part of the Los Angeles legal establishment, want its name associated with such a cause? The answers came quickly and emphatically. Each of the O'Melveny & Myers senior partners to whom I spoke told me graciously and unhesitatingly to step up to the challenge.

As I later came to appreciate more fully, the response of the O'Melveny & Myers leadership was fully in keeping with the firm's tenor and history. It was and is a place that encourages its lawyers to test the limits of their intellectual abilities and to devote a meaningful part of their professional lives to the public good, even when the public good involves matters of controversy. It has also historically been a place where political and social ideology play no part in decision-making.

As one of the law firm's first active Democrats, I had personally tested these propositions once before. In 1952, I organized a group that sponsored a controversial public statement condemning Wisconsin senator Joseph McCarthy. When the *Los Angeles Times* quoted the statement in a front-page story, I braced for a lecture from the firm's hierarchy. The only reaction I got, however, was one sentence from the head of the firm: "Nobody who makes any difference is upset, and I am not."

With the firm's blessing in hand, I was off and running. On June 24, 1957, less than a week after I had taken the call from the chief justice, the Supreme Court entered an order appointing me a friend of the Court in the Lambert matter. The case file reached me shortly after my appointment, and it quickly revealed that victory was far from assured. Virginia Lambert's principal defense at her trial was that she did not know that the City of Los Angeles required her to disclose to the police that she had been convicted on a forgery charge four years earlier. The trial court had refused even to let her tell the jury that she was unfamiliar with the law, relying on the well-established proposition that ignorance of the law is no excuse. The jury had quickly convicted her.

My only hope was to show that, notwithstanding reams of cases holding that not knowing of a particular law was not a defense to its violation, Ms. Lambert's case should be treated differently. The more deeply I investigated the facts of her arrest, the more I came to believe that for the Court to hold otherwise would be to elevate hoary legal maxim over what was right and fair. Virginia Lambert had been taken into custody on a Los Angeles street corner without explanation. She was moved to a police station, strip-searched for narcotics, and interrogated for two hours. When this invasion of Lambert's person and privacy produced no evidence of a crime, she was charged with failing to register as a convicted felon in violation of the city ordinance.

It would have been a miracle if Virginia Lambert had ever heard of the ordinance that established her duty to register. It was adopted in 1936—when she was only nine years old—and was published only once in a small-circulation legal newspaper. Los Angeles officials had made no effort to publicize its provisions, and at the time of her conviction for forgery, the judge had said nothing to her about a duty to register.

When lawyers argue to courts, they typically rely upon the decisions of other courts in similar circumstances. Here, however, there was no prior published court decision on the validity of such an ordinance. As a result, I had to base my argument on fundamental legal principles. In the brief filed with the Court, I argued that because Ms. Lambert's conduct was entirely passive and she had no knowledge of the law, her conviction could not pass muster under the due process clause of the Constitution. I urged that because she had neither the belief that she was engaged in wrongdoing nor reason even to inquire about the existence of such an arcane regulation, she was morally innocent. Finally, I argued that punishing this woman's innocent, passive status would violate her right of privacy.

To bolster the idea that the Los Angeles regulation was out of step with the reasonable expectations of free people, I undertook a survey of the practices of other English-speaking countries with respect to the registration of felons. With the creative help of another young O'Melveny & Myers associate, Dick Sherwood, I dispatched letters to chiefs of police in thirty-nine major cities in twenty countries with common law systems comparable to our own. The replies—demonstrating that no city in those countries had a registration ordinance similar to that of Los Angeles—gave me a tool to draw the Court to my position that it was fundamentally unfair to enforce the Los Angeles ordinance against a person in Ms. Lambert's situation. To bring the point home more forcefully, I showed that onerous registration requirements similar to this were common only in totalitarian countries, such as the Soviet Union and Nazi Germany.

Like "location" for a real estate salesman, "preparation" for a litigation attorney is the first, second, and third most important contributor to success. As one who has from time to time been accused of over-preparing for key performances, I can honestly say that I have never come away from such a moment regretting that I spent too much time getting ready. In the case of my first appearance before the U.S. Supreme Court, my preparation time was measured in weeks, not days. My colleagues and I rehearsed every permutation of every question and answer we could conjure up.

By the morning of October 16, 1957, the day set for argument in the Lambert case, my head was filled with facts, case histories, and purpose—with a little room left over for nerves. As a former clerk to a Supreme Court justice, I had, of course, been inside the Court's chamber many times before. I had not, however, previously experienced the sensation of stepping before the collective eyes and ears of the Court in response to the chief justice's calm, firm announcement that "we will hear from you now, Mr. Christopher."

To ensure that I would have something to say even if my brain was not working well at the outset, I had memorized the first section of my argument. I had barely begun when I was interrupted with a question from the venerable Felix Frankfurter. Justice Frankfurter had befriended me when I was a law clerk and had captivated me by talking knowledgeably of articles I had edited for the *Stanford Law Review*. As I stood before him listening to his question, however, it was evident that enhancing our collegial relationship was not his priority today.

"Counsel, where do you find the 'right of privacy' in the Constitution?" he asked brusquely, leaning for-

U.S. Supreme Court chamber.

ward across the bench. The question was not unexpected. Our brief had, after all, argued on behalf of Lambert's right to privacy. I replied that the right was found in the shadow—the penumbra, as lawyers called it—of the First, Fourth, and Fifth Amendments, a right applicable to Lambert by virtue of the Fourteenth Amendment. Frankfurter was not pleased by my response, though he knew it was the answer I would give and had to give. The Supreme Court had sidled up to the right of privacy in a series of prior decisions, but Frankfurter was offended by the notion that something as important as a constitutional right would be "discovered" in the interstices of the words of the Constitution.

On this occasion, his reaction came not in words but in a gesture for which he had become famous among aficionados of Supreme Court oratory. As I completed my answer, Frankfurter abruptly spun his swivel chair around, 180 degrees from its starting point. I continued my argument, directing myself to eight faces and the back of Felix Frankfurter's balding head, until he swiveled back around, completing his protest trip.

After a few more sentences, I was interrupted again, this time by Justice William Brennan. Thankfully, his was a friendly question, giving me an opportunity to elaborate on how implausible it was that Lambert could have been aware of the ordinance. I then returned to my prepared remarks but was interrupted again and again by questions from the bench, twenty in all. In the middle of one of my responses, the red light went on, signaling that my half hour had expired.

As I moved away from the lectern to take my seat, my first thought was that I had not made a dent in my prepared remarks. Though I believed I had handled the questions fairly well, it was difficult not to feel that I had failed to complete the job I had come to do. Then I recalled what an experienced Supreme Court advocate had told me many years before: "The best argument is one shaped by questions from the justices." The premise is that if the justices are actively engaged, they will get it right. Maybe things had gone better than I thought.

It usually takes months after oral argument for the Supreme Court to prepare its opinions. I had seen the process from the inside and knew that there would likely be months of writing and exchanging of alternative drafts among the justices. So I steeled myself for a long winter of uncertainty. But, to the surprise of professional Court watchers, on December 16, 1957, only two months after my appearance before the Court, the clerk called with the news: "*Lambert* came down today. She prevailed." I asked for the vote count. Virginia Lambert's conviction had been reversed by a vote of 5–4.

The majority's opinion drew its main themes directly from my brief, holding that a conviction violated due process of law when a person did not know of the duty to register and where there was no proof that she should have known of that duty. The decision observed that the Los Angeles ordinance would be violated by even the "mere presence" of a previously convicted person in the city, even though such a person would have no reason to inquire as to the necessity of registration. In these unusual circumstances, ignorance of the law was held to be an excuse.

When you're on the winning side, the world looks pretty good, even if your margin of victory is the narrowest possible. From my personal perspective, the result was all I could have hoped for. Beyond winning for Virginia Lambert, I had repaid a vote of confidence from a man who had gone out of his way to help me. That the majority opinion in *Lambert* was written by that same man—Justice William O. Douglas—was icing on the cake.

A GLIMPSE OF ANOTHER WORLD

On November 5, 1958, Edmund G. "Pat" Brown, a Democrat and the attorney general of California, defeated William F. Knowland, a Republican and a U.S. senator from California, for the governorship of the Golden State. The event marked a defining moment both for California and for me. For California, it was the beginning of an era of extraordinary growth and prosperity. For me, it was an opportunity to witness firsthand the unique interaction of people, politics, and policy that produces a working government.

My relationship with the new governor had begun in late 1953, when I was drafted by a senior partner in my law firm to help Brown prepare himself for an argument before the U.S. Supreme Court. The case involved the validity of a federal law that declared California to be the owner of the seabed extending for three miles off its coastline.

Brown and I began his preparation in California, but to avoid distractions, three days before the scheduled argument we flew to Washington and holed up in a hotel suite. For forty-eight hours it was just the two of us: I attempting to simulate the smartest, meanest, and most persistent Supreme Court justice imaginable, and he trying to respond with intellect, depth, and a lack of irritation. By the end of our preparation marathon, though Brown was ready to kill me, he was also ready for anything the Court might throw at him.

On the day of the argument, February 3, 1954, Brown appeared at Court loaded for bear. Primed by me to be ready for nearly immediate and then continued interruption, he began his prepared argument with one eye on his notes and the other on the justices. As he proceeded, he looked to the right, then the left, waiting for the first challenge. It never came. Perhaps out of deference to Brown's status as a prominent political figure as well as California's chief law enforcement officer, the Court accorded him thirty rare uninterrupted minutes to make his case. As a result, Brown was limited to delivering an obviously canned speech.

He returned to his seat fuming. He had spent two

days and nights cramming for this ultimate final exam, only to be denied the opportunity to display most of what he knew. Though Brown remained grumpy for a few hours, by the time we boarded our plane to head back to California, the clouds had lifted and he was his gregarious, engaging self again. Over a glass of wine we reviewed with amusement our travails of the preceding three days, talking the kind of familiar, been-through-the-war talk that characterizes two people who have worked intensely together trying to get something absolutely right.

Four months later, the Court handed down a decision in favor of the State of California. Attorney General Brown soon suggested that we team up again, this time in his quest for the governor's office in the 1958 election. He thought I could help him as a part-time researcher and speechwriter, and I happily signed on.

My intellectual contributions to Pat Brown's campaign were modest. The most noteworthy was a long piece I wrote for him based on the records of five of the most successful large-state governors of the century: Theodore Roosevelt and Charles Evans Hughes (New York), Woodrow Wilson (New Jersey), Robert La Follette (Wisconsin), and Hiram Johnson (California). The thrust of the piece was that great governors made big plans, then made their big plans work. He liked the theme and used it in speeches in which he outlined grand ideas for California's future—plans for bold action on education, water, air quality, and the budget.

In the late 1950s, *press,* to most politicians, denoted the print media exclusively. Candidates believed that getting influential print journalists to understand and report their message was the most effective way to reach the electorate. Brown saw things a little differently. Encouraged by his campaign manager, Fred Dutton, he viewed the emerging medium of television as the best conduit to the large, growing, and geographically dispersed population of California. He consciously decided to play to this new, powerful force, choosing sites for his speeches that would make strong visual impacts, and using as accompaniments to his appearances graphics that he knew would be effective on the small screen.

Brown beat Senator Knowland by more than a million votes in the election. When the cheering died down, he asked me to come to Sacramento for a few

November 5, 1968: Edmund G. "Pat" Brown.

months to serve as his special counsel and to help draft his initial messages—in effect, to produce the architect's renderings of the big projects that would define his first term as governor.

Although both my partnership at O'Melveny & Myers and our son Scott were barely a year old, I was sorely tempted. This was a seminal moment for the new administration, and I was being given a chance to influence fundamental matters of tone and direction. At the same time, I had voluntarily and happily taken on both partnership and fatherhood. Those were responsibilities that I couldn't, and wouldn't even if I could, put aside unilaterally.

It was time to consult, first with Marie, then with the leadership of the firm. It was the first of many times I would do so in my career, and the first of many times that my partners, both at home and at the office, would do more than simply grant me license to test new waters. They would urge me on. While the sacrifice I was asking of my law partners was significant—anticipating and dealing with the gaps that appear when a colleague carrying a full calendar simply disappears—Marie's was of a different order of magnitude. Moving a family to an unfamiliar city, adjusting expectations and expenditures, and learning to accept unreasonable intrusions on family and personal privacy became a familiar part of our life together. And as each of these forks in the road appeared, Marie's reaction, in substance, was the same: "Of course we'll do it, Chris."

Marie, Scott, and I took a small apartment in Sacramento shortly after New Year's Day, 1959, temporarily abandoning the new home we had just occupied in Los Angeles. I had already begun work on my first assignment: the governor had an inaugural message to deliver on January 5, 1959, and my job was to draft it. Brown saw the speech as charting the course for his first term. During December, I wrote a draft outlining each of the major initiatives the governor planned, testing the ideas by interviewing holdover state officials who knew the realities of government. As a catchphrase to describe Brown's political philosophy, I proposed *responsible liberalism.* The modifier, I thought, would frustrate any effort to turn Brown's embrace of liberalism into the sort of indictment it became decades later: shorthand for the use of taxpayer dollars to solve any and every human problem.

In the months following his inaugural, Pat Brown, responsible liberal, became a national figure. Rumors began to circulate that he might be a candidate for the Democratic presidential nomination in 1960. Reflecting his new status, he was invited to speak at the annual Gridiron Dinner in Washington, D.C., a white-tie affair where members of the press and political leaders make fun of themselves and one another. Brown called me into his office two weeks before the Gridiron event and asked me to write something funny—something *really* funny—for him. I did not respond as I should have: that "funny" was not a part, nor was it ever likely to become a part, of my oeuvre.

I was sweating bricks as I left his office. Where to turn?

My first thought, actually my only thought, was that I quickly had to find someone I knew to be funny and pick his brains. My candidate was Art Hoppe, humor columnist for the *San Francisco Chronicle*. I contacted him, and three days later, we met for lunch at his home in the bay district of San Francisco. Sitting in his backyard, we had a pitcher of martinis, then a second pitcher of martinis. As the afternoon progressed, we were positive we were getting funnier and funnier. I wobbled away from the session with lines I was certain would put the Gridiron crowd in the aisles.

The next day I picked up my notes to begin drafting the speech and found them definitely funny. Unfortunately, what was truly funny about them was that they were not entirely legible. I did the only thing I could: I called Hoppe for help. Once I had his attention, and he his wits about him, we managed to recall enough of our conversation of the previous day for me to produce something that looked like a speech.

I turned the product over to the governor and held my breath. To my enormous relief, he laughed, and a few days later, the Gridiron audience laughed, too. I had survived, but I swore to myself that I would never again take on an assignment that required me to produce something that was supposed to make someone else laugh.

The serious part of my work for Pat Brown

remained fascinating and instructive, giving me an opportunity for an unvarnished look at the intricacies of state government. In addition to working on drafts of various messages to the legislature, my job expanded to include the nitty-gritty work of the governor's office: contacting legislators, helping prepare the budget, reviewing clemency petitions, and advising on judicial appointments.

What I saw, close up, was the creation of a legend and a legacy. Pat Brown, master politician, forged and successfully sold to the California legislature landmark laws that eased Southern California's desperate need for water; expanded the state's renowned university system; attacked the critical problem of air pollution; and created a Fair Employment Practices Commission to deal with serious discrimination in the private sector. These benchmark items of legislation shaped California's path and extraordinary growth trajectory for the remainder of the century.

Our second son, Thomas, was born in Los Angeles on July 24, 1959, and I returned to O'Melveny & Myers at about that time. For me, it had been a seven-month high-yield experience. Not only had I learned a great deal about the inner, undocumented workings of California government, but I had cemented a relationship with a man who, for many years thereafter, was to be one of California's most recognized and respected leaders.

MY THIRD FIRST—
A DIPLOMATIC ASSIGNMENT

John F. Kennedy's narrow victory over Richard Nixon in the 1960 presidential election presented me with a new opportunity. A former law-clerk colleague alerted me that it was coming. President Kennedy's undersecretary of state, George W. Ball, was looking for a lawyer to help him in a difficult international textile negotiation, and friends of mine in Washington had put my name forward. Though I had no experience in either diplomacy or trade, my colleague said this actually gave me an edge for the job. The Commerce and Labor Departments, both bastions of protectionist sentiment, were going to flyspeck the backgrounds of the candidates for any hints of free-trade leanings. To have no views on the public record on such matters, I was told, was an advantage.

George Ball, brilliant Washington lawyer, political wise man, and free-trade advocate, was appointed undersecretary of state by the newly elected president and was simultaneously handed a hot potato. To drum up votes in textile-manufacturing states, candidate Kennedy had promised relief from the flood of low-cost textile imports, mainly from Asian countries, that had plagued the industry. Now it was time to deliver.

The president told Ball to find some way to persuade those responsible for the cheap imports—such countries as Japan, Korea, and Thailand—to restrain themselves. If they didn't, we risked the specter of

George W. Ball.

America having to press for unilateral import quotas, something the administration plainly wanted to avoid. Though the assignment ran directly against his free trader's grain, Ball knew that orders from the commander in chief were not invitations to debate. He set out to reach an international agreement that would mollify the American textile industry sufficiently to mute the pressure for import quotas.

Ball's invitation to me to join him came at the conclusion of a long discussion we had in his office in the early summer of 1961. After explaining the mission, he candidly confessed his uneasiness with it, but said he was sure a solution could be found without the need for harsh protectionist measures. I returned to Los Angeles impressed with the man, excited by the mission, and concerned about imposing again on my firm and family. Once more, however, I quickly received the blessings of both.

When I telephoned Ball to accept his offer, he asked me to come to Washington for briefings by his staff, then to rendezvous with him in Geneva. Together we would try to convince the countries belonging to the GATT (General Agreement on Trade and Tariffs, now called the World Trade Organization) to accept an agreement that permitted countries whose markets were disrupted by low-cost cotton textile imports to demand restraint by the countries exporting those products. Silk and wool would follow. This was sure to be a hard sell, not only with the relatively poor producing countries but with our major trading partners, such as Britain and France, who wanted to preserve the open trading system at almost any cost.

Ball and I arrived in Geneva to find a welcoming committee of American textile manufacturers, all determined to ensure that free trader Ball and his untested assistant Christopher negotiated the most stringent possible protection for their products. Ball successfully sold them his strategy: negotiate separately for the cotton, silk, and wool sectors, beginning first with cotton. His approach had the dual virtue of enabling us to focus our energies on a particular market segment and simultaneously to ease the pressure from American manufacturers who were interested only in silk or wool imports.

Watching George Ball move from group to group in Geneva was a revelation to me, a personal seminar in the art of negotiation. He had mastered both the rules and customs of international trade, as well as the economics of the textile industry. He also knew his various audiences—their attitudes and expectations, their habits and eccentricities.

In pursuing his goal to provide balanced relief for the U.S. textile industry, Ball had important credibility with those on the other side of the table. As a protégé of Jean Monnet, exponent of trade liberalization and father of what was to become the European Union, Ball had established a sterling reputation with trade negotiators from other countries. They knew he wanted to preserve the international trading system and therefore believed him when he said that his proposals were the minimum necessary to avoid more draconian action by the U.S. Congress.

I used my occasional moments in the sun to try to emulate Ball's example. When he sent me to brief industry representatives and seek their concurrence in some new position, I always thought first about what he would do in my place. However, even when I came up with what seemed like the right answer, I sometimes lacked the confidence or nerve to pursue things Ball's way. For example, when he personally briefed U.S. textile industry representatives, he delighted in appearing in a beautiful English suit, Egyptian cotton shirt, shoes made in Hong Kong, and a French silk tie. The message was clear: George Ball was not a captive of the American textile industry. I knew, though, that I was simply too young and inexperienced to deliver anything that looked or sounded like an in-your-face message.

After many days of hard bargaining in Geneva, we produced an international agreement on cotton textiles that permitted countries able to demonstrate that their markets had been disrupted by low-cost imports—such as the United States—to demand restraint from exporting countries and, failing voluntary restraints, to impose import quotas. With this umbrella structure agreed upon, Ball sent me to Tokyo to persuade the Japanese to voluntarily limit their cotton textile exports to the United States. If they refused, I was to leave no doubt that we would invoke the new agreement to impose such limitations. In truth, Ball and I wanted desperately to avoid resorting to the import quota alternative.

I spent August 1961 in hot, humid Tokyo, haggling over cotton shirts, socks, shorts, and T-shirts. The negotiations marked my maiden experience as a first-chair negotiator with someone from a different culture. Initially, I was just frustrated. My Japanese counterpart had an absolutely maddening technique, repeating over and over again without change in substance or, it seemed, inflection, his opening hard-line position that Japan had no intention of further restraining its exports. It seemed as if he was waiting for me to give up and go home.

After six days of this mindless formality, I began to ready myself mentally for failure. I told our ambassador to Japan, former Harvard professor Edwin

Reischauer, that I believed the Japanese intended to force us to impose import quotas. Reischauer, a leading scholar on Japan and a consummately wise man, responded with a to-the-point lecture on patience and persistence. The Japanese, he said, were expert at making their negotiating adversaries weary and frustrated. The mission entrusted to me was simply too important to let them succeed.

I returned to the negotiating table determined to mask my irritation and frustration. By word and expression, I let the Japanese negotiator know that I was not going to take stonewalling for an answer and that I had the stamina, patience, and resolve to wait him out. Two days later, suddenly and without explanation, my adversary came to the table with a new proposal. He was ready to negotiate new voluntary restraints.

The gates had opened, and within a week I was en route home with an agreement that bound the Japanese to pare their cotton exports in specified amounts. We had done our best to preserve the essence of the free-trade regime while redeeming the president's campaign promise. More important to me personally, I had delivered for George Ball, another person who had given me a leg up.

Bill Douglas, Pat Brown, and George Ball had vastly different personalities and talents, but they had one important thing in common: the ability to inspire, and the inclination to nudge forward and upward a younger person in whom they saw some promise.

They sought neither repayment nor even credit for their help, apparently satisfied by the feeling that came in having linked themselves to someone else's future. In addition to what they taught me about law, politics, and diplomacy, they also showed me that an inseparable part of being an accomplished person is helping others to accomplish.

3

THE JOHNSON TREATMENT

I T WAS JUNE 14, 1967. I WAS SITTING BOLT upright on the front edge of a sofa in the Oval Office when Lyndon Johnson, the president of the United States, walked in. In the high fashion of the day, he presented an uncharacteristically subdued image: a gray suit, gray shirt, and a matching gray silk tie. He appeared several inches taller than I expected him to be, but, as I have come to appreciate over time, all presidents look tall in the Oval Office. My nervousness was compounded because in contrast to his dapper appearance, I knew I was red-eyed and rumpled, having flown overnight from Los Angeles in a small government plane, with no time to shower or change clothes before heading immediately to the West Wing for our scheduled meeting.

The trip had come up suddenly. I was hosting a dinner in Los Angeles for presidential assistant Joe Califano and a group of Los Angeles–area academics, discussing the administration's 1968 legislative program. In midmeal, Califano was summoned to a telephone call. When he returned to the table, he asked to speak to me privately. We adjourned to an alcove where Califano told me that the caller had been the president. He wanted Califano to bring me back to Washington so he could interview me for the job of deputy attorney general.

Ramsey Clark, Johnson's attorney general, had sounded me out about the deputy position a few weeks earlier, but I hadn't known that the idea had reached the president. While the prospect of interviewing with Johnson without sleep or preparation was troubling, I also instantly realized that this might be my one chance at the job. Lyndon Johnson was famous for changing his mind if an appointment was delayed or leaked. After a few moments' thought, I told Joe I'd go.

We landed in Washington at 8 A.M. local time. En route to the White House I pleaded with Califano for a chance to get myself presentable. He brushed me off, saying that if I got the job, I'd get used to appearing before Johnson after staying up all night. As the president approached me in the Oval Office, it crossed my mind that he might have planned it this way. My guard was down, and it was a good moment to find out what I was made of.

Whatever Johnson's intentions might have been, he opened with a good line: "Ramsey thinks he wants you to be attorney general when he goes fishing." While I knew Ramsey Clark had not gone fishing in years, I also knew better than to deflate a presidential effort at a bon mot. He paced in front of me, never quite looking me in the eyes, talking about the role of the deputy attorney general, the importance of the position, and the good things he'd heard about me. As if he'd timed his performance, he ended the monologue directly in front of me, looked into my eyes, and said he wanted me to take the job. I was astonished but not speechless. I told him I'd be pleased to serve.

Having gotten what he wanted, Johnson then did a very Johnsonian thing. He put me in my place. In congratulating me, he mentioned that he normally preferred former district attorneys for high Justice

July 1967: Being sworn in by Justice Abe Fortas, with President Johnson, Marie, Kristen, Thomas, and Scott.

A conference with President Johnson
and Joe Califano.

Department jobs, but had concluded that even
though I hadn't been a DA, I would probably be up to
the challenge.

What leads a president to decide on a particular
person for a particular position is a frequently debated
question in Washington. As I departed the president's
office, my dominant thought was "Why me?" Walking from the West Wing, I came up with a possible
answer. I had handled sensitive matters for California's governor during the riots in Los Angeles two
years earlier. With recent disorders at three Southern
black universities, as well as racial trouble in Tampa
and Cincinnati, Johnson must have sensed that
America's urban ghettos were ready to ignite, and he
wanted people close at hand who had experience in
dealing with racially charged situations. I was one of
those people.

LOS ANGELES

I'd earned my degree in the unusual subspecialty of urban riot control in 1965, when disturbances had broken out in the Watts area of Los Angeles. I saw the first televised pictures of the rioting on Friday, August 13, while on vacation in the Bahamas. As I was not yet a sophisticated viewer of such events, I, like millions of other Americans, subconsciously extrapolated from the footage of burning buildings and roving bands of looters the conclusion that all of Los Angeles was in chaos. Marie and I immediately made plans to return home to our three young children.

As our plane descended toward Los Angeles International Airport on Saturday evening, August 14, I saw fires burning out of control in large areas under and around our glide path. I struggled to find some context, something in my experience that could help me relate to what was going on below us. Though as a young naval officer I had seen the destruction in war-ravaged Tokyo, that situation was really not parallel to this one. When I'd left Los Angeles to go on vacation, it was intact, stable, and by all appearances at peace with itself. I was returning to something else, and it was not at all clear what that something else was.

Our taxi driver was scared. He was white and, I suspected, even in normal times suspicious of blacks. We gave him our address and he grimaced—he knew that reaching our home by the shortest route would require him to cross zones in which fires were burning. He said he would take us home only if we could go *his* way. We agreed, and by a circuitous route, and in twice the usual time, we threaded a path home. Given the television pictures of the day before, we braced ourselves for what we would find. But when we arrived in our neighborhood, it was the picture of normalcy. It was as if we lived in a city far from the one we had seen the day before on television.

First thing the next morning I called Governor Pat Brown, who had also just flown back to California from a trip. After my stint as special counsel in 1959, I had remained a close friend and adviser. He told me he was forming a team to deal with the riots and asked me to join it. I immediately agreed. A few hours later I was in the midst of the riot area, touring the hardest-hit neighborhoods in a police car, passing buildings still smoldering from the prior night's firebombings. The most frequent targets had been white-owned businesses. In the first news cycles following the outbreak, the burned-out hulks of stores known to be owned by whites had quickly become a kind of visual embodiment of the frustration and hate that had driven people to the streets.

The conduct of the rioters followed what I came later to recognize as the choreography of urban rioting. A controversial arrest would trigger a demonstration that would, in turn, prompt someone to smash a store window and take whatever was on display. Then packs of looters would follow, seizing what attracted their attention, sometimes fighting with one another over prized items, sometimes transporting their loot out of the store in grocery carts. When the place was stripped clean, someone would light a match, throw a bomb, destroy what remained of someone's lifetime of work.

On the streets, I talked to National Guardsmen who had been in civilian jobs only a few days before. I found them bewildered, often frightened, and uncertain of their mission. Because they were inadequately trained for their task, their immediate response to any challenge was to use their weapons.

Order was restored by the following Tuesday, six days after the rioting began and thirty-four lives had been lost. The National Guard deployment, increased police presence, and pleas from African-American leaders finally brought a semblance of peace. When the immediate threat abated, Governor Brown turned to longer-term issues. He called me to his office to deliver a personal pledge, one that he wanted me to help him fulfill. He was determined not to preside over a repetition of what had happened in Watts— now or ever. He wanted to know what had caused it, what had been done right or wrong in handling it, and what could be done to prevent a recurrence. He asked me to assemble a bipartisan commission to study all of these questions.

John McCone, a Republican business leader who had served as CIA director under Presidents Kennedy and Johnson, had just returned home to California and agreed to serve as chairman. We chose for the remaining six slots an ethnically diverse group of prominent locals. When the governor announced formation of the commission, he took me by surprise by adding me to the group as its vice chairman.

I plunged into the investigation, helping to arrange sixty-four hearings by the full commission in three months. We set up offices in the Watts area and interviewed dozens of residents about what had led to and happened during the riot. John McCone and I were determined to go beyond law enforcement issues to probe the underlying causes. At the same time, to capture public attention, we knew the report had to be issued quickly, before memories faded. We also recognized that, given its highly controversial subject matter, it had to present conclusions with a single, unequivocal voice in order to have a real impact on the public consciousness. One hundred days after the rioting in Watts ended, we delivered a report to the governor entitled *Violence in the City—an End or a Beginning?* It was, as we had hoped, a bipartisan and unanimous product.

Each of the commission's members doubtlessly had his own view of the most important facts and conclusions we reported. I took four key lessons from our investigation. First, an early display of massive, well-trained force is the best way to contain a riot. In Watts, delay by the lieutenant governor (who was acting in Governor Brown's absence) in calling in the National Guard produced a corresponding delay in bringing the riot under control. Second, police forces and, to an even greater extent, National Guard troops need special training to deal with urban disorders. The generic drills to which "weekend warriors" were subjected did not enable them to deal with the provocations and fears that arose in riot situations. Third, the Watts rioters primarily threatened property, not people. Human casualties stemmed from responses to attacks on property, and tragically and ironically, the responses fell much harder on the black than the white population. Fourth, riots like Watts were going to recur so long as we failed to address the underlying causes: too few jobs, poor schools, substandard health facilities, and distrust of law enforcement within the minority community.

In addition to providing some invaluable lessons about handling urban unrest, my work on the 1965 Watts riot brought an unexpected opportunity: a chance to work with Ramsey Clark. Then deputy attorney general under Nicholas Katzenbach, Clark was put in charge of a federal inquiry into the riot. In that role, he contacted me several times for facts we had unearthed in our investigation and to discuss conclusions we had reached. Two years later, I stood in the Oval Office as the man who, according to Lyndon Johnson, Attorney General Clark had said he wanted to stand in for him "when he goes fishing."

By the time I reported for work at the Justice Department on July 3, 1967, major racial disorders had broken out in Tampa, Cincinnati, and Atlanta. In each case, the scenario was much as I had seen in

Watts. It was evident that the summer would bring more outbreaks, and Ramsey Clark made clear from my first day on the job that I was on the riot watch until further notice.

On July 12, nine days after I arrived, the first test came. The streets of Newark erupted in deadly conflict, one that led to twenty-three deaths. That toll included one white fireman, one white detective, and twenty-one black Americans. The conflict was brought under control after four days, with the infusion of massive numbers of state police and National Guardsmen. My own role in dealing with the outbreak was a delicate one. Because I had yet to be confirmed by the Senate, and because senators view any official action by a nominee prior to confirmation as presumptuous or worse, I had to keep a low profile. I stayed on top of events in Newark from the department and chaired meetings with federal and local officials to define the character and quantity of federal assistance that would be needed to rehabilitate the city. On July 24, the Senate confirmed my nomination, and later the same day I found myself front and center in handling the next, and by far the most serious to date, of the urban disorders of 1967.

DETROIT

It was late Sunday, July 23, 1967, when I heard the first radio reports of rioting in Detroit. I was up to my shoulders in packing boxes. My family had reached Washington the night before, and we were trying to settle into our new quarters in a Virginia suburb.

Ramsey Clark, knowing my family had just arrived, didn't call me that day, but I could divine from the radio reports what was going on. He was up most of Sunday night talking with our people in the field and with Michigan's governor, George Romney, a leading Republican candidate for president in 1968. When I reached the office early Monday morning, I learned that Romney was angling for federal help but did not want to take the step necessary for federal intervention—certification of a state of insurrection in Michigan that the state could not control.

By midmorning on July 24, Clark and I were on our way to the White House to discuss with the president whether to send federal troops to Detroit to restore order. On entering the Cabinet Room I was startled. In addition to the president and Defense Secretary Robert McNamara, both of whom I had expected to see, Supreme Court associate justice Abe Fortas was sitting at the table. Fortas, whom I had last encountered as an antitrust litigator in private law practice, was holding forth on the sensitive and constitutionally significant issue of whether troops could be dispatched to Detroit without a certification by Romney. In other words, a justice of the Supreme Court was providing informal legal advice to the president of the United States.

You don't have to be a lawyer to understand my

feelings at that moment, but it helps. Like other Americans, I was taught from the first day of civics class that under the Constitution the federal government is organized so as to separate the functions of the executive, legislative, and judicial branches. The lesson was reinforced in law school. As a result, I carried as part of my intellectual baggage the belief that high government officials understood and conformed themselves to this overarching principle. To put it mildly, I was shocked to find a Supreme Court justice opining to the president on whether a request from a governor was necessary before the president could dispatch federal troops to a riot area. In addition, although Fortas's advice was couched in legal terms, it had an obvious political subtext: the president should not deploy troops without the political cover of a request from his possible adversary in the next election, Governor Romney.

By the end of our meeting it was clear that federal troops were likely to be needed in Detroit. But in addition to a certification by the governor, Johnson also believed that the troops should not be deployed unless a nonmilitary official representing the president determined they were necessary. He decided that he wanted Cyrus Vance, a private citizen, to go to the riot scene to make that call. Vance had recently resigned as deputy secretary of defense and was a Johnson favorite. Ramsey Clark objected. He said that sending a private citizen to Detroit on behalf of the president would be interpreted by the press as a negative reflection on those serving in the administration. Fortas and McNamara defended the president's decision, praising Vance's role in prior crises, such as dispatching federal troops to quiet racial tensions in Oxford, Mississippi, in 1962 when he was secretary of the army. The president ended the debate by saying to Clark, "Why don't you send Warren along with Vance?"

When the president called, Vance accepted the assignment without a pause. What Vance did not say to the president in that call speaks volumes about the man. He was suffering from a herniated disk; the pain was so severe that he had to sleep sitting upright in a chair and needed help getting dressed. The pain was compounded by grief. He had just returned from his mother's funeral. But Cy Vance comes from a tradition that does not yield to mere physical or emotional pain and that never says no to the commander in chief. A few hours later, he and I were en route to Detroit.

Immediately after landing, Vance and I joined U.S. army general John Throckmorton in an open jeep for a tour of the riot areas. President Johnson had ordered five thousand paratroopers into Selfridge Air Force Base near Detroit. He was awaiting our report before sending them into the city.

The commander of the Michigan National Guard joined us on our tour. Although he was fully empowered to act, and although the streets had been under siege for more than a day, he said he had waited for us to arrive and counsel him before deciding how and where to deploy three thousand additional National Guard troops. His indecision took Vance, me, and General Throckmorton aback. As in Los Angeles, the failure to make an early, massive show of force in the face of widespread rioting had undoubtedly prolonged and encouraged lawlessness. Throckmorton, the first to respond, barked, "Get them on the streets as fast as you can."

When darkness came, it was clear that the state's response was too little, too late. Vance's military aide maintained a graph tracking the hourly rate of riot incidents, and by 9 P.M. it had shot up like an out-of-control fever chart. Vance, General Throckmorton, and I believed the situation was veering out of control, and Vance telephoned a gloomy report to the White House. But the standoff between the president and

Late-night press conference in Detroit with
Cyrus Vance and General Throckmorton.

the governor continued. Urged by Justice Fortas to await a formal request from Romney, Johnson said he would not insert federal troops until the governor made the necessary certification. Though Johnson pinned his decision on the law, he obviously wanted to avoid sole responsibility for having federal troops shoot at black Americans.

Governor Romney continued into the evening to refuse to certify that a state of insurrection existed in Detroit. He told me that he was worried that if he made such a certification, insurance companies would be able to avoid compensating homeowners for their losses. The temptation was strong to remind Romney that lives, in addition to property, were at stake. I resisted that impulse in favor of giving him legal advice. I suggested he might avoid triggering the escape clause in homeowners' policies by spelling out in his certification precisely what was happening in the city while avoiding use of the word *insurrection*. He still wasn't satisfied.

By about 11 P.M., the president had decided, based upon further legal research by the White House counsel, that he could act on his own constitutional authority. He had been swayed by a precedent from the Roosevelt administration, when FDR had deployed federal troops during the 1945 Detroit race riots. Having decided that he would no longer wait for a certification from Romney, Johnson ordered federal troops into Detroit and took to the airwaves to explain his action. When he addressed the nation at midnight, he was crystal clear as to what action had been taken, but the casual listener might well have concluded from the president's phrasing that he had responded to a request from the governor.

In the early-morning hours, the phone rang as I manned the makeshift federal control center in Detroit. It was the president asking for Cyrus Vance and wanting to know what was happening in the streets. When I told him that Vance was out inspecting the city, Johnson decided I would have to do. "Was it worse than Watts?" he asked. I told him it was at least as bad. He then rattled off at machine-gun speed a dozen questions that I had no time to get on paper, much less answer without further investigation: How many policemen were on the streets? How many National Guardsmen? Had the federal troops been deployed? How many injuries? How many dead? How many arrested? And on and on. Before his call I'd thought I was on top of the facts. By the end I knew that the next time I talked to Lyndon Johnson I had to be better prepared.

That next call came the following night. I steeled myself for the Johnson onslaught but felt I had in my head the answers needed to survive the experience. I was wrong. Johnson had gotten his hands on an early edition of the *Washington Post*, containing an editorial criticizing him for failing to dispatch federal troops while awaiting Vance's report on riot conditions. Contrary to my expectations (and planning), the president didn't pepper me with questions. He simply railed at me about the editorial. He damn well didn't like it and damn well wanted me to know it. By the end of the call, I was definitely clear on how he felt. I struggled to end the one-way exchange by promising to find the *Post* reporters covering the riot and educate them on the constitutional principles involved in using federal troops to quell an urban disturbance.

I was shaken by what I experienced in Detroit. The death toll was forty-three: thirty-three black, ten white. Clearly, law and order had a tenuous hold in major urban ghettos, and anarchy was a real threat. The roots of the problem were the same as I had discerned in Watts: not enough jobs to go around; not enough schooling for the disadvantaged; poor housing; a deep resentment of largely white police forces. Compounding all of this in 1967 was the discriminatory operation of the Vietnam War draft. College-going sons of the wealthy found exemptions easy to come by; black Americans in the ghetto found it impossible to avoid military service. It was hardly surprising to find despair of a depth and breadth that inspired widespread violence.

I returned from Detroit determined to use what I had learned to head off or mitigate civil disorders elsewhere in the country. My most urgent goal was to share our information and conclusions with city officials across America. The attorney general called a conference of mayors and chiefs of police from twenty-five cities with large black populations and told them that training of local police needed to begin immediately to prevent and contain outbreaks. A comparable message went to state commanders of National Guard units. We told local and state officials that, with the first signs of civil disorder, the right response was to deploy all available manpower and to ask for federal help at the moment it became clear that local action would not suffice. Beyond this wake-up call, Clark and I beefed up the Justice Department's Community Relations Service, organized interagency emergency teams, pressed the Defense Department to make contingency plans for the deployment of troops, and created a package of materials to facilitate local authorities in asking for federal assistance.

Against all predictions, the balance of 1967 passed without another urban disorder, although the nation stayed tense through the remainder of the summer. On many evenings, Ramsey, Community Relations director Roger Wilkins, and I camped at the department to monitor reports of threatened disturbances and to offer advice to local authorities if violence broke out. As a Californian, I am no fan of cold weather, but I was relieved when winter came, bringing temperatures too chilly for people to gather in the streets of most of America's cities.

In October of 1967, I came face-to-face with a different kind of disorder. Approximately 100,000 young men and women came to Washington to demonstrate against the Vietnam War, many with the avowed purpose of shutting down the Pentagon. Secretary of Defense Bob McNamara asked me to join him in the difficult task of devising protection for the building and its operations while upholding the rights of free assembly and expression. The Pentagon is approachable from so many directions that we decided to surround the building with soldiers.

On Saturday, October 21, a cordon of hundreds of soldiers stood shoulder to shoulder around the Pentagon. U.S. marshals from the Department of Justice joined in the effort to maintain the lines and to make arrests if warranted. The soldiers carried unloaded rifles, but reinforcements with loaded weapons were stationed in the Pentagon's central courtyard for deployment if the demonstrators broke through the lines and reached the building.

After gathering at the Lincoln Memorial, twenty thousand of the most militant demonstrators marched across the Memorial Bridge toward the Pentagon. I had great empathy for their idealism, but concern for their tactics and apparent disregard for the law and national security.

Part of the time, I monitored events from McNamara's office or from the roof of the Pentagon, but mostly I was on the lines with the soldiers. I stood behind them, reporting my observations by walkie-talkie to the command post inside the Pentagon. When they reached the troops, the protesters hurled insults and abuse on them. They called the soldiers "queers" and "creeps" and burned facsimiles of draft cards. While making obscene proposals in stage whispers, young women rubbed their breasts against the

October 21, 1967: Protesters confront
troops outside the Pentagon.

soldiers and tried to unzip their flies. The troops, under orders not to respond to such provocations, held the line.

After several hours of trying to provoke the soldiers, a knot of protesters rushed the north entrance to the Pentagon. Standing behind the line, I was worried that the entire band of protesters might join in the rush and reported my concern to the command post. The soldiers were ordered to fall back to the northern doors, where reinforcements from inside the Pentagon's core joined in pushing the protesters back. The troops, highly disciplined and forewarned of the tactics that would be used against them, were able to restore the protective line without firing a shot or causing serious injury.

I stayed all night at the Pentagon, monitoring the ten thousand or more remaining protesters. Some left, but most remained until Sunday morning. When the threat finally abated that afternoon, the Pentagon was secure and there had been no disruption of operations.

I had been determined to preserve the civil liberties of the demonstrating students, but I was equally determined that the government not be shut down. I came away with great admiration for the unflinching discipline of the soldiers in the face of enormous provocation. Pentagon officials, who were under heavy criticism for the conduct of the war, earned my respect for the lengths to which they went to preserve the protesters' rights. Most of the crowd behaved in a peaceful and positive manner. A militant core bent on closing down the Pentagon had been dealt with firmly but carefully. Overwhelmingly, the event brought home to me, as only firsthand contact can, the depth of the animosity and disdain that young Americans harbored for the war and the "Establishment."

4

A YEAR ON THE EDGE

PERHAPS THE RELATIVE QUIET OF THE WINTER months of 1967 and early 1968 made what happened next seem more dramatic. But even from the perspective of thirty years, I still feel that the period between March and August of 1968 was one of the most shocking and dispiriting I have lived through.

It began with the evening of March 31, 1968. Lyndon Johnson was about to conclude a televised speech from the White House on the Vietnam War. Today I cannot remember anything about the speech except its conclusion. He had written a peroration that took everyone by surprise: "I shall not seek, and I will not accept" the nomination for another term.

I can't vouch for the reaction in other living rooms in America, but the president's statement knocked me back on my heels. Only a few days earlier at the White House, he had quizzed me about California politics, leaving me convinced that he planned to reassemble the coalition that had carried him to victory in 1964. While I'd also noted that the strains of the job had left distinct marks on him—deep lines in his face and a slightly depressed air—it hadn't crossed my mind that Johnson might not run for reelection.

As I sat staring at the television screen trying to absorb what I had heard, my first reaction was concern over how Johnson's lame-duck status would affect legislation and judicial nominations pending on Capitol Hill. My second thought was that it would not be a good idea for me to give up my California driver's license.

In normal times, the announcement by a president that he will not run for reelection is the story of the year. Everything flows from and relates back to that moment. But 1968 was far from a normal year, and what we did not and could not know on that evening in March was that more, much more, was to come. Only a few days later, the LBJ announcement was overtaken by an event that shook the country to its foundations.

On Thursday evening, April 4, 1968, as I sat in a meeting with the attorney general, a secretary brought in a note. Martin Luther King Jr. had been shot in Memphis. Shortly after 8 P.M. we learned he had died of his wounds. I knew immediately that we had to prepare ourselves. In addition to the search for the killer, I was certain we would soon be dealing with violent outbursts all across America.

The eruptions were quick in coming. Rioting started within blocks of the Justice Department in Washington, subsiding temporarily before dawn. In black ghettos all across the country, looting and fire-bombings were reported. I stayed at the department all night to monitor those reports for signs that federal help might be needed.

At the White House, the president took command, making a televised appeal for calm and issuing a stream of orders to Joe Califano and other aides. He directed Ramsey Clark to go to Memphis to show that the federal government was on the job. When Clark left at 2 A.M., I became acting attorney general and started to plan in detail for dealing with an escalation of the violence.

I started with a call to the undersecretary of the army, David E. McGiffert. He was point man for determining the readiness of the army troops and installations across the country that might be called upon. I told him to expect the worst and to plan for federal deployments to several cities at the same time. By the time the post-King assassination riots had run their full course, major disorders had broken out in twenty-six cities. Federal troops were sent to three: Washington, Chicago, and Baltimore.

At 11 A.M. on April 5, the day after King's murder, the president convened a meeting of black leaders at the White House. As we gathered in the Cabinet

Room, I was amazed at the number of prominent African-Americans who had assembled on short notice—Thurgood Marshall, Roy Wilkins, Leon Higginbotham, Whitney Young, Bayard Rustin, and several others. The event featured Lyndon Johnson at his best. He preached, he cajoled, he pleaded for at least temporary acceptance of the conclusion that the shooting was the work of one deranged man, not a manifestation of white society's attitude about race.

As he spoke, I looked around the room at the faces of the assembled leaders. They wore expressions ranging from bewilderment to despair. Without speaking a word, they were communicating what I suspected everyone in the room already knew: no one could do much of anything to head off the destruction that was about to come. King's death would be treated by young blacks as more than enough justification to vent their rage. But in doing so, they would do more than destroy property and imperil human life—they would reveal the magnitude of the loss of the most influential black leader of the century.

By midmorning, rioting had erupted again in Washington, D.C., but on a much larger scale. At 2 P.M., the president called and directed me to make a personal inspection of the streets in anticipation of a request for federal troops from Washington's Mayor Walter Washington. The commissioner of public safety, Pat Murphy, drove to the White House in a police car to pick me up. Joined by army general Ralph Haines, I left at about 2:45 P.M., amid reports

April 5, 1968: Rioting in Washington, D.C.,
following King's assassination.

that disorder was spreading. At one point, we left the police car to get a look at the rioting from a hill near one of the neighborhoods under siege. As we tracked the erupting fires, General Haines was hit hard on the shoulder by a flying rock, which spun him around. Though plainly shaken, he insisted he was unhurt and we continued on.

We had been on tour for less than an hour when I concluded that the rioting was beyond the control of the D.C. authorities. The District's 2,800 police officers simply could not cope with the roving bands of looters and firebombers. I needed to talk to the president immediately. I tried first to contact the White House via police radio, but emergency police traffic had jammed all the circuits. With the monstrous traffic tie-ups, our car's siren and flashing lights had almost no effect. Finally I decided to look for a pay phone.

We stopped three times, finding only ransacked, inoperative phones. On the fourth corner we got lucky—in an abandoned service station was a working telephone. General Haines, Pat Murphy, and I, in suits and ties, surrounded the instrument. I borrowed a dime from Murphy, called the White House general number, asked to speak to the president, and in less than a minute heard the voice of Lyndon Johnson on the line. It was 4 P.M.

"Where have you been!" The words were civil, but the tone demanding. "I've been trying to reach you for an hour!"

A line was now forming behind me of people as anxious as I had been to find a working phone. As I struggled simultaneously to keep the conversation private and to mime to those in line that the call wouldn't be long, I hastily explained to the president where we were and the problems we had encountered in trying to reach him. I gave him my impression of the situation on the street and, despite frowns from those waiting in line, handed the phone to General Haines for his appraisal.

After three or four sentences of description, the president interrupted. He said he was going to deploy federal troops and would immediately sign the executive order I had drafted and delivered to the White House before leaving for the inspection. By law, the wording of such an order must be precise. It includes a pro forma appeal to the people, originally intended to be read aloud in the streets, to cease and desist from rioting and other unlawful conduct. That public appeal is the origin of the phrase *read the riot act.*

Mayor Walter Washington asked for the help of Cyrus Vance, and the president leaned on Cy once again to come down to Washington from his home in New York. Once the president had ordered federal troops onto Washington's streets, I went to the District of Columbia offices in the late afternoon to brief Vance. Vance took charge with his customary firmness, and I went back to the department for another long night of monitoring reports of the disturbances in other cities.

On Saturday, April 6, the rioting intensified in Chicago. Joe Califano called me at the department and said the president wanted me to fly to Chicago immediately and report back to him on the situation. After landing at O'Hare in the early evening, I took an hour-long helicopter tour of the areas under siege. I quickly realized that traveling above the chaos deprived me of the feel of events below and conferred a false sense of order on the scene. But even at a thousand feet, it was evident that the situation was grave.

After conferring with National Guard officials and spot-checking the affected neighborhoods, I sped to City Hall. There I was ushered into the presence of Richard J. Daley, Chicago's fireplug of a mayor. I told him I was going to recommend that the president deploy federal troops to South Chicago. Daley, normally quick to challenge any incursion on his territory, was upset, but he was angry at the situation, not with me. He said he understood the reasons for my conclusion and wouldn't fight me.

I put in my call to the president. It was 1 A.M. in Washington, but Johnson came on the line immediately. He sounded weary and disheartened. It had been a terrible two days since the King assassination. Nevertheless, he was on top of the situation and said he would at once sign the order for deployment. Federal troops were in the streets of South Chicago by the next morning, and the rioting was under control by the end of the day.

The tragedy of King's assassination gave the president an opportunity to reinvigorate his civil rights agenda in the Congress. His fair housing proposal, barring racial discrimination in the sale and rental of properties, had passed the Senate in March, but was bottled up in the House. Immediately after King's death, Johnson pressed the Congress to make a renewed commitment to equal opportunity and justice. The House responded by sending the fair housing law to the president's desk on April 10, just six days after King's death.

THE KENNEDY ASSASSINATION

I—and the country—had just begun to absorb the shock of the King assassination when another earth-shaking tragedy occurred. In the early hours of Wednesday, June 5—barely two months after Martin

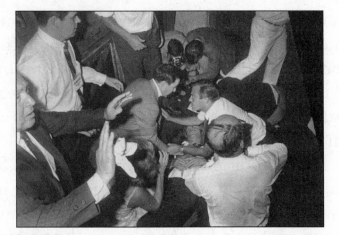

June 5, 1968: Robert F. Kennedy lies
mortally wounded in the kitchen of
Los Angeles's Ambassador Hotel.

Luther King's death—the Justice Department watch
officer woke me to report that in Los Angeles, Senator
Robert F. Kennedy had been shot in the head a few
minutes after midnight, California time, and that the
wound was grave. The shooting had come just after a
postelection celebration at the Ambassador Hotel, as
Kennedy was being led through the hotel kitchen to
an exit. I had gone to bed about three hours earlier,
when the first results indicated that Kennedy would
win the California presidential primary. There was no
sleeping after the dreadful news came, and I dressed
and went to the department to be ready for whatever
the next day might bring.

Throughout the day, Kennedy barely clung to life
in a Los Angeles hospital. Conditioned by the violent

reaction to King's death, I feared another round of urban disorders. However, on checking with the FBI and local sources, I was relieved to find that calm prevailed in the big cities. Even after Kennedy's death on Thursday, June 6, the streets were quiet. It was almost as if the country was too shocked to react.

Los Angeles police took Kennedy's assassin, Sirhan Sirhan, into custody at the Ambassador Hotel immediately after the shooting and launched an intensive investigation. Since Los Angeles was home territory for me, I volunteered to fly to the West Coast to make sure that every stone would be turned. Ramsey immediately agreed.

I arrived at Los Angeles International Airport on Thursday night and was met by U.S. Attorney Matt Byrne, a longtime friend. In the next twenty-four hours, I met with top officials of every law enforcement office in the city, who impressed me with their thoroughness and aggressiveness. The police and the prosecutors knew the world was watching.

Remembering what had happened to Lee Harvey Oswald after President Kennedy's assassination, I wanted to see for myself the conditions of Sirhan's detention. I traveled with Byrne to the county jail on Friday and was ushered by him and Los Angeles County sheriff Peter Pitchess into the hospital wing where Sirhan was kept. Security was so tight that when Byrne and I approached the hospital wing with Sheriff Pitchess, the head guard directed Byrne and me, whom he did not know on sight, to a separate locked chamber. After we had separated from Pitchess, the guard questioned him to make sure we had not brought him to the jail under some form of coercion.

When we were finally admitted to the area in which Sirhan was kept, I saw that significant thought had gone into the arrangements. Sirhan was the sole prisoner in a ten-by-ten cell, kept company by one unarmed deputy who sat in the cell with him on suicide watch. Another stood outside the cell looking through the window of the cell door. The cells on either side of Sirhan were empty, and five armed deputies patrolled the corridor.

From the county jail, I traveled to the Ambassador Hotel, where Kennedy had been shot. As we walked into the kitchen, I felt a chill rise inside me. The floor was strewn with police markers and still smeared with bloodstains. The huge metal steam tables that bracketed the path where Kennedy had walked and fallen were still askew. Though security procedures have become much more sophisticated and reliable in the thirty years since June 1968, whenever I am escorted through a hotel kitchen to avoid crowds at a speaking engagement, I never fail to experience an echo of the feeling I had that day.

As I flew back to Washington, I considered whether this latest shock would become a healing and unifying point for the country in general and for the Democratic Party in particular. The assassinations of Martin Luther King and Robert Kennedy were stigmata for all Americans, bigger and more important than political or ideological differences. It seemed impossible that the Democrats could remain at odds with themselves in the face of such tragedies.

As we neared the 1968 convention, I realized I had been wrong. Robert Kennedy's supporters did not bond well to the party; many tuned it out. In retrospect, election night in California proved to be a kind of Greek tragedy centered on the Democratic Party— a dramatic victory by a promising young leader, murdered at the moment of his triumph.

THE POLICE RIOT

In late August of 1968, I returned to Chicago, this time as the president's law enforcement representative at the 1968 Democratic convention. Johnson had dispatched me because he believed that the gathering of thousands of antiwar demonstrators in the city held the potential for trouble. The King and Kennedy assassinations and their aftermath had left me drained, but I felt little apprehension. This event promised to be more like the march on the Pentagon than the Detroit riots. But in fact, it was like neither. It was a bald display of lawlessness by public servants sworn to uphold the law.

The Conrad Hilton Hotel was jammed with conventioneers. I was housed in a large room on the third floor, commanding a clear view of Michigan Avenue. Late on Wednesday afternoon of convention week, thousands of demonstrators gathered for a march down that street. Joined by a group from the Poor People's Mule Train, led by the Reverend Ralph David Abernathy, the demonstration became both an anti-war and antidiscrimination event.

From my room, I saw the protesters assemble and move down the street toward a phalanx of burly Chicago policemen. When they reached the police line, "Chicago's finest" set upon them almost immediately. They tried to flee, but club-swinging police pursued them, catching and beating the less agile.

I had never seen before, nor have I since, police so completely out of control. I put in an urgent call to Chicago's Chief of Police Conlisk, imploring him to do something to restrain his officers. He seemed surprised by my call and calmly said he would look into it. But as the evening wore on, the brutal abuse of

August 1968: Chicago police beating
young demonstrators.

demonstrators and, in some instances, members of the press continued unabated, spreading to other venues in the city. I called the commander of the federal forces in the area and told him that deployment of troops might be necessary. Ultimately it was not. The fury of the Chicago police was spent before the situation reached that point.

The Chicago police riot was fully documented on television. It played and replayed on TV sets all over the convention hall, as the delegates prepared for the roll call on the presidential nomination. Worried about the possible need for federal troops at the convention that night, I watched TV only intermittently. When Senator Abe Ribicoff placed George McGovern's name in nomination, he shouted down from the podium that there would be no Gestapo tactics in the streets of Chicago when McGovern became president. A red-faced Mayor Daley, sitting in the Illinois delegation, leapt to his feet, shook his fist, and shouted an obscenity at Ribicoff, which for those watching on television required little in the way of lip-reading skills to decipher.

At the outset of the Chicago convention, President Johnson had harbored the secret hope that the delegates might turn to him despite his earlier withdrawal from the race. Holed up at his Texas ranch, Johnson kept tabs on the proceedings through constant telephone calls to aides in Chicago. But the roll call, unlike the rest of convention week, proceeded more or less as predicted. By about midnight on Wednesday, Hubert

Humphrey had prevailed over Eugene McCarthy and George McGovern by more than a thousand delegate votes. Humphrey had won the prize, but given the events of the day and the week, whether it was worth having was questionable. Beyond the violence and disarray that had been broadcast to the world, many Democrats saw Humphrey as shackled to the failed Johnson war policy. No one could remember a convention that had evoked so much bitterness or a nomination that generated so little immediate enthusiasm.

A JUSTICE DENIED

The series of seismic events that marked 1968 went beyond disruption in the streets. On the morning of June 13, 1968, Supreme Court chief justice Earl Warren paid an unnoticed visit to the White House. Alone with the president, he said that after fourteen years as its leader he wanted to step down from the Court.

I had known Warren slightly in California when he was governor and came to know him better after I became deputy attorney general. White-haired and barrel-chested, he was larger than life in both physical and historical stature. He was revered for leading the Supreme Court to the unanimous, epochal desegregation decision in *Brown v. Board of Education* in 1954. It was a decision I had hoped for and fashioned in my mind while clerking for Justice William O. Douglas in the 1949 term of the Court.

Lyndon Johnson realized instantly that Warren's decision to leave the Court gave him one last opportunity to make history, a chance he did not intend to miss. When Warren's written statement of resignation was delivered, Johnson responded with a note: "I will accept your decision to retire effective at such time as a successor is qualified." Johnson wanted to ensure that Warren would remain at the helm of the Court if something went awry in the confirmation process. This strategy ultimately raised more problems than it solved.

To succeed Warren as chief justice, Johnson chose Supreme Court associate justice Abe Fortas, his close friend and, as I had witnessed during our Detroit-riot deliberations, his regular adviser. Years earlier, I had encountered Fortas when each of us represented defendants in a major antitrust case in Los Angeles. His performance was equal to his reputation as one of the most brilliant lawyers in the nation. Johnson's decision to tap him for chief justice was hardly a surprise. It was an open secret that Abe Fortas had the inside track for the job if Johnson was ever given the chance to appoint him. Now that chance had come.

On June 26, the president announced the nomination of Fortas for chief justice, and that of Federal Circuit Court of Appeals justice Homer Thornberry to replace him as associate justice. The Fortas nomination seemed headed for quick success. He had friends and admirers on both sides of the aisle. Republican senator Robert Griffin of Michigan announced his opposition, grounded principally in a desire to save the chief justice nomination for what he hoped would be a Republican president after the November election. Few other Republicans joined him. However, when the Judiciary Committee met to discuss the upcoming hearings, Democratic senator Sam Ervin of North Carolina, a former state supreme court justice and a constitutional expert, questioned whether there was, as a matter of law, a vacancy in the chief justice position. He claimed that a resignation conditioned on the confirmation of a successor was no resignation at all. When powerful Republican senator Howard Baker echoed Ervin's concern, the issue was joined.

One of the duties that fell to me as deputy attorney general was to process and support judicial nominations to the federal courts. The vast majority of those nominations involved nominees at district court and court of appeals levels. But on June 27, 1968, shortly after Senator Ervin fired his shot across the bow of the Fortas nomination, the president called to ask for my help. He wanted legal support for the proposition that Chief Justice Warren's resignation was valid and effective.

Following the president's call, I immediately turned to one of my law school professors, Charles Fairman, who was regarded as one of the leading authorities on the history of the Supreme Court. After a week of intensive research, Fairman produced an analysis concluding that the wording of Warren's resignation was not only appropriate but was the "mode of succession most in the public interest." Fairman anchored the argument with a showing that Justice Horace Gray, who had left the Court after a debilitating stroke in 1902, had resigned on about the same terms as Warren, and that President Theodore Roosevelt had accepted the resignation with substantially identical language to that used by President Johnson. Johnson directed me to deliver a copy of the Fairman material to Everett Dirksen, the Republican minority leader, and it was published in the *Congressional Record*. Dirksen then telephoned Fairman and afterward reported the exchange on the floor of the Senate. When Florida senator George Smathers asked if Fairman was a crony of his, Dirksen said, "He was a second lieutenant in the artillery in World War One. So was I. That makes us close cronies."

Attorney General Clark, as the first witness at the Fortas/Thornberry confirmation hearing, relied on the Fairman material and seemed to put the resignation question to rest. By the time Abe Fortas strode to the table before the Senate Judiciary Committee on July 16, 1968, everyone expected smooth sailing. But while Fortas conducted himself well, certain uncomfortable facts emerged. Senators questioned him about published reports that he had continued his relationship as a friend and adviser to the president while serving on the Supreme Court.

Fortas's answers about when and why he talked to Lyndon Johnson were disingenuous, evasive, and sometimes wrong. Under heavy fire, Fortas tried to defuse the charge that he had improperly stepped beyond his constitutional role by saying he had only helped the president by summarizing arguments, pro and con. In a deliberative body where the right to summarize someone else's argument was known to spell the difference between victory and defeat, the answer did not help, and the grilling continued.

When he was not under questioning about his relationship to Johnson, Fortas was subjected to exquisitely detailed questions from three Southern senators—Sam Ervin of North Carolina, Strom Thurmond of South Carolina, and John McClellan of Arkansas—about his Supreme Court decisions. In keeping with the practice and wisdom of the day, in the face of these questions Fortas generally refused to comment on his judicial performances or philosophy. The Judiciary Committee members fumed. After thirteen days of questioning, they still refused to vote on the nomination.

In the midst of this contretemps, I was called before the committee to explain a Department of Justice memorandum that had been prepared at the request of Democratic senator Phil Hart. The memorandum, intended to fill the gap left by Fortas's refusal to discuss his votes on the Court, addressed and placed in context the key controversial decisions. Though intended for use by Hart without attribution to the Justice Department, for some reason the senator credited the department as author when he introduced the memorandum into the record. Senator Ervin then demanded that someone from Justice appear to answer questions about the memorandum. Enter that "someone": Warren Christopher.

As the representative of the Justice Department, I instantly became a surrogate punching bag for Justice Fortas. To mix the metaphor, I was red meat for the Southern conservatives, who saw Fortas as a dangerous liberal. Senators Ervin and Thurmond came to the hearing table on Tuesday, July 23, 1968, my day in the hot seat, licking their chops.

The festivities began with questioning by Ervin. He was agitated, very agitated, that Fortas had voted with the Court's majority in holding that the Sixth Amendment guarantee of a right to jury trial extended to criminal contempt cases. The decision, said the senator, flew in the face of twenty prior Supreme Court decisions on the question, spanning a period of 178 years. That, said Ervin, was characteristic of the Warren Court's practice of "tak[ing] precedent after precedent and cast[ing] it into the judicial garbage can."

Ervin then tried to extract from me an endorsement of the view that the Court had exhibited shameful disregard for precedent. I first tried something resembling a direct response. I referred to an instance in which Ervin as a justice of the North Carolina Supreme Court had himself overruled an earlier decision, noting that "the importance of being right sometimes overwhelms the importance of following prior precedent." Ervin, ignoring his own precedent, persisted in asking variants of the same question, hoping for a less guarded answer. In response, I withdrew to variants of the statement that my views were irrelevant to the question of Justice Fortas's competence to serve as chief justice.

First I tried: "Senator Ervin, if I may, I would like to indicate what I regard to be the unimportance of my views on that subject." That was not successful. In the next go-round I said: "I would be delighted to talk with you about those legal questions. But I would say that I would not want the expression of my personal views to delay the hearings." Again, Ervin would not move on. He was absolutely determined to show that Fortas was what he called "a judicial activist," defined by him as "an occupant of a judicial office who is willing to interpret the Constitution, not according to what the Constitution says, but according to what the Constitution would have said if he had written it."

I made one more effort: "Senator, with all due respect, I would like to say again that whether I agree with you does not seem to me to be the issue here. The issue here is whether or not a majority of this committee regards the nominee as qualified." Though Ervin persisted, he was eventually convinced that I was not going to share my personal views on the merits of Fortas's decisions. After a sarcastic rebuke to me ("I did not bring you down here to examine you about the flowers that bloom in the spring, tra-la"), Ervin took a different tack. He pressed me to say whether Justice Fortas himself should have taken the heat of the questions to which I was being subjected.

With mock Southern gentility, he asked whether there was "any obligation on the part of the man who held a judicial office to remove from a senator's mind what may possibly be a misconstruction of his position on an opinion?" I replied, "[A] justice's highest duty is to honor the independence of the judiciary by declining to be called to answer by another branch of the government, sir."

Ervin was displeased with my response but shortly thereafter concluded our exchange, at least for the moment. Though yielding to allow other senators to question me, he soon returned to the fray, embarking on a soliloquy that started with a prolonged, historically footnoted attack on Fortas's inappropriate assistance to the president and ended with Ervin's announcement of a proposed constitutional amendment to alter the process for approving Supreme Court justices, an approach that would have required the president to make his choices from a list generated by federal judges. When Ervin had finished, it was lunchtime.

I hurried back to the department for a moment of repose. As I nursed a chicken sandwich, I did what any trial lawyer does when there's a pause in a hostile cross-examination of his witness: figure out where the questioning is going next. Because in this case I was also the witness under siege, I had something less than a clear head. I was able, however, to check off the various topics covered in the morning session against a mental checklist of issues I had believed might be raised. It took a little while to realize what was coming, but when it came to me, it put a charge up my spine. No one had asked me about Fortas's decisions on obscenity, and more to the point, Senator Strom Thurmond, the self-appointed ringmaster of the obscenity issue, had not yet had his moment in the sun. It was going to be a long afternoon.

When the hearing resumed, Thurmond lost no time in getting to his favorite subject. He read aloud graphic descriptions of films that had been ruled "hard-core pornography" by a Los Angeles federal judge, a decision subsequently reversed by the Supreme Court, with Justice Fortas voting in the majority. When Thurmond finished, he looked up from his reading material. Then he looked down at me:

Q. "I just want to ask you this. You probably have a family, don't you?"

A. "Yes, sir."

Q. "You would not want your wife or daughter to see a film that was [like the film I have just described], would you?"

A. "Well, I have not seen the film, Senator. The description does not make it sound like a family entertainment."

Thurmond was neither entertained by nor particularly interested in my answer. I was, in effect, a prop to be used in facilitating his performance. He summarized other material banned as pornographic by lower courts but held by the Supreme Court to be within the protection of the First Amendment. Again I was called upon to register my personal revulsion. I tried a version of my "Ervin deflection":

"Senator, with great respect, I would like to reiterate what I have said this morning. The issue in this hearing, as I understand it, is not what my views are, or what the views of the lawyers of the Department of Justice are. The issue is whether or not a majority of this committee thinks that Justice Fortas . . . [is] qualified [to be chief justice]. The hearing has gone on for a number of days, longer, I believe, than any other hearing at which justices have appeared as witnesses. I would not want to protract it by a statement of my views, which I think to be quite irrelevant to the purpose for which the hearing is being held, sir."

Thurmond was diverted, for the moment, from further pursuing my personal reaction to pornographic material. We moved to the subject of the law, on which I felt on somewhat firmer ground. Thurmond wanted me to explain how Fortas could have voted twenty-six times to reverse lower-court findings that material was obscene and suggested there was apparently no subject matter on which Fortas would sustain an obscenity conviction. I saw an opening—a chance to discuss substance—and I ran for it, serving up a discourse on the three kinds of cases in which Fortas had demonstrated he was prepared to sustain obscenity convictions.

Thurmond was drawn temporarily into the discussion, but soon realized that the afternoon was waning and he had allowed the record to wander from the material of which newspaper stories were made. So he drew the discussion back to the stuff, rather than the law, of obscenity. He complained to me:

"[A] magazine that came through the mail to me is obscene, it is foul, it is putrid, it is filthy, it is repulsive, it is objectionable, it is obnoxious, and it should cause a flush of shame to the cheeks of the members of the Supreme Court who affirmed decisions that allow such material as this to go through the mails. This is called the *Weekend Jaybird,* which was handed to me—I believe yesterday—by an interested citizen. Now, I want to hand that down to you.

"[I] want to hand you that and ask you if the Justice Department approves of publications of this kind, obscene publications, being sent through the mail."

The faint taste of chicken sandwich materialized at the back of my throat as an aide to the senator approached me with *Weekend Jaybird.* I looked at it briefly, then spoke:

"Senator, the question is not whether the Justice Department approves of this material. The question is whether or not a prosecution can constitutionally be mounted. But I would want to say again it seems to me we are straying a long way from the central issue in these proceedings, and that is not whether I or any other lawyer in the Department of Justice is outraged or made to feel nauseated by particular material, but rather whether Justice Fortas [is] so well qualified that [he is] entitled to receive the favorable view of the majority of this committee."

Thurmond would not be diverted:

Q. "Do you think this material that I have just handed to you from the newsstands is wholesome material to be sold to people on the streets?"

A. "With all respect, Senator, what I think about it is almost totally irrelevant. I do not think it wholesome. But I really implore you to permit me to answer the questions which are relevant to this hearing."

Thurmond had his audience now, and he was not about to lose it:

Q. "Why are you not surprised at this filthy, obscene material which you are looking at . . . ?"

A. "Because it has become commonplace in our society, not only in the United States but elsewhere, for there to be magazines of a girlie character."

Perhaps the muted chuckles from the audience, responding to the unintended primness of my phrase, turned the tide. Whatever the cause, shortly after our exchange Thurmond receded, and thankfully, the hearing ended.

Thurmond and like-minded senators rode the pornography issue for further delay, and the Senate adjourned for its August recess with the Fortas nomination still languishing in the Judiciary Committee. The delay provided just enough time for detonation of a time bomb that further undermined Fortas's chances.

When the hearings reopened in early September, the dean of the American University Law School testified that Fortas had been paid $15,000 for teaching a substantively modest seminar at the law school. The funds for the seminar had been donated by six prominent businessmen from New York whose widespread interests might well have evolved into Supreme Court litigation. If handled properly, the teaching and even the payments might not have been a problem, but the last-minute disclosure and the identities of the donors added new weight to the opposition.

As the struggle continued, the president grew increasingly fretful. One night the telephone rang at my home well after midnight. I jumped out of bed to stop the ringing before it woke our children. In my haste, I banged my toe hard on the bed frame. As I hopped around the dark bedroom on one foot, the White House operator informed me that the president was calling. When Johnson came on the line, he told me he had in hand the early edition of the *Washington Post*. My toe throbbed.

The president complained that although the editorial of the day addressed the matter of the Supreme Court nominations, it had failed to acknowledge the excellence of Judge Thornberry, his nominee to replace Fortas upon elevation. I listened while trying not to convey that I was in excruciating pain. Somehow I managed to get through several more exchanges with the president without letting on. I told the president that in the morning, first thing, I would call my contact at the *Post* and try to convince him that Judge Thornberry was unusually well qualified. I hung up and spent the rest of the night waiting, in pain, for first light. When it came, I delayed a call to my friend at the *Post*. Instead, I went directly to an emergency room, where I learned that my toe was fractured.

The Judiciary Committee sent the Fortas nomination to the floor on September 17, much later than Johnson had hoped and planned for. Support for Fortas had sharply eroded, and by early October it was clear that friends of the nomination could not gather the sixty votes to stop a threatened filibuster. In fact, they could probably not even muster a majority. Lyndon Johnson knew how to count noses, and he knew when to cut his losses. On October 10, the Fortas nomination was withdrawn.

The tragedy of Abe Fortas was not over. Following the election of Richard Nixon as president, a second bomb exploded. William Lambert, a *Life* reporter, revealed that Fortas had a complex financial relationship with a convicted financier, Louis Wolfson. Fortas had accepted a $20,000 payment from the Wolfson Family Foundation (returned eleven months later) and had entered into a lifetime contract to advise the foundation on educational and civil rights projects. With his credibility gone and Nixon in hot pursuit, Fortas sent his resignation from the Court to the White House on June 14, 1969.

The relationship between the president and Attorney General Ramsey Clark was another casualty of the Fortas wars. Ramsey, son of Johnson's intimate friend U.S. Supreme Court justice Tom Clark, had been a Johnson favorite, but in the Fortas fight Ramsey Clark made a tactical error. Senator Richard Russell, now in the twilight of his legendary career, was Johnson's mentor and closest friend in the Senate. As the acknowledged leader of the Southern Democrats, his commitment to support Fortas was a linchpin of Johnson's strategy. In the midst of the Fortas controversy, Russell proposed Alexander Lawrence Jr. for a federal judgeship in Georgia, assuming the nomination would be processed promptly. However, Clark had reports of segregationist speeches by Lawrence and refused to be rushed. Johnson was furious. After receiving an angry letter from Russell, Johnson stepped in and virtually ordered the nomination made, but it was too late. Russell said he felt released from his commitment and announced his opposition to the Fortas nomination.

THE END OF A YEAR OF TUMULT

By tradition, top Justice Department officials do not take an active role in political campaigns, and I did not. However, as election day loomed closer, I fully understood that my future was riding on the results. If Humphrey won, we might well be staying in government. If he lost, we'd be heading for the private sector.

On election night, November 5, Marie and I watched as the lead seesawed back and forth between Humphrey and Nixon, with Wallace running strong in the South. We turned in at about 1 A.M., with the race undecided. The next morning, the *Today* show told us that key states had shifted to Nixon, who was now projected to win by less than 1 percent of the vote.

I went to work on that gloomy Wednesday morning with only a vague notion of what I was going to do next. Before I had finished my first cup of coffee, a call came from Los Angeles. It was John O'Melveny, the head of the law firm I had left eighteen months earlier, O'Melveny & Myers. He had been my mentor and friend from nearly the day I'd arrived at his firm in 1950. He had gone to great lengths to make me, a committed Democrat, comfortable in his overwhelmingly conservative firm. His efforts had succeeded. When he called me that Wednesday morning in November 1968, I was overwhelmed by nostalgia and a desire to get out of Washington. O'Melveny, probably knowing he had reached me at a vulnerable moment, told me he wanted me back at the firm and had a generous proposal to make it happen. I nearly said yes on the spot, but realized it was a bad time to commit to anything. I told him I had enormous affection for the firm and for California, but I needed time to decide.

After a few weeks, I'd been approached with offers by several law firms in the East, putting urgently before me the question of where I was going next. It was a hard call. Despite the tumult of 1968, I was still high on government service and wanted to keep open the possibility of a return. Staying in Washington seemed the most obvious way to do that. On the other hand, California and O'Melveny & Myers were my home, a fact that my family and Mr. O'Melveny kept squarely in my sights.

Ultimately, I reasoned that my chances for a return to public service were at least as good if I lived in Los Angeles as if I stayed on the East Coast. In addition, I've had the good fortune to be attracted to public service, but not obsessed by it. So it was back to L.A.

Packing to go home was my first opportunity for personal reflection in my year and a half in Washington. Only then did the magnitude of what I had lived through dawn on me. I had been near the helm of the American ship of state as it traversed a period of urban violence unparalleled in its history. Two icons of the disadvantaged had been assassinated within a two-month period, bringing the nation close to insurrection.

The tumult of 1967–68 left me with more than the right to say that I was on the bridge at a critical moment. I came away with a strong empathy for the wretched and despairing in our society, particularly those in the inner cities, and for what they had to endure. I understood, as I had not before my Washington assignment, that short-term, violent "solutions" may seem appealing to those without hope. My own largely monochromatic life had been changed, permanently and profoundly, by my face-to-face encounters with the burdens of nonwhite Americans.

I had learned other lessons as well. Watching the

tragedy of Lyndon Johnson play out in his final excruciating year showed me that great achievements and worthy intentions are inadequate counterweights to being on the wrong side of history on a cosmic issue, and that the support of the American people is the sine qua non of an overseas commitment of American troops. When almost every element of society—the business community, the churches, the press, students, and intellectual leaders—turns against him, even a very gifted leader cannot survive.

5

♦

A NEW VENUE

"CYRUS VANCE IS CALLING," MY SECRETARY said. It was December 11, 1976. Cy came on the line and, characteristically, wasted no time on pleasantries. "Chris, the president has asked me to be secretary of state, and I want you to be my deputy."

The call threw me off-balance. Usually, stirrings in the press or thumpings on the tribal telegraph from friends give advance notice that something is in the works. This time no drums preceded the event.

Though taken aback, I was delighted by Vance's proposal. My conservative side told me, however, that rather than accept on the spot, I should talk with him about what he had in mind. I suggested that I fly to New York to see him. He agreed, but I could tell he was humoring me. As always, Cy knew exactly what he wanted and couldn't imagine there was anything left to talk about.

I was somewhat reluctant to return to Washington after nearly a decade in California. After finishing my service as deputy attorney general in January 1969, I had gone back to my Los Angeles law firm, O'Melveny & Myers, and again immersed myself in my practice and community issues.

I had not really looked for chances to return to the national stage, but one intriguing opportunity did present itself during the interregnum between the end of the Johnson administration and Cy Vance's call in 1976. In May 1973, as a result of the now-famous "third-rate burglary" at the Watergate complex in Washington, D.C., I received a telephone call from Elliot Richardson, Nixon's secretary of defense. The president had decided to name Richardson attorney general, and, to be confirmed by the Democrat-controlled Senate, Richardson would apparently have to name a special prosecutor to investigate the Watergate case. He set about finding a judge or lawyer the Senate would accept as both qualified and independent enough to produce a credible review of the facts.

I took Richardson's call without any idea of why he wanted to talk to me. I had known him through mutual friends, but certainly not intimately. He got to the point quickly. He wanted me to come to Washington to talk about the job of special prosecutor for the Watergate investigation. Calls for an independent probe filled the press, and I was interested enough that I decided to invest in a trip East.

As Richardson was still secretary of defense, our meeting took place in his Pentagon office. I was ushered into his presence by a military aide, and then we were alone. Richardson, gifted with every patrician attribute—intelligence, looks, charm—did not seem to be himself. As he explained to me what the special prosecutor was supposed to do and for whom he would do it, he stumbled and even seemed to sweat a little. On reflection, I think these were manifestations of his discomfort with trying to sell me on what he perhaps knew to be a flawed concept.

The devil in the details Richardson presented about the special prosecutor job was that the White House and the attorney general would maintain ultimate control over the Watergate investigation. While I had no reason to doubt Richardson's good faith in saying he wanted the prosecutor to function independently, he was under the thumb of a president about whom I had substantial doubts. As we reviewed the guidelines Richardson had drafted, I noted in particular that the president, if displeased with the direction of the investigation and if unable to persuade his attorney general to fire the special prosecutor, could bring about the same result by firing the attorney general. Richardson said nothing about that possibility.

After about an hour of discussion, I told Richardson I wanted to think about the proposition. I left him and took a long, solitary walk around Washington to ponder the issues. After a few hours of ruminating, I telephoned Richardson to tell him I thought the structure of the job was unworkable and that I had decided to return to Los Angeles. A reporter caught me at the airport and asked if I was going to be the special prosecutor. I told him the position did not provide the requisite independence and that I was going home.

Five months later—Saturday night, October 20, 1973—the president fired Attorney General Elliot Richardson for refusing to dismiss Special Watergate Prosecutor Archibald Cox. Deputy Attorney General William Ruckelshaus also resigned rather than do the deed, and it was left to Solicitor General Robert Bork to follow Nixon's lead and administer the coup de grâce to Cox. There but for the grace of a mind-clearing walk around Washington was I.

While I had managed to dodge that bullet in 1973, as I flew across the country to meet with Vance, I could not shake the concern that I knew little about how the State Department operated. I mentioned that misgiving to Cy at the start of our meeting in New York, but he brushed it aside. He said that qualities other than foreign policy or State Department expertise were important to him. He wanted someone he could trust without reservation, someone who could serve as his alter ego in all things. Even if I'd been inclined to do so, there was no way to turn down an offer phrased that way from a man like Cy Vance. So it was moving time again for the Christopher family.

Foggy Bottom

The offices of the secretary and deputy secretary of state on the seventh floor of the State Department are like no others in Washington. As a result of gracious donations from many Americans and canny decisions by a professional staff of curators, these large, graceful rooms are furnished with museum-quality American antiques. The setting befits a world of visiting ministers and ambassadors, a world in which démarches and protests, treaties and executive agreements, are the stuff of daily life. I had been on only the periphery of this world when I negotiated textile agreements for the State Department in the early 1960s. Because my work was done mainly in foreign capitals, I was a stranger to much of the department.

At the Department of Justice, the amenities had been principally functional and the focus of daily business easier to define—in largest part, the facts and consequences of criminal and civil litigation. But differences in furniture and subject matter were inconsequential in comparison to the differences in the missions and people of the two institutions.

In the ebb and flow of the executive branch, the Justice Department generally stands off by itself, soliciting or accepting guidance from the White House on a limited subset of the matters for which it has responsibility. The people of the department are independent, sometimes very independent, lawyers who tend to regard the pursuit of justice as a sacrosanct, lonely mission. As a result, they brook "interference" from other arms of the government grudgingly, if at all.

The State Department functions as part of a cooperative and (only theoretically) seamless foreign policy mechanism that includes the White House, National Security Council, Defense Department, and Central Intelligence Agency. State is the place where the languages of diplomacy and often arcane specialties are spoken. The air of erudition that prevails at State is heightened because the majority of those who are employed there are survivors of the demanding Foreign Service system, a merit-driven mechanism designed to ensure that only the best rise to the top of the diplomatic ladder.

It was going to be a very different life for me. When I had been appointed deputy attorney general in the Justice Department, I felt I knew and had done enough as a lawyer to hold my own. But as a deputy secretary of state drafted from outside the foreign policy apparatus, I was going to have to draw on the expertise of others in my decision-making—at least in the beginning.

After reporting for work at State in January 1977, I adopted a standard procedure when an unfamiliar problem came to my desk. I'd call desk officers, ask them to bring up the maps and give me a thorough geographic and substantive briefing. I soon came to regard the Foreign Service people at State as a kind of living diplomatic encyclopedia. They were uncannily accurate and usually free of political agendas, although as part of their seminars I was occasionally treated to efforts to revive already decided issues. I found great advantage in working with the Foreign Service, rather than in trying to insulate myself from it, as presidential appointees sometimes do when joining this vast, able bureaucracy.

PANAMA CANAL TREATIES

Early in the Carter administration I was severely tested by an intense struggle to persuade the Senate to exercise its constitutionally mandated responsibility by ratifying two treaties on the Panama Canal. The agreements were needed to replace the anachronistic and tainted 1903 treaty that had given the United States perpetual sole control of the Canal and the Canal Zone. This ugly remnant of colonialism had long cast a shadow over our Latin American policy.

We were not the first administration to notice this problem. In 1964, President Johnson had launched negotiations intended to produce a new relationship with Panama, but they stalled over political issues in both countries. Henry Kissinger had achieved a major breakthrough in 1974, when he and the Panamanian foreign minister had agreed on a set of principles to guide further negotiations. But the process got sidetracked by the fight over the 1976 Republican presidential nomination, during which Ronald Reagan

The Panama Canal.

charged that the Ford administration proposed a give-away of a strategic U.S. asset. Reagan's slogan on the Panama Canal issue—"We bought it, we paid for it, it's ours, and we're going to keep it"—never failed to draw applause on the stump. Though he failed to win the nomination, his campaign succeeded in generating concern and skepticism within the American public about the wisdom of "giving back" the Canal.

Notwithstanding Reagan's poisoning of the well, in his first weeks in office in 1977, Carter decided to tackle the issue. He recognized that although the public did not want to give up the Panama Canal, holding it without a change in the treaty risked acts of sabotage and threatened our relations with the hemisphere as a whole. The president picked two tough negotia-tors—senior ambassadors Ellsworth Bunker and Sol

Linowitz—and gave them broad authority to forge a solution.

Bunker and Linowitz conceived the idea of negotiating two treaties, one that would give the United States the permanent right to defend the Canal (the Neutrality Treaty) and a second that would transfer control of the Canal to Panama on January 1, 2000 (the Panama Canal Treaty). There were obvious political advantages to pinning down our right to defend the Canal before addressing the transfer of control. Vance asked me to help supervise the negotiators. After months of talks with the Panamanians, they had agreed on treaties that accomplished both goals. The documents were signed—the first step to ratification—on September 7, 1977.

A firestorm was not far behind the signing ceremony. Senate hearings that started in late September 1977 revealed powerful opposition, and the Panamanians exacerbated our problems by leaking questionable interpretations of the treaties to the press to deflect their own domestic opposition. The outcry in the Senate grew so loud that Majority Leader Robert Byrd of West Virginia decided to postpone until early 1978 bringing the treaties to the floor for debate.

In the interim, President Carter and Panamanian president Omar Torrijos had addressed one of the key issues that enflamed the opposition: U.S. defense of the Canal. Opponents claimed that the Neutrality Treaty left the United States without a clear right to protect the Canal from a hostile takeover. The Carter-

Torrijos statement confirming that the United States would have a permanent right to defend the Canal became the centerpiece of speeches that Vance, Defense Secretary Harold Brown, and I made across the country to rally support for the treaties. While we did manage to increase public support, progress came slowly. When the debate opened in the Senate on February 8, 1978, we calculated that we were a dozen votes short of the sixty-seven needed for ratification.

Carter and Vance made me the point man for rounding up the remaining votes. Though I had never regarded myself as a lobbyist or even a good salesman, I devoted nearly two months of my time to the care and feeding of U.S. senators. At the outset,

Rallying support for Panama Canal treaties.
From the left are former senator Hugh Scott,
former president Gerald Ford, Averell Harriman,
Henry Kissinger, and the author.

twelve votes didn't seem like so many, but as time passed they began to look unattainable.

The Neutrality Treaty—the document intended to ensure that the United States would have the perpetual right to keep the Canal open—was the first to be debated. I soon learned that various senators wanted to offer amendments to the treaty, any one of which, if passed, would have required us to return to the Panamanians for approval, and likely doomed our efforts. Some of the proposed amendments were designed by die-hard opponents simply to kill the treaty, but we believed we had the votes to beat these efforts back.

Other proposed amendments came from senators who were looking for a way to cover themselves politically while voting for the treaties. They needed some way to tell constituents that they had ensured that America's security interests would not be compromised by returning the Canal to Panama. In speaking to senators in this group, I urged that they frame their proposals as "reservations" or "conditions" attached to the resolution of ratification, rather than as amendments. By doing so, they could protect themselves while sparing us the need to go to the Panamanians for a new round of negotiations and another plebiscite.

On March 10, I met for lunch with the leading Senate supporters of the treaty in the office of Majority Leader Byrd. I had drafted a condition, intended to respond to concerns expressed by several senators, stating that nothing in the treaty precluded the parties from agreeing that U.S. military forces could remain in Panama after the year 2000. I argued that this condition gave senators a way both to put their stamp on the treaty and to clarify its intent. Because Georgia's Senator Sam Nunn was up for reelection that year, Senator Byrd suggested he be given the opportunity to offer my condition on the floor. He did so, along with his Georgia colleague, Herman Talmadge, and both took the occasion to announce their support for the treaty.

Every one of the remaining ten votes needed to bring us to sixty-seven seemed to be a special case. I had many meetings with Dennis DeConcini, a freshman Democratic senator from Arizona, who had not decided how he would vote but was leaning toward no. He was under intense pressure from his fellow Arizona senator, Barry Goldwater, the Republican presidential nominee in 1964, to oppose both treaties on the ground that they didn't adequately protect U.S. interests in keeping the Canal operating. Though I persuaded DeConcini to abandon plans to offer a "killer" amendment, he demanded in return that he be permitted to sponsor a condition. It appeared that if I could satisfy him, we would win not only his vote but that of two other senators who were inclined to follow his lead. I suggested he offer a condition that stated in general terms that if the Canal was closed, either party could take steps to reopen it or restore its operations. DeConcini said that might be acceptable, but only with the addition of the phrase *including the use of military force in Panama.*

Though consistent with the intent of the condition I had suggested, I knew the addition of DeConcini's phrase would be read by the Panamanians as a license to intervene in their internal affairs. Late on March 15, as he dressed for a congressional dinner, I visited him to discuss the problem. I urged him to remove, at a minimum, the words *in Panama,* as they could easily sink the treaties. DeConcini finished dressing and, as he exited for the dinner, said he'd think about it.

I received a call from DeConcini at eight-thirty the next morning as I sat waiting to see the president at the White House. DeConcini said he had turned the matter over in his mind overnight but could not agree to delete any part of his phrase. Faced with the hardest facts of all—the numbers—the president decided to accept DeConcini's words and hope for the best.

As we expected, when the Panamanians learned of the DeConcini condition, they exploded. We explored various ways to soften the words but without success. Eventually, the problem solved itself, at least temporarily, when the Panamanians soberly concluded that the Senate vote count was simply too fragile to enable them to insist on an immediate fix. To help them save face, we agreed to try to address the problem of DeConcini's language in the second treaty.

The March 16 roll call on the Neutrality Treaty was nerve-racking. The president had pulled out all the stops in his efforts to sway undecided senators, but no one knew for sure whether we had the votes. Vance and I paced back and forth in the vice president's office in the Capitol as the roll was called. Only when the last names were called did we know we had won— by one vote more than the necessary two-thirds.

Debate on the second treaty, the one that would return the Canal to Panamanian control on January 1, 2000, had barely begun when on March 21 Carter heard from President Torrijos. He was calling in our commitment to try to insert language in the second treaty that would "fix" the DeConcini condition in the first. Unfortunately, things were headed in the opposite direction. Senator DeConcini wanted his condition repeated in the second treaty.

To reassure the Panamanians and to pacify DeConcini, I conceived the idea of using a repetition of the condition in a way that would also restate the principle that the United States would not intervene in the internal affairs of Panama. With the help of the Senate Democratic leadership, over the next few weeks I produced several drafts of proposed language, but none satisfied DeConcini. If we were going to pass the second treaty, something or someone had to budge.

Finally the Senate Democratic leadership asserted itself. Senator Byrd asked me to arrange for him and key treaty supporters to meet with Panama's highly regarded ambassador, Gabriel Lewis. We gathered in Idaho senator Frank Church's office on Sunday morning, April 16, most of us dressed in sports coats and sweaters. With Ambassador Lewis looking on, the senators argued over my latest draft, then began to produce a version of their own.

With no secretary in sight, Senator Church sat down at a typewriter and began to bang out a new document. At one point he was relieved at the keyboard by Maryland senator Paul Sarbanes. By the time the typing ended, the assembled senators had both an intellectual investment and substantial sweat equity in the product. Their version provided that any exercise by the United States of its right to keep the Canal open would not be interpreted as a right of intervention in the internal affairs of Panama or as interference with its political independence. Senator DeConcini's interest in keeping the Canal open with force, if necessary, would be preserved, while the Panamanians had face-saving language to cite to their constituency.

With the new draft in hand, Vice President Mondale and I flew to Camp David to brief President Carter. At about 9 P.M. that night, the Panamanians

With Vice President Mondale,
helicoptering to Camp David.

called Camp David to accept the new version, describing it as a "dignified solution to a difficult problem." When I called to report this development to Senator Byrd, he asked me to return to Washington to brief the Senate leadership on Monday morning.

I wasn't present when the Democratic leadership met with DeConcini, but I imagine they told him that, as a freshman senator, he had made a name for himself in the Panama Canal negotiations and it was now time to accept his victory gracefully. Whatever they said, DeConcini publicly endorsed the leadership draft the following day, and on that same day, April 18, the second treaty passed by the identical 68–32 vote as the Neutrality Treaty.

CHINA NORMALIZATION

With the Panama Canal fight behind him, President Carter turned his attention to another foreign policy priority, China. Six years earlier, during the Nixon administration, the United States and China had agreed that their goal was to normalize their relations—that is, to exchange ambassadors and to establish all of the other indicia of full diplomatic ties. Neither Nixon nor Ford had been able to make that happen; Jimmy Carter wanted to be the one who did.

The path to normalization revealed the tension between Secretary Vance and National Security Adviser Zbigniew Brzezinski. When they were appointed, the two had vowed to work together harmoniously, but their agendas and styles were so different that confrontation was all but inevitable. Vance was determined to build a U.S.-Soviet relationship that would enhance prospects for arms control. Zbig, with his Polish heritage, was hostile toward the Soviets and looked for any opportunity to thwart them. He saw enhanced U.S.-China relations as a potential counterweight in the struggle between Washington and Moscow. Vance was polished and courtly, while Zbig was colorful and feisty. Zbig loved media attention; Vance barely tolerated it.

One of my first instructions from Vance was to tamp down any moves by our subordinates that would abrade the NSC staff. He refused to play the bureaucratic games of the Washington insiders, the tricks seen with unusual frequency in dealings between the State Department and the NSC. While I followed Cy's instructions to the letter, I could not eliminate the fundamental friction that characterized his relationship with Zbig. In the case of China, that friction manifested itself as a dispute over the announcement date for a normalization agreement, a seemingly simple decision fraught with significant diplomatic meaning.

Vance made his first visit to China as secretary in August 1977. Though normalization was at the top of his agenda, he realized this was not the moment for definitive negotiations on the issue. The Panama Canal treaties were front and center in the Senate, and he and Carter calculated that neither the public nor the legislative branch could digest major changes on two important national security issues simultaneously. Vance handled the problem by taking a position on normalization that he knew the Chinese would likely reject. He told them he wanted to preserve an official U.S. consulate on Taiwan while establishing formal relations with the PRC. Characterizing Vance's proposal as a retreat from positions taken by Presidents Nixon and Ford, the Chinese responded as expected and rejected it.

Following Vance's visit and the successful conclusion of the Panama Canal debates, Brzezinski implored Carter to give him a chance at China normalization talks. Over Vance's objections, Carter agreed, and Brzezinski arrived in Beijing on May 20, 1978. Zbig, in the role of suitor, told the Chinese that if normalization proceeded, we would sell them previously withheld U.S. technology and help them acquire advanced weapons from our European allies. The Chinese were plainly impressed with this news and indicated that Zbig's advances were welcome. By the end of the meetings, there was an agreement to complete normalization negotiations by mid-December 1978.

Carter chose Leonard Woodcock, head of the U.S. liaison office in Beijing, to handle the negotiations in China. At the State Department, Vance was able to share details on the progress of the talks only with me and Dick Holbrooke, then the young assistant secretary for East Asia. Through the summer and fall, we inched toward agreement, agonizing over every nuance. For example, we tried to get China to say that it was committed to a peaceful outcome on Taiwan, but the best we could do was an understanding that the United States would call for a peaceful resolution at the time of normalization and China would not dispute the U.S. position.

When Vance left for the Middle East in mid-December 1978, he believed he had an understanding with the president that if agreement was reached with China on normalization, there wouldn't be an announcement of the breakthrough until after January 1, 1979. The timing of the announcement was of great importance because Vance was scheduled to meet with Soviet foreign minister Gromyko in Geneva on December 21 to complete details of a new arms limitation treaty and set a date for a Carter-Brezhnev summit for early 1979. Vance wanted to accomplish all of this in advance of any announcement of normalization of relations with China. He believed that if word of the change in our relations with China leaked, the Soviets would immediately dig in their heels.

Zbig had other ideas. The final details of the normalization agreement were settled on December 13, 1978. Brzezinski then argued successfully to the president that, notwithstanding Vance's concerns about the Soviet talks, the deal should be announced two days later, on December 15. Carter called Vance, then on a mission to Jerusalem, to tell him what he planned to do. Vance, taken by surprise, argued vehemently for a delay in the announcement. Carter heard him out, then turned him down.

When, after the fact, we pieced together what had happened, it was clear that Zbig had achieved his coup by seeing that Holbrooke and I were blacked out of the final six critical hours of discussions. This ensured that Vance would not know what was under consideration until it was a fait accompli. During those six hours, Zbig had argued to the president that an early announcement was essential to avoid leaks. To those who knew his history, however, it seemed likely that his real purpose was to demonstrate that U.S. relations with China took precedence over those with the Soviets.

The president announced the normalization agreement with China on December 15, 1978. A week later in Geneva, just as Vance had predicted to the president, Gromyko erupted in anger over the timing of the announcement. As a result, Vance could not complete the SALT II agreement with the Soviets, and the anticipated Carter-Brezhnev summit meeting had to be postponed.

The Zbig-driven early announcement exacted another price: Congress was angered because there had been no time for consultation, even with key leaders. Earlier in 1978, Senator Robert Dole had gained Senate approval of a resolution calling on the administration to consult with the Congress before China normalization. Later, he and other leaders on both sides of the aisle reminded me of this slight when I was trying to avoid language in the Taiwan Relations Act of 1979 that would inflame the Chinese. This illustrated again the axiom that if you succeed in circumventing the Congress on a foreign policy issue, Congress will neither forgive nor forget your success.

For me, the China normalization announcement proved to be the gift that kept on giving. Shortly after the announcement, President Carter decided that a high-level U.S. representative should go to Taiwan to put the best face on U.S. termination of official relations and removal of its official representatives from the island. Not surprisingly, there was little competition within the upper levels of the administration for the assignment. Six days after the normalization announcement, the president announced that I would leave for Taiwan on Christmas Day.

As I sat aboard the navy aircraft, alternately looking up at the sad little Christmas ornament dangling from the bulkhead and down at the Pacific moving slowly below me, I tried to imagine what the Taiwanese were likely to say and do during my visit. It was hard to make a credible case to myself that I would be a welcome visitor. Everything about the normalization decision and the way it had been handled was bound to have infuriated the Taiwanese. I suspected I was in for nonstop verbal abuse. As things played out, I undershot the mark.

The first opportunity to test the temperature of the Taiwanese came at the bottom of the ramp as I descended from my plane at the Taipei airport. There, Frederick Chien, Taiwan's vice foreign minister and my official greeter, laid out for me, and not coincidentally, for a spray of microphones and cameras, just what the next few days held in store. He announced in an angry voice that future relations could be maintained only on a "government-to-government basis," rather than on the unofficial basis we proposed. He added, ominously, that during my stay I would gain a clear understanding of the position of the government and the feelings of the people.

As I moved toward the embassy car with U.S. ambassador Leonard Unger for the drive to my hotel, I wondered how the Taiwanese government planned to top what must surely have been one of the most hostile official welcomes ever extended to a visiting official. The answer came sooner than I'd anticipated. Outside the airport grounds our car turned onto a road lined with an angry, jeering mob of about twenty thousand people. As we moved through the middle of the crowd, eggs and ripe tomatoes began to fly at us from both sides of the road. Following these relatively benign missiles came cans and rocks encased in mud. Within three or four minutes, every window in the car was shattered, Leonard Unger's glasses were broken, and we were both nursing cuts from flying glass.

As the car inched down the road, the protesters moved in and surrounded us. Some held bamboo poles that they jammed through the car's broken windows, forcing Unger and me to perform a panicked limbo dance in the backseat. Next, demonstrators jumped on the bumpers and fenders, violently rocking the vehicle, while hands grabbed at us through the windows, attempting to pull us into the mob. We looked around for help, but none was to be had. The Taiwanese police in the vicinity did nothing more than stand quietly, staring impassively at us and the surrounding chaos.

After what the press later reported was nearly an hour-long traverse of only five blocks, our car finally escaped the crowd and sped onto an expressway. We decided on the spot not to go to the hotel where I was scheduled to stay, because it was obvious that I'd face another demonstration there. Instead, Unger told the driver to take us to his summer house in the hills above Taipei.

By the time we arrived at Unger's place, word of my

December 28, 1978: Eggs, tomatoes, and
rocks greet me in Taiwan.

reception in Taiwan had reached the White House. President Carter and Secretary Vance called me on a secure line, saying I should come home immediately if I felt I was in personal danger. Had the call reached me while I was still in the car, I might already have been on the plane heading back. But over a stabilizing Scotch in a pleasant house overlooking the city, the situation seemed a bit more manageable. I did ask Vance to call Marie and tell her that despite what she would see on television, I was fine. True to form, Cy had already thought of that and reported that Marie was, to say the least, relieved.

After a night of calls back and forth to Washington and to Taiwan authorities from whom I not-so-politely demanded protection, I decided to proceed with my mission. I readied for a morning meeting with Taiwan's president, Chiang Ching-kuo.

When I came face-to-face the next morning with Chiang, I was still angry over the prior night's events. He tried to clear the air with a perfunctory apology, but I couldn't let the matter pass. Instead, I monopolized the first few minutes by recounting in detail the actions of the mob and the curious inaction of his police. He fidgeted, seeming to know the story before I told it, but finally said he would ensure our safety. I asked for the name of his security chief so that we'd have someone's name if the promised security arrangements failed to materialize. I was stunned when his translator refused to translate my question and, instead, began reciting a demand from Chiang that the United States reconsider the decision to nor-malize relations with China.

Though concerned about security, I also realized that I had to respond on the substantive point. I told Chiang that the U.S. decision was final and not sub-ject to reconsideration. I tried to describe how our relationship might flourish on an unofficial basis, but this fell on deaf ears. I left with the sense that Chiang intended to take up the matter next with Taiwan's friends in the U.S. Congress.

I stayed on for a second day in Taipei to explain to officials at lower levels of Taiwan's government how our new "unofficial" relationship could work through an American Institute on Taiwan staffed by former U.S. diplomats. Though the atmosphere of these talks was somewhat better, the substance was the same. The official litany was that Taiwan would deal with the United States only government to government. I begged off a farewell dinner and, to avoid demonstra-tions on my departure, left the country on such short notice that some of my party had to leave personal belongings in the hotel.

The return to the United States did not end my involvement with Taiwan. Once back in Washington I was assigned as point man in seeking congressional enactment of the Taiwan Relations Act, the measure that established the structure for continuing unofficial ties between the United States and Taiwan. The assignment was only slightly less perilous than my trip to Taipei. Congressional supporters of Taiwan, outraged by our normalization agreement and by our failure to consult with them in advance, tried to use debate over the legislation as an opportunity to alter the terms of the U.S.-China agreement. After prolonged, rancorous negotiations, we limited the damage to the agreement to vaguely worded guarantees of future arms sales to Taiwan and support for its defense. On April 1, 1979, a bill was presented to the president for his signature.

My turbulent experience in Taiwan proved to be a harbinger of things to come. Taiwan remains the most neuralgic issue in U.S.-China relations. During my four years with President Clinton, China's angst over Taiwan's status arose again and again as an impediment to improving U.S.-China relations. In that sense, normalization has yet to be completed.

6

Americans in Captivity

Shortly after 3 a.m. Washington time, on Sunday, November 4, 1979, Ann Swift, the senior political officer in our embassy in Tehran, was on the line reporting to the State Department's Operations Center. A mob of Iranian students had poured into the embassy compound and was threatening to enter the main building. The embassy's small contingent of marine guards was trying to hold the mob at bay, but Swift believed they couldn't stem the tide for long. Embassy security forces are equipped to keep order and deflect trouble, not to handle significant hostile confrontations. Without the help of Iran's revolutionary government, the embassy was certain to be overrun.

Swift next telephoned the Iranian foreign ministry for help. As she spoke, the rioting students, using a

November 4, 1979: The first of 444 days
of captivity for American hostages in Iran.

truck to pull iron bars off a window on the embassy's
ground floor, stormed into the building. The badly
outnumbered marine guards backed up the stairs to
the second floor as the attackers lit fires below them.
By 4:25 A.M. Washington time, sixty-five Americans
were huddled together on the embassy's second floor,
and the mob was poised to attack.

With no prospect of immediate help from the Iranian government, the group had no choice but to yield.
At 4:50 A.M., in her last communication with the
Operations Center, Ann Swift said that the group was
going downstairs to surrender peacefully.

In retrospect, these events had been building for
more than a year. During 1978, the shah of Iran, a
longtime ally of the United States, had rapidly lost his
domestic support and, in January 1979, was toppled

from power by a revolutionary Islamic government led by the Ayatollah Khomeini. When the shah asked to come to the United States, he was initially refused entry because of the risk to Americans in Iran and the availability of other places of sanctuary. Not long afterward, he asked again for permission to enter, this time on humanitarian grounds. He had cancer and needed sophisticated treatment in an American hospital. President Carter decided that he should be allowed to travel here for that purpose, and on October 22, 1979, he arrived in New York.

The shah's arrival touched off significant anti-American student demonstrations in Tehran. While the Iranian government assured us of continued protection for our embassy and its people, Khomeini simultaneously called on the students to increase pressure on the United States to return the shah to Iran. The November 1979 attack on the embassy was the ultimate product of that plea.

Alerted by the Operations Center, Secretary Cyrus Vance and I arrived at the State Department before dawn that Sunday morning to take charge of the crisis. Notwithstanding the ayatollah's recent hostile tone, we still hoped that the Iranian government would step in and restore order. It soon became clear, however, that the Khomeini government was the problem, not the solution.

Once we realized that we would have to find our own way out of the dilemma, Vance and I set out to explore every possible diplomatic channel to win the freedom of the hostages. Never before nor since has any foreign policy problem engaged me so intensively for so long. For the next five months, we pursued all conventional and unconventional diplomatic contacts we could conjure. Our efforts ranged from communication with every government that had any conceivable influence with the Iranians to missions to Tehran by former attorney general Ramsey Clark (aborted before he could enter the country) and later by a specially composed team of United Nations negotiators.

Between November 1979 and early April 1980, we tried more than a score of different approaches. Although these initiatives showed some promise, all ultimately failed. After Iran unilaterally decided, two weeks after the hostages were taken, to release thirteen black and female embassy employees, fifty Americans remained in captivity in the embassy, while three others continued to be held at the foreign ministry. One hostage, Richard Queen, was permitted to leave in July when he became seriously ill with multiple sclerosis, leaving fifty-two who remained to the end.

Though Vance and I held firmly to the belief that we should avoid a military mission unless the hostages were in imminent danger of physical harm, the demand grew for bolder action as the first quarter of 1980 passed without progress. The president's announcement on April 7, 1980, that the United States was severing diplomatic relations with Iran and imposing new, harsh economic sanctions on the Iranians seemed to us the right approach. Others in the government, however, had something more dramatic in mind.

THE RESCUE MISSION

On Thursday, April 10, 1980, Cy and Gay Vance left Washington for a weekend's rest in Florida. Late that afternoon, I received a call from Zbig Brzezinski's office summoning me, as acting secretary of state, to a Friday-morning meeting with the president and the other members of the National Security Council. I was not told what this urgent, high-level meeting was about, and efforts to learn its specific purpose through other means were unavailing.

At the appointed hour on Friday, I entered the Cabinet Room in the White House to find the president, vice president, defense secretary, national security adviser, CIA director, chairman of the Joint Chiefs of Staff, the White House chief of staff, and presidential press spokesman all in place. The president opened the meeting saying he was frustrated with the hostage situation and wanted to take some action. He then asked me to respond. I cycled through our options for increasing diplomatic pressure on Iran. When I finished, the president called on Harold Brown, the defense secretary, who quickly dismissed the diplomatic options I had outlined and said that a rescue mission was the only way to get the hostages home. Vice President Mondale immediately voiced his support for a rescue mission, as did CIA director Stan Turner and David Jones, chairman of the Joint Chiefs of Staff.

There are relatively few behavioral absolutes in Washington, but one widely recognized commandment is that it is rarely a good thing to be out of the loop. As I sat there, a surrogate for the secretary of state, it could not have been more obvious to me that I had not even been within shouting distance of this particular loop. The subject of a rescue mission was so secret that, as I later learned, Vance had not been permitted to brief me.

I knew Vance was strongly opposed to military action as long as the hostages were unharmed and credible diplomatic possibilities remained for ending the crisis. But I had never explicitly discussed a rescue mission with him and did not know his views on it. I resorted to the comment that I had not been briefed and could not therefore take a position on a rescue mission as such, but that I continued to feel that political and diplomatic options should be pursued before we undertook such a risky step.

The president then spoke at length, saying that our national honor and the lives of the hostages were at stake. He said he had talked with Vance prior to his departure on vacation, describing their conversation in a way that suggested Vance had not been firmly opposed. Carter then concluded the meeting by saying that we would proceed with the rescue mission. As I walked from the meeting in a daze, press spokesman

Jody Powell pulled me aside to say that, contrary to the impression the president might have given, he thought Vance was opposed.

As soon as Vance returned on Monday, April 14, I told him what had transpired at the White House. His reaction was volcanic—the angriest I'd ever seen him. Not only did the idea of a rescue mission infuriate him, but also that a matter of such moment had been raised and decided in his absence. He immediately called the president, and they arranged to talk the following morning.

When they met the next day, Vance spelled out his objections in clear and forceful terms. The president heard him out, then said he would reconvene the National Security Council to enable Vance to present his views. The meeting took place that very afternoon, Tuesday, April 15. Though Cy tried mightily to persuade the group that the risks of a rescue operation far outweighed its potential benefits, the die was cast. When he returned to the department that evening, he briefed me on the meeting, then said he was thinking about resigning.

As the two of us sat in the study behind his formal office, I had difficulty concentrating on what Vance was saying. I felt that things had been spinning out of control since my meeting of the prior Friday at the White House. Cy said that while in the past he had sometimes disagreed with the president, he'd had no difficulty going along with the president's decisions out of loyalty. But this was different. He said he simply couldn't play the role of defender of a decision that he believed to be so very wrong. Over the next two days, his resolve to resign as secretary increased, despite my best efforts to turn him around. On Thursday, April 17, Vance told the president he would resign if the rescue mission went forward. In anticipation of that moment, he delivered his formal letter of resignation on April 21.

As plans for the rescue mission proceeded, we were alerted to a troubling development that threatened to compromise the operation. A British colonel on a training assignment in Oman on the Arabian Peninsula reported that U.S. military aircraft—planes that, unknown to him, were part of our planned rescue force—had mysteriously landed there. The British had not been briefed on our rescue plan. We feared that if they began investigating the presence of our aircraft in Oman, the communications could provide advance warning to Iran or its friends about our intentions.

When the president learned of this development, he called me to the White House and said we had to stop the British from inquiring further on the subject. He wanted me to fly to London immediately to brief Prime Minister Thatcher and her foreign secretary, Peter Carrington, about the rescue mission and to ask them to maintain silence about our aircraft movements in the Mideast. He said he would give me a personal note to Mrs. Thatcher making clear I was speaking for the president of the United States. As I stood beside his desk, he wrote in large script a message that asked her to treat the oral request I would be making as coming from him personally, and to hold it in the strictest confidence.

This was not to be a trip on an attention-drawing U.S. military aircraft. I would fly commercially, and because the flights to London were heavily booked that night, I made the trip in a center seat on TWA sandwiched between two businessmen. Apart from considerations of comfort, these arrangements meant I couldn't deal with any of the highly sensitive material in my briefcase. I was going to have to prepare for my meeting with Mrs. Thatcher entirely in my head.

I landed in London in the early morning and, after a quick shower and change, was driven to Chequers, the prime minister's country residence about an hour out of the city. It was a cold April day, with patches of snow still on the ground. I was greeted at the door by Thatcher and Carrington, who escorted me to a chair in front of a roaring fire.

I told the prime minister that I wanted first to give her a note from the president. She read it, showed it to Carrington, then took it to the fireplace and tossed it into the heart of the flames. I winced at the thought that she had destroyed a document of great historical moment, but I was simultaneously impressed with her discretion. When she retook her seat, I outlined the rescue mission in detail, leaving out only the exact date of the operation.

When I finished, Carrington jumped to his feet and uttered, nearly shouted, "Capital!" The prime minister was a bit more cautious, saying only, "Good, if it works." Both agreed that any further communication by British military sources about our Mideast preparatory activities had to be curtailed immediately. Carrington said he would take steps at once to shut down the communication stream.

My mission accomplished, I rose to leave. Keeping her chair, Mrs. Thatcher asked if I would stay a moment more to share a rhubarb pudding with her and the foreign secretary. The offer obliterated every other thought from my mind. Rhubarb is a North Dakota kind of food, a vegetable that thrives in harsh Plains weather but, when heavily sweetened, can pass for dessert. It is a perennial that enables a mother to rationalize the giving of a treat by the thought that she is also doing her duty. Perhaps it was just light-headedness from the overnight flight, but as I looked at Mrs. Thatcher's slight smile and spooned the warm pudding into my mouth, I could think only of home.

I finished my pudding, caught the first flight back to Washington, and immediately gave the president a full report on my Thatcher meeting (without the pudding). He seemed relieved and pleased and told me he wanted me to be involved in the final planning meetings.

The rescue operation was complex and risky. It called for eight helicopters and six C-130 transport aircraft to depart from various locations in the Persian Gulf area, fly hundreds of miles to the center of Iran, and rendezvous at a remote desert location (called

Desert I). At Desert I, the helicopters would be refueled and loaded with equipment brought by the C-130s. With the assault team on board, they would proceed under cover of darkness to a remote site in the mountains near Tehran. The team would hide at this spot, then proceed to Tehran, fight their way into the embassy, and free the hostages from their captors. The helicopters would pick up the assault team and the freed hostages and fly them to an abandoned airfield near Tehran (Desert II), where they would rendezvous with transport aircraft for their departure from Iran.

The mission failed almost before it began. Two of the helicopters malfunctioned before they reached Desert I, while a third was found unfit to continue after it arrived there. I was with Carter at the White House on April 24, 1980, as he received the news from the ground commander. The leader of the mission had concluded it was too risky to proceed with only five functioning helicopters. Carter paused a moment to think, then, at about 5 P.M. Washington time, gave the order to abort.

It seemed that things couldn't get worse, but a short time later we learned we were wrong. The phone rang, the president picked it up, and the blood drained from his face. A collision had occurred between one of the remaining helicopters and a refueling aircraft, killing eight American crewmen. A failed mission had become a disastrous one.

The president had to decide when to announce this

April 26, 1980: Wreckage of a U.S. helicopter
involved in the aborted hostage rescue attempt.

bad news. CIA director Stan Turner pled for as much
time as possible in order to extract from Tehran our
agents who had been secretly deployed for the rescue
mission. Though Vance had delivered his letter of resignation three days earlier, he was a part of the team
keeping vigil. He remained with me at the White
House until after 11 P.M., assisting with the drafting
of the president's statement. At 1 A.M., eight hours
after the mission was aborted, the president delivered
his televised statement, describing what had happened
and taking full personal responsibility.

The failure of the mission had important diplomatic consequences that we had to deal with even
before the president told the nation what had
occurred. Late in the evening, Vance and I returned to
the State Department and began calling the congressional leadership. We also dispatched messages to our

posts around the world, setting out the facts and warning certain of them, particularly those in the Middle East, of possible Arab retaliation. The cables instructed the embassies to brief representatives of their host governments as soon as possible.

As Vance and I worked over these details, a part of my brain was focused on another issue—how to persuade Vance to withdraw his letter of resignation. Shortly after the president delivered his statement, with the ministerial tasks behind us, I went to Cy's office to make my argument. Though I knew he was as weary as I was, I thought this might be my last clear chance to turn him around.

I argued that the failure of the mission, though terrible, did not produce the results that had prompted him to tell the president he couldn't remain in the job. He had predicted that the mission would inflame the region against us and place the hostages' lives at peril. I pointed out to him that because the loss of life had been exclusively American, the diplomatic fallout and the risk to the hostages would likely be minimal.

As I spoke, Cy put his fingertips together and nodded occasionally. When I finished, he said he was touched by my effort to persuade him to stay, but still felt resignation was his only realistic choice. He said there would be postmortems over the rescue attempt on Capitol Hill, and he did not feel he could give the president's decision the support it deserved. His mind was made up, and sometime after 2 A.M. we left his office together, exhausted and dispirited, knowing that we were unlikely to feel much better for some time to come.

The second-guessing began immediately. The failure was a devastating blow to our military reputation. Monday-morning quarterbacks lamented the lack of backup for the helicopters. Some said it was lucky the mission had failed before it reached Tehran, as it would likely have resulted in the deaths of the hostages and many Iranians as well. Some of our allies joined the legion attempting to distance themselves from our actions, claiming they had assumed their willingness to enforce economic sanctions meant that the United States would take no unilateral action. When the smoke cleared, one thing was clear: the president had suffered a grave political wound, handing Ronald Reagan, who would be Carter's opponent in the fall, a large, perhaps decisive, campaign issue.

A NEW SECRETARY OF STATE

As rumors of Vance's resignation began to leak in the days following the rescue disaster, the press anointed me a leading candidate to succeed him. It was pretty well known within the White House and State Department that Vance had recommended me, and with only eight months left in Carter's first term, the pundits speculated that I was the logical choice. I had enough experience with the ways of Washington to know that nothing was really done until it was officially done, but I felt reasonably hopeful that I might soon be changing offices.

I was attending a meeting at the White House on Monday, April 28, when the president asked me to step into the Oval Office with him. As we stood near his desk, he said he had chosen Ed Muskie, the prominent senator from Maine, to be secretary of state, and that he and Muskie hoped I would remain as deputy. I was stunned and said something anodyne about his having made a good choice and that I would carefully consider the question of whether to remain. The whole exchange took no more than a minute.

I left the White House deeply disappointed. After going home and breaking the news to Marie over dinner, I decided I needed some time by myself to think through the situation. Though it was a cold, rainy night, I took a long, stumbling run through my neighborhood. As I threaded my way through the streets, I tried to sort out in my mind what I had or hadn't done to cause the president to make this choice, and what I ought to do now. After pondering the first of these questions for about a mile and a quarter, I concluded that the most obvious answer was probably the right one. Washington is a place of political, not sentimental or even merit-driven, decision-making. The president's decision was dictated by his need to bolster his standing on Capitol Hill in a presidential election year.

I moved on to the question of what I would do next. I could go back to practicing law in California or

May 2, 1980: With President Carter and
Secretary of State–designate Muskie.

could remain in a job I had found rewarding. But how to choose between these and at what cost? On the one hand, I felt that if I stayed I would be viewed in this hard city as a wallflower who had never quite made it to the dance floor. On the other hand, I had accepted the job of deputy without reservation or promise of advancement. I'd agreed to serve the country in the number two position at the State Department—period. To leave now out of disappointment at my failure to advance would be to elevate ambition over commitment, pride over duty. By the time I jogged to the steps of our house, I had decided to stay.

I had been a local campaign chairman for Ed

Muskie when he sought the Democratic nomination for president in 1972. I liked him and believed he had the stuff of a leader. In public appearances, he demonstrated a compelling speaking style, an engaging manner, and a deft sense of humor. I felt we could work together and that he could adjust to life in "the building," as Department of State veterans referred to the institution. But not long after he was sworn in as secretary, we all began to see that the ingrained habits of a senior U.S. senator did not mesh well with the synchronized order of march at the department.

Muskie's patented style of asking questions as a means of demonstrating substance contrasted dramatically and negatively with Zbig Brzezinski's confident, rapid-fire lectures. Muskie also had little experience with executive-branch hardball. Though he thought Zbig grabbed too much of the limelight, Muskie kept it more or less to himself. Zbig, on the other hand, backgrounded to the press that Muskie was a newcomer who had failed to master the nuances of foreign policy.

Muskie exacerbated the negative press problem by failing to discourage supporters who wanted to keep him in the political spotlight. As late as the week before the Democratic convention in August, he refused to take himself unequivocally out of the running for the Democratic presidential nomination against the incumbent president. The result was a growing Beltway buzz that Muskie was somehow half in and half out of the job of secretary of state, an impression that stuck to him during the entire eight months he was in office.

DIPLOMACY AGAIN

Once the dust had settled over the transition at the top of the State Department, the hostage crisis resumed its place at the front and center of our foreign policy agenda. The failed rescue attempt had changed the facts on the ground. When news of the aborted mission reached the Iranians, they quickly dispersed the hostages to various locations around Tehran and other Iranian cities to ensure that no similar mission would be attempted. Though at Zbig's insistence planning was undertaken for another rescue, it was clear almost from the outset that such an effort would be vastly more complicated and would pose daunting risks for all involved.

Through the late spring and early summer of 1980, we pursued several diplomatic leads, but partly because Iran was focused on parliamentary elections for much of that period, there was no real progress. Only after the election on July 20 of Ali Akbar Rafsanjani as speaker of the parliament and the choice on August 11 of Mohammed Ali Rajai as prime minister did we have any new diplomatic contact of substance.

On September 9, 1980, more than three hundred days after the hostages had been taken, an official of the German embassy in Washington delivered a dramatic message from his government. The German ambassador in Iran reported that an unidentified high-ranking Iranian official had been authorized by Ayatollah Khomeini to meet secretly in West Germany with an American counterpart to discuss an end to the hostage crisis. Muskie and I hurried to the White House to report the news to the president. After we'd repeated the German message to Carter, he turned to me and said, "I want you to go yourself. Anyplace. Anytime."

I returned to the State Department energized by my mission and ready to do what had to be done. First, however, I wanted to confirm that this contact was what it appeared to be. There had been too many dead ends to invest ourselves in a full-court press, once again, without independent verification of the bona fides of the contact.

Through the German embassy, we sent a message asking for some proof from the still-unidentified Iranian emissary that he was, indeed, authorized to act for the Iranian leadership. We promptly received a reply that a forthcoming speech by the ayatollah would include a recital of four conditions for the hostages' release: (1) that the United States pledge not to intervene in the internal affairs of Iran; (2) that the United States permit the return of all Iranian assets that had been frozen by U.S. sanctions; (3) that we cancel all U.S. claims against Iran; and (4) that we repatriate to Iran the shah's wealth in the United States.

On September 12, three days after the initial message and only two after my response, Khomeini appeared on Iranian television to address his nation. In the middle of his long speech, he included a paragraph that specified, in the same order, the four conditions for the hostages' release that had been transmitted to us by the anonymous Iranian. Those conditions remained at the heart of our negotiations until the end.

Following the ayatollah's speech, the Germans informed me that the name of my Iranian counterpart was Sadegh Tabatabai, and that my first meeting with him would be on September 15. We immediately set about learning all we could about Tabatabai, but our urgent inquiries yielded only that he was the brother-in-law of Khomeini's son and that he had studied extensively in West Germany.

We had three days to formulate and vet the U.S. response to Iran's four conditions. To that end, I formed a hostage-negotiation team that met in my back office. Though it can be more difficult negotiating a position within the U.S. government than with a sworn international adversary, this group managed to produce bureaucratic progress at unheard-of speed. By September 14, the date of my departure for my meeting with Tabatabai, I had in my briefcase a set of responses that passed muster with every involved arm of the U.S. government.

To ensure that the press would have no clue about the true purpose of my trip, it was announced that I was traveling for one of my regular consultations with German foreign minister Hans-Dietrich Genscher. My official itinerary also included meetings with Prime Minister Thatcher in London, Chancellor Helmut Schmidt in Bonn, and President Giscard d'Estaing in Paris to talk about a threatened Soviet invasion of Poland.

The Germans put me and my negotiating team up in Schlock Gimmick, a lovely old palace set in a beautiful private park. I had been there only an hour when word came that the Iranian had arrived and was ready to talk. I hurried to another guesthouse, to be greeted by Foreign Minister Genscher and Tabatabai.

Tabatabai certainly didn't fit my mental picture of an Islamic radical. A good-looking, dark-haired man in his midthirties, he wore gray flannel slacks and a handsome tweed sport jacket. After introductions, we repaired to a dining room and seated ourselves at the table. I spoke first: "Look, I have a lot of speeches I could make to you, and you probably have some, too. But let's put them aside." Through his translator, he agreed.

I then addressed each of the four Iranian conditions for the hostages' release. First, I told him we had no objection to making a statement that it was contrary to U.S. policy to intervene in Iran's internal affairs. Second, I said we were prepared to release several billion dollars of frozen Iranian assets, perhaps as much as $5.5 billion, when the hostages were released. On the third point, I proposed that we establish an international arbitral tribunal to adjudicate claims of Americans and Iranians against our governments.

Finally I turned to their demand that we restore the shah's wealth to Iran. This was the most difficult issue to discuss, both because our respective perceptions of reality were markedly different and because American law allowed only so much latitude. The Iranians had the illusion that the shah had squirreled away billions of dollars in the United States. We believed he was much too sophisticated to have transferred significant wealth to America. Even if the shah did have substantial U.S.-based assets, however, the most the U.S. government could do was promise to facilitate any litigation that Iran might bring to recover those assets. Our Constitution simply did not permit the seizure of private property in the pursuit of foreign policy interests. When it appeared that I might be losing Tabatabai, Genscher came to my aid, commenting that what I was proposing was more than what Germany would have been able to offer under its laws.

Having heard me out, Tabatabai asked if military spare parts that Iran had on order in the United States, some of them already paid for, could be part of the deal. I told him such an arrangement would be difficult, and he didn't press the matter again. After two hours of discussion, we parted, agreeing to meet again sometime in the next few days.

The next day I learned Tabatabai was ready to meet for breakfast the following morning, September 17. We met again at the German guesthouse and spent the time reviewing and clarifying our respective positions. Tabatabai said he had reported to Tehran on our first meeting and that our position was "not unwelcome." He said he was returning to Tehran for further instructions and that I would hear from him again soon. I flew back to Washington and reported to the president that we seemed to be in business.

Over the next few days I operated in the belief that we might soon have the hostages home. Tabatabai appeared to be an authentic emissary, and he reflected no indecision about his principals' desire to close the hostage chapter. But on September 22, war broke out between Iran and Iraq. Communications with Tabatabai ceased and, despite our best efforts, could not be revived. The Germans, our intermediaries, reported that the Iran-Iraq war now occupied the Iranian ministries full-time and that contacts on other issues were simply ignored.

During this difficult period, the president telephoned me shortly after 7 A.M. almost every morning to ask about overnight developments. Our calls had a kind of fixed architecture. He would invariably open with "Any good news this morning, Chris?" I would respond with a variant of either "Well, maybe, Mr. President" or "It doesn't look that way right now." I would then deliver filigree on the variant of the day, reviewing our actions and any responses received. The conversation would close with my reassuring Carter that we were doing everything imaginable to bring the hostages back. I don't know whether the president was comforted by these exchanges; they certainly did nothing to ease my anxiety.

As the November 1980 election drew nearer, Carter began slipping in the polls, and his political advisers began to share a sense of desperation. They pled for any shred of positive news out of Iran, but it became painfully apparent that, even if some new and unexpected diplomatic initiative appeared, there was little hope of reaching a settlement by the day America's voters would elect their next president.

ENTER THE ALGERIANS

On November 3, the day before the U.S. election, there was important news. The Algerian ambassador in Washington, Redba Malek, wanted to deliver personally a resolution that the Iranian parliament had adopted the preceding day. Though we had already seen the text of the resolution and had found little in it that was new or hopeful, I suspected the ambassador had something important to add between the lines. I was right. In a meeting on the afternoon of November 3, Malek told me the Iranians had asked Algeria to serve as an intermediary in the hostage negotiations. This was the kind of news we'd been awaiting for nearly a year. The Iranians had officially turned to a third party for help.

President Carter's decisive loss to Ronald Reagan in the November 4 presidential election cast a gloomy spell over our administration, but fortunately, I had my hands full with hostage matters. Although some speculated that the election loss might weaken our negotiating position, I sought to turn it into an advantage. I reminded the Algerians that the incoming Republican president, Ronald Reagan, had taken a hard-line position against negotiations in the campaign, and so, I argued, the Iranians would be better off dealing with me rather than taking their chances with the new administration. Despite rumors that the Republicans had made a deal with the Iranians not to release the hostages before the election, I never saw any evidence of it. The bellicose statements emanating from the Reagan transition team helped to make my point that the Iranians might as well deal with the devil they knew—me.

Immediately after the election, we went to work formulating the U.S. response to the Iranian parliament's resolution. We had to address the same four conditions that I'd discussed with Tabatabai in Germany, but now we had to do so on paper, with precision and detail. My goal was to produce a brief, simple document that could be understood and discussed by nonlawyers, even after it was doubly translated, first into French (for the Algerians) and then into Farsi (for the Iranians).

The State Department lawyers didn't immediately get the message. Their first partial draft—dealing only with the international arbitral tribunal for U.S. and Iranian claims—ran to twenty-five mind-numbing pages. I told them they had to do better. Two days later, inspired by legal adviser Roberts Owen, they presented me with a three-page version that did the job nicely. With this exercise as our precedent, we ultimately produced a settlement package that totaled only eleven pages.

A few days later, we presented to President Carter our proposed written response to the four Iranian points. Since the documents were mainly elaborations of what I had presented to Tabatabai, he approved them immediately and authorized me to fly to Algiers to begin negotiations. I left on November 9.

I had never been to Algiers, and although my mission didn't include sight-seeing, I got a fleeting first impression as I headed from the airport toward the ambassador's residence. The city sits, almost hangs, on the Mediterranean, at the edge of a half-moon-shaped bay. From a distance it appears clean and uncluttered, with classic white buildings and tile roofs. As I entered the heart of the place, I quickly became aware that the streets were filled with young people, milling aimlessly about. The feeling, however, was not festive or playful, but ominous and uneasy. Later, between meetings, when I walked through the Casbah, I got a closer look at these idle youths, who stared warily and anxiously back at me, as if waiting for a provocative word.

Almost immediately upon arrival I went into a negotiating session. The meeting convened in a Moorish government villa, where we arranged ourselves around a long rectangular table with a green maize cover. Under other circumstances, one might have seen poker chips at each place. The country's foreign minister, Mohammed Ben Yahia, sat in the principal's chair, assisted by Ambassador Malek, by Abdul Karim Gharaeib, Algeria's ambassador to Iran, and by Seghir Mostafai, governor of Algeria's Central Bank. Clearly, Algeria was making an extraordinarily high-profile commitment to the success of these negotiations.

Ben Yahia, a chain-smoker in precarious health, was so thin he made me look overweight. As we warmed to each other, he gave me hints about his style. "I am a night person," he said. "Be careful of me at midnight." In the months that followed, we did most of our work at midnight—either literally or figuratively—and Ben Yahia's creativity at those moments was critical to resolving every one of the problems we confronted.

I began by distributing a notebook to each of the Algerians, containing, in English and French, a statement of the Iranian demands and the U.S. responses. I then explained the U.S. positions, pointing out the obstacles in U.S. law that prevented us from accepting each demand as it had been made. When I finished, the Algerians pressed for detailed elaboration of what I had said. They asked me the toughest possible questions to ensure that they'd be prepared to respond to the same questions when they faced the Iranians. After two days of this exercise, the Algerians said they were satisfied and would leave at once for Tehran.

After a few anxious days, the Algerians came to Washington to report on their Tehran meetings. They were circumspect about revealing with whom they had talked or what had been said, but they came armed with questions and reformulated demands. This procedure—U.S.-Algerian meetings followed by Algerian-Iranian meetings—continued through mid-December. Awkward as the process was, we seemed to be making progress and slowly closing the gap between us.

Then on December 20, five days before Christmas, the Algerians forwarded to me in Washington a startling message from the Iranians. The captors now demanded $14 billion in frozen assets and $10 billion in cash guarantees—about $18 billion more than what we had previously discussed.

As a matter of principle, I felt firmly that the United States should not pay a ransom to Iran for release of our people. I was prepared, however, to negotiate the return of a portion of the Iranian assets that had been frozen in U.S. banks shortly after the hostages were taken. Given what seemed to me a deal-breaking increase in their demand, I bounded down the hall to talk to Arnie Raphel, a Foreign Service officer who had served in Iran and had been a key part of our effort since my trip to Bonn in September. Raphel sagely reminded me that the Iranian negotiating style is grounded in the bazaar tradition, where the making of outrageous demands and haggling up to the last minute are routine. He predicted that this latest Iranian move was a tactic, not a reversal of position. I went back to work, resolved to submerge the angst that this new message had evoked.

In diplomacy, the form and style of documents are often more important than the content. Up to this point, we had drafted and redrafted the U.S. position, given it to the Iranians via the Algerians, then received in return redrafted forms of the Iranian position paper. The U.S. team decided to try accelerating the negotiations by breaking this cycle. We worked through the holiday season to create a new form of document that set out a series of mutually dependent promises that would be made to Algeria by both the United States and Iran.

During the last week of 1980, the Algerian team came to Washington to discuss the new approach. President Carter, though in great pain from a broken collarbone that he'd suffered in a skiing accident, invited them to Camp David. There he spent more than an hour with the Algerians, reviewing the status of the negotiations and urging on them the merits of our alternative. Carter was at his best—quiet, firm, simple, knowledgeable—and the Algerians were deeply impressed. On the return trip from Camp David to Washington, one member of the Algerian team turned to me and said, "Don't give up; you may be closer than you think."

Shortly after New Year's Day, 1981, I received a message through an Algerian channel that the Iranian financial demand had dropped from $24 billion to $9.5 billion. Arnie Raphel had been right. However, while the reduction to $9.5 billion was good news, we had the capacity to free only somewhat more than $7 billion, due to lawsuits pending in U.S. courts. I tried to explain the problem in a cable to Algiers, but the response that reached me on January 7 made it clear that I was not getting the message across.

That same afternoon—January 7—I met in the Oval Office with the president, Muskie, and Brzezinski to review the situation. We quickly concluded that if the negotiation was to be wrapped up by January 20, the day of Ronald Reagan's inauguration, a face-to-face meeting with Algerian foreign minister Ben Yahia was essential. President Carter told me to make that happen as quickly as possible and to call him, "day or night," if I needed his personal assistance.

On my return to the State Department I immediately contacted the Algerians and learned that Ben Yahia could see me the following morning if I could make it to Algiers. I left Washington at 9 P.M., believing I'd be back in two days. In fact, I didn't touch American soil again until after Ronald Reagan became president.

THIRTEEN DAYS IN ALGIERS

As I descended the aircraft steps in Algiers on January 8, the U.S. ambassador, Rick Haynes, a tall, handsome man with a well-trimmed beard, was there to meet me. Haynes stayed at my side for the next thirteen days—mobilizing his embassy, advising on Algerian sensitivities, acting as interpreter when necessary, and though simultaneously packing to return to the United States after inauguration day, making our team at home in the 150-year-old Moorish compound Villa Montfeld, his official residence. He and his attractive wife, Yolaunde, scavenged from their shrinking supplies to feed us, and by the time our forty-eight-hour trip had stretched to a week, the cupboard was nearly bare. One day as Haynes and I walked in the embassy compound, he pointed to a chicken walking across our path and said, "That's dinner for tomorrow."

Upon arrival in Algiers on January 8, I went directly from the airport to Ben Yahia's office. My urgent task was to convince him that the $9.5 billion demand was beyond our reach because it included Iranian deposits that had been tied up by orders from U.S. courts, prohibiting transfer without judicial approval. I told Ben Yahia that if the president tried to order the transfer of these funds to Iran, the U.S. bank involved would go to court and ask for direction as to whether to obey the president or the existing court order. That kind of question, I said, would take months to resolve.

While even sophisticated foreigners often have trouble understanding our separation of powers, Ben Yahia quickly saw the point. In due course, the Iranian monetary demand was reduced to $7.955 billion, the precise cumulative value of unencumbered frozen Iranian deposits, plus interest, in branches of U.S. banks abroad, and gold and other assets held in the Federal Reserve Bank in New York.

As we worried over money, we also continued to negotiate over the language of the settlement documents. On the nonintervention pledge, the Iranians pushed us to concede that we had intervened in their internal affairs in the past. We resisted and they eventually settled for a pledge saying "it is and from now on will be the policy of the United States not to intervene . . ." The language for describing how claims of Americans and Iranians would be handled by an international arbitral tribunal produced nonstop technical discussions. The key breakthrough on this demand was the Iranians' agreement to establish a $1 billion revolving fund to pay arbitral awards against them. Regarding the repatriation of the shah's assets in the United States, we held our ground, reiterating that the most we could do was "facilitate" Iranian lawsuits by, for example, ensuring that the shah's property, if there was any, would remain in the United States.

In the days prior to January 15, executives of various American banks met in New York with Iranian bank officials, attempting to work out a basis to "bring current" (that is, make all overdue payments on) the $3.6 billion in outstanding loans to the government of Iran. Only if the loans were brought current were the banks prepared to free up the $5.5 billion in Iranian deposits and interest in their overseas branches.

The discussions with the bankers seemed to have no prospect of concluding before inauguration day. But suddenly, on January 15, I received a startling message in Algiers. The Iranians had decided to pay off the

$3.6 billion in loans from the U.S. banks rather than continuing negotiations to bring them current. I could scarcely believe the news and took it as a sign that we had truly reached the end game. Though the new approach required us to work through the night to restructure our settlement, we figuratively whistled while we worked.

Amid the frantic redrafting activity, I was called to the embassy radio room on January 16 and told that the president wanted me to hear something. I put on the headphones and, at first, got only static. Slowly I was able to make out what sounded like a ceremony. The president was awarding me the Medal of Freedom at the White House, and Marie was there to accept it on my behalf. Though someone had hinted that this might be in the works, I had no idea it was really going to happen. While delighted, my main thought was to get the job done for which I was receiving the award. The president obviously had the same priority. After the ceremony was completed, I called the White House to thank him. He responded gracefully, then said, "Of course, it's on the condition that you get the hostages out."

I presented the revised documents to Ben Yahia that same day in a long and difficult session during which he examined our restructured proposal with meticulous care. Finally, late on the night of the sixteenth, he said he was satisfied that we were on the right track. Then he turned to me and said quietly, "Tomorrow we will talk about transportation." This was his first reference in our two months of negotiation to arrangements for bringing the hostages home.

The next morning, January 17, Ben Yahia told me that the Algerians planned to use two 727s of Air Algérie to fly the hostages out of Tehran, but that the planes did not have "long enough legs" to return from Iran without refueling. He asked me to propose the best place for a safe refueling stop. After consulting with the Pentagon, I suggested alternative stopover points of Athens, Malta, and Ankara, in that order. We settled on Athens.

On January 17 and 18, I dealt with last-minute problems in the documents, but with Ben Yahia's help—and unstinting efforts from President Carter—we found ways to surmount these final hurdles. Meanwhile, in a room next door to Ben Yahia's office, State Department legal adviser Roberts Owen and the translator Alec Toumayan undertook a painstaking, word-by-word review and translation of the settlement material with lawyers from the Algerian foreign ministry. I pushed for a quick finish, but in the great tradition of bureaucrats from developing countries, the Algerians played their ministerial role to the hilt. They would not be hurried.

Late on the eighteenth, President Carter authorized me to sign the settlement for the United States. Ben Yahia advised me to hold off until Iran had approved. Dawn came without word from Iran, and at 6:30 A.M. I went back to the residence to shower and get ready for another day. Before the shower water got warm,

January 19, 1981: Algerian foreign minister Ben Yahia
and I sign the hostage-release agreement.

Ben Yahia called to say that Iran's approval had finally
come. It was 7:08 A.M. Algiers time, on January 19,
the day before Ronald Reagan's inauguration would
take place.

Without a moment's delay, I rushed back to the foreign ministry, straightened my tie, and went down to
sign with Ben Yahia before a hundred cameras—in
clothes I had not taken off for forty-eight hours. The
U.S. and Algerian teams stood behind us. One of my
exhausted aides fell asleep on his feet, teetered, and
was caught by a colleague.

Although the documents had been signed, tension
remained high. Later in the day, Ben Yahia told me
that the Iranians had thrown up a new obstacle. They
were refusing to accept a vital technical annex to the
basic documents. This was the last straw. While I am

The press in Washington watch the signing
of the agreement in Algiers.

generally prepared to negotiate at infinite length prior
to the signing of an agreement, postsigning negotiation, in my experience, produces no good. I directed
an aide to call the airport on an open line and tell our
crew to prepare my plane for departure. I also made
telephone calls telling my colleagues to get ready to fly
home. As I intended, the Algerians intercepted my call
and immediately passed the word to Iran that the deal
was crumbling. The obstacle suddenly evaporated.

After all was finally agreed, there was the matter of
moving $7.955 billion in frozen Iranian funds into the
escrow account of the Bank of England on the morning of January 20. Only after this was accomplished
and verified to the Algerian Central Bank would the
Iranians be obligated to release the hostages. Always
wary of Iranian commitments, I had insisted that no

funds actually be transferred to Iran until the hostages had cleared Iranian airspace.

I paced the halls of the Algerian foreign ministry as the sums flowed from U.S. banks into the Bank of England. The deputy governor and the cashier of the bank sat on the floor of an office, toting up the sums as they were reported from London. The total reached five billion, then six, then seven, finally hitting the magic number at 6 A.M. Washington time.

As the day unfolded, Ben Yahia told me about the Algerians' elaborate security plans. All of the hostages would be placed on one of the two 727s. The second 727 would carry the highly trained Algerian security unit that surrounded the planes at the Tehran airport. When they left Tehran, one aircraft would file a flight plan for Damascus, Syria, and the other for Ankara, Turkey. Only after they were airborne and out of Iran's airspace would they change their flight plans and head for Athens. I later learned that the Algerians had also refrained from taking on fuel in Tehran for fear it might be contaminated.

Ben Yahia told me the Iranians had promised that the planes carrying the hostages would leave before noon Washington, D.C., time (5 P.M. Algiers time), the hour of President Reagan's swearing in. As it turned out, they did not leave until 12:23 P.M. Washington time. After the fact, there was broad speculation that the Iranians intended the delay as a final affront to President Carter. I am not so sure. In the chaos of that last day, and given the Iranians' habit of procrastination, it may be impossible ever to know for sure whether the delay was by accident or design.

I went to the Algiers airport at dusk to await the arrival of the hostages. Because of the depth of the animosity harbored by the Iranians for the United States, I had long felt that the hostages would be at most physical risk in the last hours before their departure. As darkness fell and rain poured down on us, we squinted toward the south. At first there was nothing. Then we saw tiny dots of light that quickly grew into what were plainly the landing lights of aircraft. As the two 727s descended, the television lights lit up the tarmac and the last act of the drama unfolded.

When the door of the plane opened, the first two faces to appear were those of the women hostages, Ann Swift and Katherine Koob. Fifty more Americans—the men—followed. Holding a checklist of names in my hand, I ticked off a name after greeting

January 20, 1981: The hostages are freed.

each one. As I looked into the eyes of these brave people, some of whom had been in solitary confinement for months, I could barely speak. I felt that we had been together, in a sense, for the last year, but I knew that I could never fully appreciate the darkness of their experience.

My instructions from Ben Yahia about that evening were definite. There were to be no political speeches, no emotional statements that would compromise Algeria's role as neutral intermediary. I was to accept custody of the hostages and that was all. I did not think I violated the rules when I said to him in front of the arrayed cameras and reporters: "You have answered our prayers."

The next few days were a blur of activity and emotion. I flew back to Washington almost immediately after the hostages departed Algiers and was met at Andrews Air Force Base by Marie. We headed straight for home.

I was almost asleep on my feet, but wanted to have something to eat before I turned in. We decided to walk to a nearby neighborhood place to grab a quick bite. As we walked along, some city workers were digging a trench in the street. Though Marie and I were conversing, I noticed as we passed that the workers stopped what they were doing, smiled, and flashed a V sign in our direction. I thought it a little odd, but said nothing.

We entered the restaurant a few minutes later and approached the dining room, which was nearly full.

By the time we reached the maître 'd's post, all conversation had stopped. Then, with all eyes on us, a man on the far side of the room began to clap. He was joined by a few other diners, then by everyone in the room. Soon all the people rose from their chairs, applauding.

I was very tired. My first and only thought was that someone famous must have entered behind me. Turning to see who it was, I saw only Marie. Beaming at me, she said, "It's for you, Chris. It's for *you*."

I would like to say that a great and worthy thought entered my mind at that moment, one suitable for quoting at the conclusion of a chapter of a book. In the cause of historical accuracy, however, I must be candid. What struck me then, as it does now, is how very strange, nearly magical, life can be. Who could have predicted only nine months before that one of the luckiest things ever to happen to me would be *not* being named secretary of state? *Not* finding myself in a job that would have kept my feet firmly planted in Washington?

The lesson I draw from this chapter of my life is simple, and a little ironic: the chance of a lifetime is not necessarily the next rung up the ladder. It may be the one on which you already stand.

—— ✦ ——

7

POLICING THE POLICE

TOM BRADLEY WAS A KIND OF HUMAN ANALOGUE to the City of Los Angeles. Big and quietly self-assured, he was willing to embrace people and ideas of all stripes. His gentle, self-deprecating style was a surprising counterpoint to his imposing physical presence. But when Tom spoke, people listened, not because they feared what would happen if they did not, but because he spoke words of uncommon common sense.

Bradley, the son of a sharecropper and a maid, was the grandson of slaves. In 1937, he escaped from the ghetto by winning a track scholarship to UCLA and, three years later, left UCLA to become a police officer. After twenty years on the force, he had risen to the rank of lieutenant, but had concluded that he was unlikely to rise further in the mostly white, highly seg-

Tom Bradley.

regated LAPD. Having made a variety of friends in the city power structure, and armed with a night-school law degree, in 1961 he ran for the Los Angeles City Council and won. Twelve years later, in his second run for Los Angeles mayor, he ousted the incumbent, Sam Yorty.

I had known Tom Bradley before joining the Carter administration in 1977 and resumed our acquaintance when I returned to my Los Angeles law practice in 1981. I confirmed firsthand his growing stature with all of the city's diverse constituencies. When I called Bradley's office for an appointment in March 1991, he was serving an unprecedented fifth term as the city's mayor. He had seen Los Angeles through hard moments and magical ones, the most notable of the latter being the extraordinarily successful 1984 Olympics. He had built his reputation in parallel with that of his city. But in the first week of March 1991, events occurred that put the fruits of his hard work at serious risk.

After a high-speed chase in the early hours of Sunday, March 3, Los Angeles police officers, using extreme and excessive force, apprehended Rodney King, a twenty-five-year-old black motorist. The event might well have passed into police records as a routine weekend drunk-driving arrest with a reckless car chase as its denouement, but this particular chase ended in front of the apartment house of George Holliday, an amateur photographer. As Holliday stood on his second-floor balcony, new Sony camcorder in hand and rolling, four uniformed LAPD officers pounded King with fifty-six power strokes from their batons and savagely kicked him in the head and body. As this terrible scene unfolded, fourteen other law enforcement officers simply stood there watching.

Holliday did not take his videotape to the authorities until the following day. Then he went to the Foothill Police Station to describe what he had seen and to offer up the tape. The LAPD desk officer brushed him aside, but Holliday, feeling that what he knew and had on tape were too important to ignore, took the video to a local Los Angeles television station. Within hours, the images of Rodney King's beating had traveled around the world, becoming the most-watched piece of news footage since the 1986 *Challenger* spacecraft disaster. The Los Angeles Police Department, and with it the city it was sworn to serve and protect, were immediately under siege from a world that wanted to know how such a thing could possibly have occurred in the America of 1991.

I saw the Rodney King footage for the first time on Tuesday, March 5, after word of its content had begun to spread. While my experience in the Detroit, Chicago, and Washington, D.C., riots of 1967–68 had given me insight into the psychology and necessary tactics of police officers when faced with tough situations in the field, the video (that is, the portion of the tape repeatedly played on television) tested the limits of my objectivity.

My eyes told me that a black man, apparently subdued and surrounded by a score of uniformed officers, had been viciously beaten with batons wielded by several of them. Others casually watched, almost as if the event were a performance staged for their private benefit. At the same time, I knew that Holliday and his camera had been some distance away, making it difficult to assess what the officers closest to King had seen, said, and heard as they delivered the beating. Even this tempering thought, however, didn't keep me from feeling sickened and angry by what I saw. And I knew that if I was having trouble controlling my response, the rest of Los Angeles, America, and the world were not likely to be looking for ways to explain why they should not believe their eyes.

The Rodney King beating threatened everything that Tom Bradley had worked for during his five terms as mayor of Los Angeles. It had the power to replace the glow that the 1984 Olympics had brought to the city's reputation with a dark cloud that could last for decades. While I knew there would be competent investigations of the beating event itself, I suspected that no one had yet mobilized to deal with the broader question of how Los Angeles would analyze and act on its implications. That concern brought me to Tom Bradley's office.

We met in the mayor's formal sitting room in City Hall. Dressed impeccably, as always, he rose to greet me and enveloped my hand in both of his. I knew he had many claims on his time, so I got quickly to the point. I said something had to be done to make clear that the city was not going to treat this as an isolated event but rather as evidence of a potentially broader set of problems that required study and, if appropriate, remedy. I suggested he appoint a citizens' commission to investigate the underlying causes of excessive force by police and to suggest ways to prevent it. Bradley was equally direct. "If I do that," he said, "you'll have to be chairman." I had not come to volunteer, but was not so naive as to have thought I'd get away without further commitment. "Let's talk about it," I said, "if you decide to go in that direction."

The Chief

Bradley's next step depended, in part, upon dealing with a personality that was the antithesis of his own—

that of Chief of Police Daryl Gates. Where Bradley was calm and conciliatory, Gates was cocky and aggressive. While Bradley was laid-back, letting the spotlight come to him, Gates thrust himself front and center.

From the day I arrived in Los Angeles, it was clear to me that the chief of police and the mayor were the two most important public officials in the city. Daryl Gates, after thirteen years as chief, could claim, at least in some quarters of the city, that he was as well known and as influential a public servant as Tom Bradley. With a tough-guy charm, he had a passionate following among the white population in the upper-class suburbs, particularly the San Fernando Valley. He also had a flair for controversy, sometimes unfortunate, sometimes just dumb. For example, he'd once sought to explain unusual injuries to black suspects from officers' use of the choke hold by speculating that the veins or arteries of some blacks did not open as fast as they did in "normal people." He'd created resentment in another slice of the population by saying that Latino officers weren't interested in advancement.

As mayor, Bradley had testy relationships with a series of white chiefs of police, but nothing else came close to the antipathy between him and Daryl Gates. They had clashed over police tactics, such as the use of the choke hold, and over periodic allegations of racism directed at the LAPD.

On March 27, 1991, roughly three weeks after the King beating, Gates announced that he had asked retired California Supreme Court justice John Arguelles to form and chair a panel to study the LAPD's training and procedures concerning the use of force. Arguelles quickly named two prominent local lawyers to join him.

In the meantime, however, Tom Bradley had contacted me, saying he intended to form a commission and wanted me to chair it. I accepted the job and began to assemble what I regarded as a credible, authoritative panel. Plainly, two commissions doing the same thing was both unnecessary and posed the risk of exacerbating an already grave problem, but I saw in the situation an opportunity. If I acted quickly, before either panel began its investigation, I might bring about a merger of the two, underscoring my independence and avoiding the problems inherent in permitting two finders of fact to proceed their separate ways.

THE INDEPENDENT COMMISSION

On Monday, April 1, the mayor announced the formation of a seven-member Independent Commission, charged with conducting "a full and fair examination of the structure and operation of our Police Department." The very next day, April 2, Bradley met with Daryl Gates to discuss the chief's response to the Rodney King beating. Bradley was convinced that the chief was trying to minimize the importance of the incident and, unbeknownst to me, had decided to ask for Gates's resignation. When Gates refused to quit and stormed out of the mayor's office, Bradley went on television to denounce Gates's refusal, saying he had made a bad situation worse.

I felt compromised. The man who had appointed me only the day before to conduct an impartial investigation had jumped to a conclusion on a fundamental issue: whether the chief of police should stay or go. If a commission under my leadership ultimately endorsed the mayor's view, wouldn't the press simply characterize our effort as a rubber-stamping of Tom Bradley's preordained conclusion? Was it now impossible to claim convincingly that the commission was operating independently of the political apparatus?

As I pondered these questions—and gave myself unsettling answers—I contemplated resignation. But after thinking about the matter, I decided to do what I had told Mayor Bradley I would do. The possibility of merging the two commissions into a serious and impartial inquiry now held an extra attraction for me. It provided a chance to show that, whatever the mayor might think or believe were the problems that gave rise to Rodney King's beating, a group was assembling that would examine the facts before reaching, or endorsing, any conclusions.

Without consulting anyone, I called John Arguelles, the man chosen by Gates to chair "his" commission, and asked if I could drive down for lunch with him near his office in Newport Beach. Over that lunch we agreed that the public interest would be badly served by dueling commissions, and Arguelles generously accepted my invitation to join in a consolidated effort as vice chairman. Soon after our meeting, the other two Gates commission nominees, Richard Mosk and Willie Barnes, also agreed to come on board. By week's end, we had assembled a ten-member group of people with diverse and impeccable credentials.

I turned to two exceptionally able lawyers, John Spiegel and my law partner Gilbert Ray, to fill the key positions of general counsel and staff director, respectively. Together we contacted the leading law firms in Los Angeles, asking each to lend the commission, pro bono, a top trial lawyer for ninety days. By keeping the commitment short, we managed to elicit an overwhelmingly positive response. We also enlisted the gratis help of the accounting firms Price Waterhouse and KPMG Peat Marwick, and the statistical consultants Freeman & Mills. Within a matter of days, we had assembled a staff that money couldn't, and hadn't had to, buy.

I was determined to penetrate the surface of official statements and training manuals. I wanted to know the real attitudes of officers toward the use of force and racial issues, and how they acted when they were on the job. These facts could come only from the lips of the officers themselves and from the records of the department.

I directed our staff to talk to every available LAPD officer to probe attitudes toward racial issues and the

use of force. Over the next ninety days, they interviewed nearly three hundred current and former
police officers, providing the commission detailed
reports on what was said. The commissioners also
heard the oral testimony of more than thirty current
and former officers about management and discipline
within the department.

Within a few weeks of beginning our investigation,
a troubling picture had begun to emerge. In the eyes
of many of its veterans, the LAPD was torn by infighting, handicapped by Gates's isolation, and hobbled by
poor communication among its top officers. Each of
these generic problems was a cause for concern, but
they paled in comparison to what we learned from the
LAPD's own files.

Shortly after the King beating story reached the
press, the LAPD released patrol-car computer messages exchanged by the involved officers just before
and after the incident. The messages were damning.
They revealed both extreme callousness about the use
of force ("I haven't beaten anyone this bad for a long
time") and chilling racism (a dispute between an
African-American couple was characterized as being
"right out of *Gorillas in the Mist*").

Spurred by the thought that similar statements
might be contained in other LAPD patrol-car transmissions, I directed our staff to determine whether the
department maintained records of such exchanges.
The LAPD responded that such files did exist but
indicated initially that it was unwilling to yield them

for our review. We bore down. After protracted hard-ball negotiations, the department finally agreed to provide tapes of all computer transmissions from and between patrol cars for the six-month period preceding the King incident.

Reviewing and evaluating this material was a Herculean task. Accountants and lawyers worked in tag teams for a month, eventually examining more than one hundred thousand pages of patrol-car messages. The LAPD itself had never undertaken this, and as we soon learned, it was tragically overdue. By the time we completed our work, we had found 693 computer messages in the six-month period that demonstrated that the pernicious attitudes revealed in the transmissions at the time of the King beating were not isolated examples.

The messages contained statements ranging in tone from enthusiasm to vindictiveness about the use of force ("Capture him, beat him, and treat him like dirt"; "We'll start with beating the drunk and go from there"; "They give me a stick, they give me a gun, they pay me fifty g's to have some fun"). They also contained highly disturbing racial slurs ("I would love to drive down Slauson [a black area] with a flamethrower . . . we would have a barbecue"; "I almost got me a Mexican last night, but he dropped the damn gun too quick, lots of wit") and gender slurs ("You won't believe this . . . that female called again, said suspect returned. . . . I'll check it out, then I'm going to stick my baton in her").

The other "smoking gun" unearthed in our investigation came from the department's files on the handling of citizen complaints charging officers with
using excessive force or improper tactics. The disciplinary system was heavily stacked against finding fault
with police officers. Between 1986 and 1990, more
than three thousand allegations of excessive force or
improper tactics had been made by the public against
LAPD officers, but only 3 percent had resulted in
"sustained" decisions, the equivalent of "guilty" findings. While many citizen complaints were obviously
specious, it became equally obvious as we reviewed the
disciplinary files that the system of classifying and
adjudicating complaints filtered out meritorious as
well as bogus claims.

Over a 4-year period, 183 LAPD officers had drawn
4 or more allegations of the use of excessive force or
improper tactics, and 44 had 6 or more such allegations lodged against them. Although the nature of the
conduct alleged from complaint to complaint was
sometimes eerily similar, most had resulted in no discipline for the officer in question. Of even greater concern, however, was that when annually reviewing the
performance of these officers, the department took no
apparent account of the multiple citizen complaints
lodged against them. Instead, their annual reviews
were typically positive and upbeat.

The LAPD had clearly ignored evidence that a significant number of its officers had repeatedly misused
force and had not been called to account for it. The

live testimony before the commission of Gates's top aides reinforced that conclusion. Retiring Deputy Chief Jesse Brewer told us, "We know who the bad guys are, but no one is held accountable for doing anything about it." Likewise, Assistant Chief David Dotson said, "We have failed miserably . . . holding people accountable."

By mid-June, the commissioners had reached the unhappy, unanimous conclusions that Rodney King's beating was far from an aberration; that a significant number of LAPD officers, operating without adequate supervision or discipline, used excessive force under color of law; and that racism and sexism in the ranks were problems that required urgent attention. Virtually without dissent, the group agreed on more than one hundred recommendations that addressed these issues in detail.

THE GATES PROBLEM

We had yet to grapple, however, with the toughest question of all: what to do about Chief Gates. As the leader of the department, he held ultimate responsibility for what we had unearthed. But what was the appropriate way to hold him accountable? If we failed to act decisively or proportionately in dealing with him, the press and the public would pronounce our report either a whitewash or a vendetta.

During the investigation, I had come to a conclusion about Gates that lay somewhere between the views of his most ardent advocates and most strident detractors. I didn't think he consciously approved the use of excessive force or that he was a rampant racist or sexist. Rather, I thought Gates had disconnected himself from day-to-day LAPD operations as a result of his preoccupation with personal public relations. He came in late, loaded his schedule with media interviews or phone calls, and was inaccessible to his top staff. Daryl Gates, I believed, was no longer fully engaged in his job and ought to move on.

Solving the problem was much more difficult than diagnosing it. The job of chief of police had become a lifetime position. The Los Angeles Police Commission's ostensible authority over the chief was undermined by a city charter that gave him a legal property right in his job, making it virtually impossible to remove him. Those serving on the Independent Commission all believed that this needed to be changed— that the charter ought to be amended so that the job of chief would have a five-year term, with no more than one five-year renewal. But that did not solve the immediate issue of what to do about the incumbent chief.

I knew that the commission members would never agree unanimously to call for Gates's dismissal on grounds of deficient performance. However, anything less than a unanimous vote would guarantee controversy and bitterness that we could not afford. I decided that a different approach to removing Gates was essential. I reasoned that the commission membership could be persuaded that if two five-year terms were the maximum that anyone should serve in the job, then Daryl Gates, who had already served longer than that maximum, should move on. This would enable us to offer Gates a dignified departure, avoiding a highly divisive debate on his competence.

Gates's long-awaited appearance before the commission gave wings to my plan. Under respectful, patient questioning by General Counsel John Spiegel, Gates initially did a brilliant job. He described police procedures in relaxed, competent detail and denounced as "deeply offensive" and "very disappointing" the inflammatory patrol-car computer messages we had reviewed. Then his charm and self-assurance gave way.

Spiegel reminded Gates that he had once favored a fixed, five-year term on the job of chief. In response, Gates sputtered, "Five years and get out of here—that was my intent. . . . You gotta be a masochist to stay here much longer than that period of time." He added, "[Chief of Police] Bill Parker stayed a long time, probably too long, and probably I've stayed longer than I should, and probably if people left me alone, I would have left some time ago."

He had given me what I needed: an admission that even a competent performer should move on after five (or ten) years as chief. When the testimony ended, I was certain that the commission could now be persuaded to apply a ten-year maximum to the Gates incumbency.

My prediction proved right. After long discussion, the commissioners unanimously agreed that our report should say that the chief had given his full measure of service. We ultimately settled on an approach that began by noting Gates's thirteen years of service as chief of police, referred to the commission's recommendation that the job of chief be limited to two five-year terms, and ended with the sentence: "The Commission believes that commencement of a transition in that office is now appropriate." Estimated conservatively, each of the fourteen words in that sentence represented at least two hours of negotiation with my hesitant commission colleagues.

The commission's message was quickly understood and trumpeted. The banner headline in the *Los Angeles Times* said: "Panel Urges Gates to Retire." But, notwithstanding that we had given him a graceful path for exit, Gates was not ready to slip quietly from the stage. The day the report was released, he told a cheering crowd that he would step down only if and when the citizens of Los Angeles voted a change in the city charter that imposed a term limit on the office of chief. Gates was betting that the commission and those who supported its efforts were not prepared to put in another six months of work to implement the commission's key recommendation. Gates was wrong.

Legislating Change

The commission's report, including the recommendation to impose a term limit on the chief, was greeted with such universal acclaim that I naively assumed someone else would step forward to lead the charge for passage of the necessary amendment to the city charter. I should have known better. After catching up on my sleep and casting my eye across the horizon, it was obvious that everyone expected me to stay at the helm until the charter amendment had passed. Thus, largely by default, I took the lead in the campaign to frame and win voter approval of Charter Amendment F.

The first and easier part of the job was to draft the language of the amendment, get it approved by the city attorney and city council, and place it formally on the June 2, 1992, ballot. The hard part was getting people to turn out to vote for it.

What was needed to get the ball rolling was a citizens' committee to raise funds and mount a campaign. I enlisted commission member Roy Anderson, the esteemed former Lockheed CEO and a stalwart Republican, to join me in cochairing the effort, which we gave the uninspiring name of Citizens for Law Enforcement and Reform (CLEAR). Though we succeeded early on in winning the hearts and minds of an impressive list of prominent citizens from every quarter of Los Angeles, what we really needed was money to enable us to get the message out to the community at large. Anderson and I were the ones who had to find it.

I loathe political fund-raising, but now there was no alternative. The payoff for the hard work of hundreds of commission volunteers, as well as those who had signed on to help with CLEAR, hung on whether we could come up with $400,000 for a media buy.

It didn't sound like a lot of money, given the millions raised and spent by political candidates with whom I'd been associated, but political candidates have something going for them that the charter amendment did not, namely, the ability to reciprocate the kindness of strangers. Charter Amendment F was good if not excellent government, but it did not have star quality. No businesses had a direct economic interest in the outcome, nor would any individual or group be catapulted to prominence by its passage. It was the hardest kind of cause to collect for—something that was just the right thing to do.

Essentially abandoning my law practice, I allowed the campaign's public relations firm, Marathon Communications, to schedule me for appearances in any respectable forum that would have me. I appeared at churches, synagogues, community halls, and schools, on radio and television shows, and places in between. In addition to reaffirming my long-held instinct that I was not cut out for retail politics, these appearances, coupled with Roy Anderson's own indefatigable efforts, pulled in the money we needed to get Charter Amendment F on the public's radar screen.

It would have been hard enough to win voter approval to amend the charter in the absence of opposition. Unfortunately, life was not so simple. An organized opposition to the charter amendment, led by Chief Gates and the police union, dogged our footsteps, turning a number of my public appearances into tense and even angry exchanges. As the June 2 election drew closer, it seemed doubtful that we would win the necessary votes.

We needed something approaching a miracle. What we got was an unexpected, terrible event that jarred voters into the realization that reform was desperately needed. On April 23, 1992, an all-white jury in Simi Valley, California, began to deliberate the criminal charges against four white officers involved in the Rodney King beating. Like most Angelenos, I believed that the videotape of the beating all but guaranteed convictions. When six days later, at 1 P.M. on April 29, the jury informed Judge Stanley Weisberg that they had reached verdicts, I assumed that some or all of those verdicts were guilty.

THE RIOTS

Judge Weisberg delayed announcement of the verdicts for two hours. This seemed prudent, given that many in the community, including Assistant Police Chief Robert Vernon, had predicted that violence might follow any verdict. The delay would presumably give the police the extra time needed to prepare for whatever might occur. No one dreamed that an LAPD under Daryl Gates, who had served as a young field commander in 1965 at the time of the Watts riots and had vowed to stop in its tracks any similar disturbance, would be unprepared.

Shortly after 3 P.M., Judge Weisberg announced the verdicts: all four defendants had been found not guilty. Everyone in the courtroom, including the defense attorneys, reacted with stunned disbelief. By the time the defendants were hustled out of the courtroom behind a protective shield of sheriff's officers, the crowd outside had already begun to demonstrate and throw rocks. Just after 4 P.M., incidents of looting and burning in South Central Los Angeles were reported.

The first serious confrontation between rioters and the police came a little after 5 P.M., roughly two hours after the verdicts were read, at the intersection of Florence and Normandy, a relatively prosperous part of South Central Los Angeles. This event provided the first sign that the LAPD was not prepared to handle a full-scale riot. Faced with a chaotic situation, the police lieutenant in charge ordered all of his forces out of the area. Worse still, they never returned, and by 6 P.M. the police had lost dominion of the streets in a wide area of South Central. Six months later, an investigation headed by former FBI and CIA head William Webster concluded, "During the first evening of the disorder, the LAPD seems to have lost all control over the demonstrators in the South Bureau, who looted and burned at will."

With rioting spinning out of control, at about 6:30 P.M., Gates made an incomprehensible and irresponsible decision. Deserting the downtown police command center, he had himself driven forty-five minutes to a private home in the elegant Brentwood neighborhood of Los Angeles. He'd been scheduled to star at a fund-raiser in opposition to Charter Amendment F, and not even civil insurrection in his city would keep him from it. An audiotape of the fund-raiser revealed that while violence escalated in the streets of Los Angeles, for twenty-five minutes Gates calmly answered the questions of wealthy, white supporters before leaving the party to return to police headquarters. As he departed, his hostess is heard on the tape to remark, "I know he should be elsewhere." In all, Gates

Los Angeles, the night of April 29, 1992.

was physically absent from his downtown command post for nearly two hours.

When the sun rose on Thursday, April 30, no one really knew what would happen next, though it was generally assumed that the rioting would subside in the light of day. Several weeks before, I had set aside this morning for a press conference on behalf of Charter Amendment F, to be held at the top-floor restaurant of the thirty-two-story Occidental Tower, located on the southern edge of downtown Los Angeles. The event was to feature various luminaries supporting our measure, ranging from Republican business leader (now Mayor) Richard Riordan to Archbishop (now Cardinal) Roger Mahony.

When the rioting had broken out the night before, we'd talked about canceling the press conference. Then we'd realized that calming messages from a gathering of diverse leaders might help to end the unrest. Overnight, I altered my remarks from a direct pitch for the charter amendment to a plea for ending the violence. Archbishop Mahony and others did the same.

The room in which we gathered for the press conference faced South Central Los Angeles and had floor-to-ceiling windows on three sides. When we entered, perhaps a half dozen television cameras and many more reporters were arrayed with their backs to the south-facing windows. As chair of the CLEAR committee, I was the first speaker. I began my remarks by denouncing the previous night's violence and imploring the citizens of Los Angeles to direct their energies to helping us make important changes in the system.

As I spoke, I noticed that one of the reporters had turned toward the south-facing window and had quietly directed the cameraman who was with him to film something going on in the streets below. That tableau repeated itself during the presentations of speakers who followed me. When we had finished and the television lights were extinguished, the leaders moved as a group to the south-facing windows and saw that, as we had been speaking, fires had broken out all across South Central. The riots were resuming and accelerating, in broad daylight.

I drove dispiritedly to my largely deserted offices in the heart of downtown. For safe measure, my law firm and other businesses in the downtown area had decided to send most of their employees home. I could accomplish little at the office, but it somehow felt better to follow the pattern of a normal day. However, as I had been advised by the police and others to take special care to leave the office in the daylight, I decided to head home in the late afternoon. As I inched along the Hollywood Freeway, I could see cars loaded with shouting rioters moving north toward the white areas of the city, and new fires breaking out close at hand.

I had been delegated no official role by the mayor or anyone else, but I had seen enough riots during the Johnson administration to recognize the familiar choreography and the corresponding danger. As soon as I walked in the door of my house, I headed for the telephone, called Tom Bradley, and urged him to ask for federal troops. Bradley agreed and said he would talk with Governor Pete Wilson immediately.

I next called the Pentagon in Washington and was soon connected to the watch officer for Colin Powell, then chairman of the Joint Chiefs of Staff. I described the situation to him and urged him to begin identifying federal troops who could quickly be moved into Los Angeles if the governor made a request and the president gave the order. I knew that if troops were eventually needed in the city, the more advance planning that was done the more lives and property that could be saved.

On Thursday night, mobs of blacks and Latinos roamed the South Central area, looting and burning at will. By midnight, Governor Wilson had formally approved Bradley's request for federal troops. Over the weekend of May 2–3, the combination of local law enforcement, the National Guard, and federal troops finally brought the riots under control. The mayor was able to lift the dusk-to-dawn curfew on Monday, May 4.

During the five days of rioting, fifty-four people lost their lives, over two thousand more were injured, and property losses amounted to nearly $1 billion. It had been the deadliest urban riot in the United States in more than one hundred years.

In the four weeks between the end of the rioting

and the June 2 vote on the charter amendment, it was difficult to assess just how the voters were going to react to the events of late April and early May. The city had plainly been shaken to its foundation by the outbreak, but whether Los Angeles would say, as we did, that passing the charter amendment represented an important step forward was not clear. Ultimately, I surmise, Gates's curious actions on the first crucial evening, paired with the obvious unpreparedness of his force, made the people of the city conclude what I had some months before: Daryl Gates was no longer doing his job.

The Biltmore Hotel in Los Angeles is a traditional gathering spot for political candidates and their supporters on election nights. Typically, the hotel's principal meeting rooms begin to fill shortly before the polls close, each a cell of milling, expectant supporters waiting for a shred of good news. On election eve June 2, 1992, the Biltmore was truly a full house. While the fortunes of the charter amendment, the focus of my life for months, had drawn scores of faithful legal and business types to one set of Biltmore rooms, a much bigger contingent, the one awaiting word of Bill Clinton's fate in that day's California Democratic presidential primary, occupied the bulk of the available hotel space. As 8 P.M. neared, closing time at California's polls, word had already filtered to both groups that they would soon have reason to celebrate.

The charter amendment carried by a 2–1 margin. It prevailed in every district of the city, with all races and ethnic groups. The victory spurred Daryl Gates to resign within the month.

Governor Clinton also fared well on June 2, cruising to victory over his nearest competitor, former California governor Jerry Brown. After making my victory statement to the charter amendment supporters, I joined victorious candidate Clinton in his upstairs suite and we reveled briefly in our mutual good fortune. It had been a good, if frenetic, evening.

On the morning after the election, June 3, the charter amendment's communications adviser scheduled a news conference, again at the Biltmore. As the moment marked both the end of a successful political campaign and the vindication of the work of the commission I had chaired, I invited fifty or more of the stalwarts of both efforts to attend. We filed into a ballroom and arranged ourselves on risers, a little like a high school choir. I made a brief opening statement, addressing myself, in part, to rank-and-file LAPD officers. I said I knew the vast majority of the men and women of the Los Angeles police force aspired to a high standard of conduct. I hoped and intended that passage of the charter amendment would make their working lives easier. Then I invited questions.

The first question, or one of the first, is the only one I remember today: "You just won an election. Why aren't you people smiling?" No one knew how to respond or even who was supposed to respond. I stood in silence, listening to the ice melt in the carafe beside me. Then I heard something from the "choir" behind me. It started as a low collective exhale, then built to a deep, loud laugh.

The reporter was perceptive. We hadn't been smiling, and it had been that way since March 3, 1991, when Rodney King was stopped by the LAPD in front of George Holliday's apartment house. We, and the city we all cared about, had been through fifteen months of fear and uncertainty. While along the way there had been brief moments of relief from the tension, none had justified any public display. But today was different, and the reporter's question helped us see the difference. We had identified what needed to be done to change the LAPD into an organization that would be responsible to all of its citizens, and we had persuaded a strong majority of the people of the city that we had gotten it right. It now seemed okay to smile again.

8

◆

THE SEARCH FOR A
RUNNING MATE

How I CAME TO CHAIR BILL CLINTON'S SEARCH for a vice presidential running mate in 1992 is another of those tales that leads you to conclude that someone up there is planning your future. Although I did not know Clinton well, I had become convinced by the end of 1991 that he was the best Democratic candidate. He knew the key domestic issues—crime and the economy—and his personal style captivated audiences. Mickey Kantor, Clinton's national campaign chairman, asked me to introduce the candidate at a major fund-raising dinner in Beverly Hills on February 28, 1992.

I was predisposed to say yes to Mickey's request. Apart from my conclusion that Clinton was the man for this moment, I knew that Mickey had recently made a considerable personal sacrifice in flying to New Hampshire to help Clinton respond to tabloid charges of an affair with Gennifer Flowers. Mickey and I were personal friends, and I was particularly grateful to him for having served on the Independent Commission that investigated the LAPD. Mickey had helped me convince a politically diverse group of citizens to conclude unanimously that the department needed reform. In short, in addition to my enthusiasm for Clinton, it would have been hard to turn Mickey Kantor down.

Clinton arrived in Los Angeles late in the afternoon. My instructions were to greet him at his hotel, walk him up to his suite, then leave him to take a nap. But he had other plans. As I came to learn, he prefers talking to sleeping. He ordered some fruit from room service, then peppered me with questions about the presidents I had served. He wanted to know what I thought had gotten them elected—was it policy or personality?—and asked what it was like to work for them. He was especially intrigued by Lyndon Johnson and plainly admired his civil rights and antipoverty legacy.

After an hour of this nonstop barrage, it was time for us to go to the dinner. Moving with him through the corridors of the hotel afforded me my first chance to observe him in action with the voting public. As we walked, he dispensed smiles and effortless charm. When he stopped to hug someone or shake hands, he locked on with laserlike eye contact, making the subject feel like the most important person on the planet.

The campaign staff had offered to help me with the introduction, but I decided to write it myself. I stressed the candidate's ability to withstand attack and to bounce back without missing a stride. It went over well with the large audience, which included many of my Los Angeles friends and colleagues. Kantor called the next morning to say that Clinton was pleased by my three minutes onstage and hoped I would stay involved in the campaign.

Not long after the fund-raising dinner, Clinton asked me to head up his search for a vice presidential running mate. He never told me precisely why he had chosen me for this key responsibility, but I suspect it stemmed from a Kantor recommendation. Whatever the catalyst, I immediately began a self-taught crash course on the vice presidency.

For much of our history, the cliché that has captured the sum and substance of the job of vice president has been that "he stands only a heartbeat away from the presidency." As the United States has emerged as a global superpower, the office has taken on a greater significance. During my earlier stints in government I watched the importance of the vice presidency grow as President Carter installed Fritz Mondale in an office in the West Wing of the White House, brought him into top-secret briefings, and consulted with him on many foreign and domestic decisions. This was in sharp contrast to the troubled and suspicious relationship that I'd observed between

Johnson and Vice President Hubert Humphrey in 1967–68.

Looking back, I am impressed that Clinton, overcoming superstition and uncertainty, decided to commence the vice presidential search at the height of the primary season and before he had locked up the nomination. Mike Dukakis did not start the process until after the last primary, and George McGovern waited until the convention itself.

Starting so early meant that my meetings with Clinton had to take place around the edges of his wall-to-wall campaign schedule. To launch the search, Kantor and I flew overnight on April 25, 1992, from Los Angeles to Tallahassee, where Clinton had been campaigning the day before. By then, his primary victories had given him the lead for the Democratic nomination, but he was still running behind both President Bush and third-party candidate Ross Perot in the polls.

When we arrived at about 8 A.M., Clinton was out running. We began breakfast in his absence, and when he joined us, he quickly caught up, consuming impressive quantities of fruit and bagels at lightning speed. We got down to work immediately. Over the next four years, this would frequently be the setting, pattern, and pace of our business sessions.

I began by telling him that the choice of a running mate was probably the most important decision he would make before the election. Since he was an untested governor from a Southern state, his choice would be studied as an important indicator of his judgment. I urged that choosing the best-qualified person would serve him better than simply perpetuating the tradition of "balancing the ticket" geographically or ideologically. In the age of television, anyone chosen becomes nationally known within days, and the statements of the candidate and his running mate are compared and analyzed instantaneously, wherever and whenever made.

I pointed out that failure both to have a disciplined process and to put substance first had been costly in recent elections. Vice President Bush's selection of Indiana senator Dan Quayle as his running mate in 1988 had proved an albatross around Bush's neck and was the product of an obviously flawed approach. Bush knew Quayle only casually and had never had a face-to-face discussion with him on campaign issues. Bush's choice of Quayle stunned his closest advisers, especially James Baker, who never had a chance to warn Bush that Quayle was widely regarded as too lightweight for the job. Plainly, no one, in advance of Quayle's selection, had probed his sitting out the Vietnam War in a National Guard desk job, or his father's role in producing that assignment. Although Bush won in 1988 despite Quayle's presence on the ticket, by the time of the 1992 election Quayle had become a lightning rod for criticism and was a drag on Bush's reelection chances.

Vice President Mondale's selection of New York congresswoman Geraldine Ferraro in 1984 had encountered similar problems. Mondale started his selection process with a highly publicized series of candidate interviews that seemed principally designed as an appeal to Democratic constituency groups rather than as a serious effort to find the best person. The choice of Gerry Ferraro was designed as a daring stroke to appeal to women voters, but her selection actually hurt the ticket when the public focused on her thin qualifications for national office. The problem was compounded in the all-important early days after the convention when the press concentrated on the questionable real estate dealings of Ferraro's husband rather than on Mondale's substantive attacks on Reagan's record.

Whoever anyone else might think was the perfect candidate, I stressed to Clinton that the choice had to be his own. It would be unwise to defer the question to the convention, as Adlai Stevenson had done in 1956, or to a roomful of advisers, as McGovern had done in 1972. Franklin Roosevelt's instruction in 1944 to "clear it with Sidney" (Sidney Hillman, a prominent labor leader) was also a poor model.

Clinton listened intently to my presentation and, after a last gulp of fruit, responded that he agreed with the general approach. He said his main criteria were that his running mate have the stature and ability to take over the presidency if necessary, and that he or she be seen exactly that way by the people. Clinton pressed us to look for possibilities from outside government, and he gave every indication of having an open mind.

With that exchange, we were in business. We turned to defining the review process and developing a "long list" of potential candidates whom I would personally interview. Kantor and I had come armed with a start on the list; Clinton added several names to it. We agreed that the interviews should have three goals: first, to solicit advice on who should be considered; second, to determine each interviewee's interest in serving as running mate; and third, to evaluate the suitability of those interviewed for the job of vice president.

By the end of our breakfast, the list held thirty-eight names. This eclectic group included women, members of minority groups, senators, congressmen, governors, mayors, former public officials, and businesspeople. Based upon his own knowledge of the candidates, the governor designated fifteen names for highest-priority consideration. He said that, when I had finished the interview process, he would personally meet with a subset of those on the list, but he did not want the kind of demeaning public parade of candidates that Mondale had arranged in 1984.

I left the meeting with a clear sense of what Bill Clinton wanted me to do and with the broad authority and flexibility to accomplish it—an approach to doing big jobs that would become familiar to me over the next four years. As I learned, one of Clinton's managerial strengths is to lay down guidelines, then give broad authority for implementing them. He wants to know what's going on but doesn't micromanage.

From Tallahassee, I flew directly to Washington to organize our research team. Victoria Radd, a partner in the Williams & Connolly law firm who had a brilliant academic record and had been involved in the Dukakis vice presidential search, agreed to head up the team that would produce profiles from the public record on each of the thirty-eight names on our list. Early in May, Clinton named Washington lawyer Vernon Jordan, a longtime friend of both Clintons, and Vermont governor Madeleine Kunin to join me as cochairs of the search. I consulted closely with them as the effort evolved.

I began my interviews on May 11, in Washington, D.C., and quickly found that some of the likeliest choices weren't interested. New Jersey senator Bill Bradley, one of the names mentioned repeatedly in the early interviews, was reluctant even to meet with me. When he finally agreed to meet, he would do so only in secret, without the knowledge of his Washington staff.

It took some time to arrange a clandestine meeting, not in Bradley's home state but in a Philadelphia hotel on May 26. At the outset of our one-on-one session, he informed me that he had no interest in being considered for vice president. Having been warned by one of his senior Senate colleagues that Bradley was a loner and might react this way, I had prepared a list of propositions to test his resolve. Would it make a difference if he was the overwhelming choice of the party? What if his presence on the ticket would have a decisive effect on the outcome of the election? He was unmoved and made it clear that he would not change his mind. He didn't spell out his reasons, but I got the impression that he had his eye on something beyond the vice presidency.

I found West Virginia senator Jay Rockefeller deeply conflicted about whether he wanted to join the ticket, and my thirty-minute appointment with him stretched into more than two hours. He liked Clinton and was interested in helping him, but felt that his wife's career deserved priority because she had so often put his interests first when they lived in West Virginia. He displayed the calm confidence that comes with inherited wealth and success, yet had an appealing sincerity and sensitivity that made his dilemma real and credible to me. When we parted, he was still agonizing over the decision, but after mulling it over for a few days with trusted advisers, he said he had decided definitely that he was not interested.

The only prospective candidate whom I did not interview personally was Colin Powell. That job was handled by Vernon Jordan, a longtime friend of Powell's. The vice presidential search gave me my first sustained opportunity to work with Jordan, and I found him wise, engaging, and dependable. Though we came from different worlds, I discovered we had similar reactions on matters ranging from policy to style. On the few occasions where we differed, I was surprised to find that he was more conservative than I. We became fast friends.

Powell told Jordan that, in addition to family and financial considerations, he felt precluded from running by his obligation to complete his term as Joint Chiefs chairman, his loyalty to his troops, and his unwillingness to appear unfaithful to George Bush, his commander in chief. So we struck off another name.

In Tallahassee, Clinton had put Senator Al Gore on the priority list of fifteen, but did not single him out as more likely than others on the list for ultimate selection. Being from adjacent states and "New Democrats," Clinton and Gore were acquainted but were far from intimate friends. I soon learned that the public figures Clinton knew best were those he had worked with at the annual Governors' Conferences, men such as Dick Riley of South Carolina and Bruce Babbitt of Arizona. Gore brought neither geographical nor ideological balance to the ticket, and his detractors said that in public he seemed wooden and brittle. However, he was clearly a man of substance, had served ably for eight years in the House and eight more in the Senate, and had run credibly, if briefly, for the presidential nomination in 1988. Clinton felt Gore deserved careful consideration.

My interview with Gore took place in the Washington apartment that his family had long maintained for their personal use in the Methodist Building, across the street from the U.S. Supreme Court. He said he often worked there and showed me the room in which he had written his widely admired book,

Earth in the Balance: Ecology and the Human Spirit.

I was impressed with Gore's personal qualities and his record. His intellectual equipment was plainly excellent, and his personal standards high. I liked the crisp but considerate way he dealt with me. He addressed the possibility of being on the ticket with unfeigned interest, but not overeagerness.

Gore's résumé admirably complemented Clinton's. He brought experience in both the U.S. House of Representatives and the Senate, where Clinton had none. Gore had worked hard to make himself knowledgeable in arms control, foreign affairs, and the environment—all areas in which Clinton needed support. Gore had enlisted in the army in 1969, served in Vietnam for five months as an army reporter, and was honorably discharged in 1971. Though he did not balance the ticket in the geographical sense, his record strengthened the capacity of a Clinton-Gore ticket to govern.

At this juncture, Clinton was still campaigning furiously, and I looked for chances to meet with him personally to supplement our telephone calls on the progress of the vice presidential search. On May 26, a month after our meeting in Tallahassee, I met him in Cleveland at the end of his long day of campaigning to deliver profiles of the fifteen top candidates and to give him firsthand impressions from my interviews. He carried the profiles around with him for days, read and reread them, and telephoned me for more discussion of the candidates.

On June 2, the day of the California primary election, I delivered the remaining twenty-three profiles and another summary of my latest interviews. We shared election-night euphoria, Clinton for having handily captured California's convention votes, and I for the decisive passage of the Los Angeles police-reform ballot measure. I told him I thought it was time to narrow the list, and he suggested that we talk the following weekend.

On Sunday, June 7, Mickey Kantor and I called Clinton from Kantor's home in Beverly Hills. Clinton told us he wanted to proceed to the next stage of the investigation with five candidates: Senator Gore, Congressman Hamilton, Governor Cuomo, Pennsylvania senator Harris Wofford, and former senator Paul Tsongas. That Tsongas was on the list, despite his sharp criticism of Clinton in the primary season, is a good example of Clinton's willingness to let his superb political instincts, rather than his personal feelings, guide him in such decisions. Presidential candidates, like presidents, receive information from myriad sources, and I am sure his choices for the priority list reflected impressions he had received on the campaign trail, as well as my reports on the interviewees.

The examination we had in mind would require intensive effort and cooperation from the five men on our list. They would complete a detailed questionnaire, submit tax returns and medical records, and give us access to other confidential records. An experienced lawyer would be designated to analyze the material and follow up on any troubling questions. We had designed the process to prevent the kind of surprises that had emerged in the Tom Eagleton, Geraldine Ferraro, and Dan Quayle cases.

I promised the five candidates that our investigations would be confidential and the results would be returned to them or destroyed after they had served their purpose. Both Wofford and Hamilton promptly promised to cooperate, though Hamilton said he could not commit to accepting the candidacy if it was offered to him. He was apparently hesitant to give up his chairmanship of the House International Relations Committee and was also concerned about policy differences with Clinton.

I reached Senator Gore in Rio de Janeiro, where he was attending a U.N. conference on the environment. He asked for twenty-four hours to reflect, and when we talked the next day, his answer was affirmative but conditional: he wanted an opportunity to reconsider the question after he returned home. Remembering the bad decisions I'd seen people make when they were far from home and preoccupied with other matters, I admired Gore's prudence rather than faulting his caution.

My call to Governor Cuomo about moving to the next stage did not go well. Although he had been amiable in our initial conversation, this call found him in a foul mood. The preceding day, on *Meet the Press,* he had advocated that Clinton meet with Majority Leader George Mitchell and Speaker Tom Foley to show that Democrats could get something done in Washington. Cuomo was miffed because Clinton, when asked if Cuomo was stealing his thunder, said he "didn't mind." Cuomo worried aloud, for reasons he did not explain, that Clinton's comment would produce a "bad story" the next day in the *New York Times*. (It did not.)

When I asked Cuomo if he would cooperate in our more intensive inquiries into his background, he replied that he knew we had already prepared a "book" on him for use if he ran in the primary. (I could find no evidence that we had.) He added that the Republicans had had three gubernatorial campaigns to find something on him without any success. Then he said, "The answer is no," and abruptly terminated the call. The exchange left no doubt in my mind that if Cuomo was to be chosen as Clinton's running mate, we would have to take him without much additional information. I promptly reported this to Clinton, and it seemed to reinforce concerns in the Clinton camp that despite Cuomo's charm and formidable political skills, he would not be comfortable in the second chair.

Paul Tsongas also asked to be dropped from the list of five. He attributed his decision to a combination of factors, including his strained financial condition, other family matters (perhaps referring to the lymphoma that took his life a few years later), and discomfort with a number two role. At that point, Clinton added two names, Nebraska senator Bob Kerrey and Florida senator Bob Graham, and both agreed to cooperate with in-depth investigations of their backgrounds.

When I met with Clinton in Little Rock on June 25, I summarized the results of our intensive inquiries and prepared him for his meetings with the five remaining candidates. I urged him to meet one-on-one with them so that he could gauge the chemistry between each one and him, and form his own undiluted evaluation. Although he had known each of them in other contexts, I said he needed to assess them in this new and unique light. He agreed, and in preparation for the meetings, asked me to provide a description of what a vice president would do in a Clinton administration.

I described the important role that Vice President Mondale had played in the Carter presidency, and I recommended a participation that could be described as "Mondale-plus." Carter's relationship with Mondale lifted the vice presidency to a new level, but the two men had come from different wings of the party and frequently had different perspectives on issues. I recommended that Clinton seek a true partnership. That would mean that, in addition to having an office in the West Wing of the White House and a role in all key meetings, the vice president should be given meaningful policy assignments that would draw on his special talents. Clinton agreed.

Clinton traveled to Washington, and we set up interviews for him at the Washington Hilton. To avoid the press, we arranged for a sports utility vehicle to bring the candidates to the hotel garage, from which they were whisked upstairs to Clinton's well-guarded suite.

Clinton was impressed with all the interviewees, but clearly there was something special about Al Gore. Scheduled for an hour on June 30, their encounter began at about 10 P.M. and continued until after 1 A.M. Clinton told me the next day that he was taken not only with Gore's knowledge of national defense, the environment, and technology, but with his commitment to the need for change. Clinton also liked Gore's national campaign experience, gained from having stumped the country in the 1988 primary season before withdrawing from the race. Clinton obviously felt comfortable with Gore on a personal level.

To check my own judgment, I reviewed all of the vice presidential choices of both parties since 1944. Based upon that evaluation, I told Clinton I was convinced that in Gore, Hamilton, Wofford, Kerrey, and Graham he had an excellent group of thoroughly investigated candidates from which to choose. Recalling the disasters that often had ensued from last-minute changes of strategy, I urged him to stick with the plan and make his choice without delay. He agreed, but nevertheless some last-minute efforts were made to derail the process.

After the names of those interviewed had leaked to the press, Democratic Party chairman Ron Brown urged the addition of a woman and an African-Amer-

ican to the list to demonstrate Clinton's commitment
to diversity. Clinton agreed with me that this could
mislead those whose names were added, and he
rejected the idea, saying that "people don't like to be
used." A group of African-American leaders also
announced that they would try to persuade Senator
Bradley to let his name go forward. That effort ultimately proved futile.

Near the end of the search process, Ron Brown said
that Cuomo was interested in being considered after
all. He was still unwilling, however, to submit to
intensive second-stage scrutiny of his background. As
the message was delivered only a week before the convention was to open on July 13, I told Clinton that
even if Cuomo agreed to a thorough investigation,
there was not enough time to do the job. That ended
the matter, once and for all.

Clinton asked me to come to Little Rock on July 8
to review our files and help him make the final decision. En route to Little Rock, I stopped by Gore's farm
outside Carthage, Tennessee, to tie up a couple of loose
ends in the investigation. We met in the comfortable
family room of their farmhome, the senator in jeans
and a sports shirt, and his wife, Tipper, in a blouse and
slacks. We had a good conversation, which left me
fully satisfied. As I was leaving, I told him that while
Clinton had not reached a decision, I wanted to assure
myself that if the call came to Gore, neither he nor
Clinton would be embarrassed. He said that though he
would give a direct commitment only to Clinton, the

odds were great that he would not disappoint us.

After leaving Gore's farmhouse, I flew to Little Rock and arrived at the governor's mansion shortly after 9 P.M. Initially, I met privately with Clinton to give him the final results of the in-depth investigations. We were then joined by Mark Gearan, Bruce Lindsey, and from time to time, Hillary Clinton. Hillary had been a silent observer during our selection discussions, though I was well aware she had opportunities to make her views known. We gathered around a table in the breakfast room where there were several telephones.

When it comes down to the wire, Clinton likes to keep several names or options in play until the decision absolutely must be made. On this night, he went through the five names on the list, saying something positive about each, then conferring by telephone with trusted advisers such as Mickey Kantor. We also discussed the best timing for the announcement of his choice.

Around ten-thirty, Clinton said he was ready to invite Al Gore to run with him. I believe Clinton had been leaning toward that decision for more than a week, at least from the time of his interview with Gore at the Washington Hilton. Clinton found their similarities in age, geography, and outlook to be pluses. And he thought, as I did, that television had made geographic ticket-balancing obsolete.

Before calling Gore, Clinton said he felt an obligation to give the bad news to Senator Graham so he could file for another term in the Senate before the midnight deadline. I knew it was a tough decision for Clinton to communicate because of his affection for Graham. He left the room to talk to the senator in private.

At 11:35 P.M., Clinton returned and placed a call to the Gore farmhouse. I chuckled when he asked, "Did I wake anybody up?" because I knew that after my visit earlier in the day no one at the Gore house would sleep before Clinton phoned. He edged into the call with eloquent comments on the need for change, then popped the question. I could tell that Gore said yes because Clinton immediately started talking about the logistics of the announcement and plans for the days leading up to the convention.

No one could have predicted the enthusiasm that greeted the choice of Gore. The country was electrified by these two good-looking young men, both under fifty, with their handsome families and five children between them. The Clinton candidacy, which earlier could not seem to shake off Bush or Perot, suddenly shot up ten points in the polls and never looked back. After a carefully choreographed and intensely reported bus trip to New York, the Clintons and Gores took the convention by storm. During convention week, people I had never met before stopped me on Fifth Avenue to thank me for my role in putting the two together.

The partnership that began so auspiciously continued throughout my time in office. The way they worked together raised the office of vice president to a

August 1993: With Vice President Gore.

new level of public awareness. Gore became a full partner, not because Clinton made a formal commitment
to make it so but because the president genuinely
respected Gore's views and talents. They enjoyed each
other's company, teasing and laughing in a natural way
that bespoke friendship rather than a number
one/number two relationship. Time and again, I found
that the president made his most important decisions
only after talking privately with the vice president.
Clinton's mantra—"It's all right with me, but let's talk
it over with Al before we decide"—became familiar to
every member of the cabinet.

POSTSCRIPT

On April 6, 2000, Vice President Al Gore announced
that I would lead the process to select his running

mate in the 2000 presidential election. On August 7, 2000, the vice president declared that Connecticut senator Joseph Lieberman was his choice. The story of what transpired during those four months is, as they say in Washington, "another lunch."

9

---◆---

BUILDING A CABINET

THE FINAL WEEK OF THE 1992 PRESIDENTIAL campaign was a marathon runner's sprint for candidate Clinton. Though the polls were moving in his direction, he continued to run like an underdog, worried that his voters might lose their nerve and drift back to George Bush. During that last week, Clinton sometimes had to let his running mate or wife pinch-hit for him to spare his failing vocal chords. Despite the help, by the last rally of the campaign, held at dawn on election day in a Denver airport hangar, his voice had been reduced to a whisper.

After flying from Denver to Little Rock and catching a few hours' sleep, Clinton was back on his feet, studying the first exit polls and receiving reports from his state chairmen. The crucial states, the ones Bush had to win to have a chance in the electoral college—Michigan, Ohio, Pennsylvania, New Jersey, and Georgia—quickly fell into the Clinton column. By midday in Little Rock, the exit polls indicated that he had won.

When all was said and done, he had scored a 43–37 percent victory over Bush and a landslide 370–168 majority in the electoral vote. Nevertheless, Ross Perot had garnered 19 percent of the vote, more than enough to deny Clinton a popular majority, and one of the largest third-party votes in history. The heavy Perot vote meant that Clinton would have to govern—and try to change the direction of the country—with a shallow mandate.

On election day, Marie flew from Los Angeles to Little Rock to join me for the celebration. It seemed as if the entire nation had converged on the town: campaigners, "Friends of Bill," journalists, foreign dignitaries, and the merely curious. The several parties in process at the Excelsior Hotel complex soon spilled out onto the streets. Even with official credentials, Marie and I could hardly find a place to stand or sit. Because I've never been high on mass celebrations, I didn't need much encouragement to flee the scene. So around eleven, I went to bed.

The confetti still lay in the streets of Little Rock when the jockeying for position among Clinton's hard-charging campaign aides began. The principal struggle centered on who would direct the transition, and ultimately, who would be White House chief of staff.

Mickey Kantor, the national campaign chairman, had begun planning the transition in September. He installed Gerald Stern, on leave from his job as general counsel of Occidental Petroleum, in a suite of offices in Little Rock and authorized Stern to develop a transition plan. Gerry, an experienced Washington hand, generated a thick notebook, replete with elaborate diagrams, as a blueprint for organizing the incoming administration. By early November, the Kantor-Stern operation was ready to roll.

A group of campaign aides, including George Stephanopoulos and James Carville, immediately made clear that if the Kantor-directed transition was in fact going to roll, it would be over their strong objection. There had been a struggle over access to the candidate during the campaign, and the anti-Kantor group worried they might be shut out of the White House if Mickey was put in charge. With sound and fury, this group made its unhappiness known to the president-elect. Not ready to choose among the quarreling aides, Clinton quickly went outside the campaign structure for transition leadership.

Two days after the election, the president-elect asked Vernon Jordan to become transition chairman and named me as transition director. I would remain in Little Rock with Clinton, and Vernon was to lead the transition in Washington, where teams of Clinton people would prepare reports on key issues and critical upcoming decisions in each of the departments. As one example, ironic in retrospect, the team with responsibility for the Justice Department looked at the question of whether the Independent Counsel Act, which was to expire at year's end, should be renewed. Its recommendation for reenactment was embraced and announced by the president-elect on December 10. The same team looked at a host of other issues within the Justice domain, reducing its findings to multiple binders that served as briefing materials for the attorney general–designate. The same pattern was followed in the other executive agencies.

When the smoke cleared on Clinton's transition appointments, Mickey Kantor had been relegated to service as a member of the Transition Board. Even in this limited role, good-soldier Kantor proved his value to the president-elect by organizing a successful economic conference in Little Rock, barely a month after the election, at which business and labor leaders, academicians, consumer representatives, and ordinary citizens delivered their views to the new executive team.

The economic conference gave the nation a chance to observe Clinton in action for the first time as president-elect. He was impressive in several dimensions: his grasp of the subject matter, his ability to articulate his views, and above all, his willingness to listen . . . and listen. While some felt the conference was an unwise diversion from the task of forming the government, it was widely reviewed as a hit.

When Clinton asked me to serve as transition director, he told me he liked the approach we had taken in the vice presidential search and wanted me to adapt it to selecting his cabinet. It was a formidable task. Clinton said he wanted to have the cabinet selected and announced by Christmas, and we were starting from scratch. The Democrats had been out of power for twelve years, and there was no instruction manual on what we were supposed to do.

The approach I developed involved almost daily meetings, beginning in mid-November 1992, bringing the president-elect and vice president–elect together with a small group of key advisers to identify the candidates for cabinet posts. The advisers included Gore's chief aide, Roy Neel; Thomas F. (Mack) McLarty, a prominent, wealthy Arkansas utility executive and a boyhood friend of the president-elect; Bruce Lindsey, a Little Rock lawyer and longtime Clinton confidant; and when he could make the trip from Washington, Vernon Jordan. Other members of the Transition Board were consulted along the way. Hillary Clinton frequently joined our sessions, usually seated in a chair a few feet back from the table or in an adjacent window seat. Except when we were discussing positions of special interest to her, such as attorney general, or when I explicitly solicited her opinion, she seldom voiced her views. When she did speak, she displayed great depth of knowledge, coupled with strong conviction. There was no mistaking her powerful influence on her husband.

Our gatherings took place in the spacious den of the governor's mansion in Little Rock. The routine was to begin with a discussion of the mission of the

November 21, 1992: Talking transition
with Clinton and Gore on the grounds
of the Arkansas governor's mansion.

particular department or agency, then move to a
review of candidates. Typically, Clinton participated
actively in discussing the mission and in assembling
the long list of people to be profiled, but he usually
grew quiet when we reached the question of who
would fill the top job. His pattern was to review the
six to twelve detailed profiles that our Washington
researchers had generated, listen to what everyone else
in the room had to say, then weigh in with his position.

The product of these meetings was a list of two or
three names for each cabinet position or agency spot.
I would then invite those two or three candidates to
Little Rock for one-on-one conversations with the

president-elect. Conscious that the mob of reporters camped out in Little Rock was desperate for information on the selection process, I took pains to keep our progress secret, but was only partially successful. Although we went to the extraordinary length of having candidate profiles delivered to us by hand rather than fax, we were seldom able to bring a prospective cabinet member to Little Rock for an interview without some enterprising representative of the press spotting him or her and reporting the sighting. After the president-elect had focused on a single name, the candidate was subjected to an elaborate vetting by a team of Washington lawyers who were tasked to unearth any surprises in the candidate's background.

As part of the transition, Clinton named Dick Riley, former governor of South Carolina, to coordinate sub-cabinet appointments. At the time of the Riley announcement, I said that these selections would be a cooperative endeavor between the president-elect and his cabinet officers. This signaled a change from President Carter's largely laissez-faire approach—allowing department heads to choose most of their own deputies—a practice that occasionally produced high-ranking staff members who pursued policies at odds with those of the White House. Although I was one of those who had benefited from Carter's practice (Secretary of State Cyrus Vance had exercised his free hand by choosing me as his deputy), I felt that, to ensure loyalty to his agenda, Clinton should have a strong say in selecting the top subordinates in each department.

CHIEF OF STAFF

Had I been given a mandate to staff the entire upper echelon of the executive branch, I would have turned first to selecting the president's chief of staff, a position described by Jim Baker, Ronald Reagan's chief of staff, as "the worst job in Washington." The chief of staff drives the president's policy throughout the executive branch as well as on Capitol Hill. Though the post is not defined or authorized by statute or regulation, no presidential appointment is more important. Whether Jim Baker had it right or not, the success or failure of the presidency depends in large measure on the skills of the chief of staff.

I joined many others in urging the president-elect to give priority to choosing his chief of staff so that the person chosen could become an integral part of the team that was organizing the government. Clinton, however, wanted to proceed with naming the cabinet while he pondered the overall organization of the White House, including the choice of chief of staff. During November and early December, while we worked through the cabinet selections, he continued to resist entreaties to fill the job. He may have been reluctant to disappoint his disputatious campaign aides, each of whom seemed to have his or her own favorite candidate. When Clinton's delay in making the choice became a topic of press and public comment, he finally acted. On December 12, he named Mack McLarty for the key position. Presidential historian Michael Beschloss said of the choice, "There is no case when a president has reached back to such an old childhood friend for his chief of staff."

McLarty, then forty-six, was bright, charming, well-organized, and deeply loyal to Clinton. But he had no significant experience in Washington, D.C., and more specifically, with the Congress. Faced with a job that daily called for decisions requiring the equivalent of a Ph.D. in political chemistry, he brought with him few lessons learned in Washington's political trenches, with no wellspring of trust or confidence established with the key congressional players.

The president stuck with his lifelong friend for more than a year in the chief of staff job, despite well-publicized deficiencies in White House operations and troubled relations with Capitol Hill. But after seventeen months, the president realized that a different kind of person was needed. Leon Panetta, a nine-term congressman who was heading the Office of Management and Budget, was appointed to the job on June 17, 1994. McLarty loyally chose to stay on in the administration until the middle of Clinton's second term, serving effectively as counselor to the president with special responsibilities for Latin American affairs. Panetta, in the meantime, armed with boundless energy and an encyclopedic knowledge of Congress, gave the White House operation the shot in the arm that it needed. He deserves much of the credit for the first-term successes of the Clinton administration.

Each of us learned his own lessons from the transition experience, and I came away convinced that the job of chief of staff should have been filled early. As with the cabinet posts, there should have been careful discussion as to what the job required, development and thorough investigations of the backgrounds of a list of candidates, and brainstorming sessions with the president-elect to narrow the field to a few people whom he then interviewed. While the comfort level between the president and his chief of staff is certainly a factor in making the choice, it should not be the defining or even a dominant consideration.

THE LOOK OF THE TEAM

During the campaign, Clinton had developed a mantra, promising across the country to select a cabinet that "looks like America." Shortly after the election he softened the statement, saying that his cabinet "would look more like America than previous administrations." I never discussed explicitly with Clinton what he meant by this pledge in either of its forms. Perhaps he knew that, with or without his urging, I would push hard to find a widely diverse group of qualified people.

In practice, in our candidate-review sessions in the governor's den, we'd ask regarding every cabinet position whether there were qualified women or members of minority groups who could be added to our list. The answer frequently was yes. Ultimately, with our help, Bill Clinton fashioned the most diverse cabinet in American history. Of the sixteen nominees, four were women, four were blacks, two were Hispanics, and a twentieth-century record low of seven were white males. In comparison, President Bush's outgoing cabinet contained eleven white males, three women, one black male, and one Hispanic male.

This special effort to find diversity generally blended well with our overall approach to candidate identification and selection. The job of attorney general, however, proved to be a stumbling point. Initially, Vernon Jordan was thought to be the president's candidate, but Jordan removed himself from consideration. We then began a hunt for the first female attorney general in American history. While male candidates were discussed, they generally got short shrift in our conversations in the governor's den.

The first front-runner was U.S. Court of Appeals justice Patricia Wald. She was intellectually strong and widely admired for her capacity to work effectively with contentious colleagues on her court. But when sounded out for the job, she said she was within a year of establishing her federal retirement benefits and didn't want to lose them. She suggested that the new administration seek special legislation to permit her to take the job without losing her retirement rights and, hesitant about leaving the bench, sent word that she wanted to be drafted. Watching Clinton respond to this situation taught me an early, important lesson about him: he was usually not inclined to plead with someone to take a job. He wanted people grateful for the opportunity to serve, happy warriors who would be undaunted by the ups and downs of official life in Washington.

We expanded our search. Two other candidates, Justice Judith Kay, the chief judge of the New York Court of Appeals, and Virginia's attorney general, Mary Sue Terry, said they preferred to pursue careers in their home states. Some other women we considered simply didn't measure up. Attention then turned to Zoë Baird, general counsel of AETNA Life and Casualty, a deputy to Lloyd Cutler during his tenure as Carter's White House counsel, and a former law partner of mine at O'Melveny & Myers. I first mentioned her name in our Little Rock sessions, suggesting she be considered for the job of White House counsel.

Zoë and her husband, Paul Gewirtz, a constitutional law professor at Yale Law School, had met the Clintons at the now-famous annual New Year's Renaissance Weekend at Hilton Head, South Carolina. As we eliminated other possible candidates for attorney general, her name began to be discussed for that position. When I contacted her to ask if she was interested in the job, I got a quick and firm yes.

I asked Baird the usual questions about what she thought her Senate confirmation risks might be. She said she felt there were no embarrassments in her background, except possibly that her husband had been a sponsor for green cards for a Peruvian couple who had been working for them, the wife as a nanny for Zoë's son and the husband as her own driver.

Lanny Davis, who later served as special counsel to the president in connection with the marathon Starr independent-counsel inquiries, conducted the vetting on Baird. Davis's investigation showed that the employment facts were more complicated. The Peruvian couple that Zoë and her husband had employed for two years were illegal aliens, and the Baird-Gewirtzes had failed to pay social security taxes for them. None of us involved in the appointment, certainly not I, fully grasped the significance or possible impact of these facts. And so on December 24, 1992, Zoë Baird—attorney, wife, and mother—was named by the president-elect for attorney general. The Baird appointment was widely heralded, the *New York Times* editorializing on Christmas Day that "Ms. Baird more than vindicates President-elect Clinton's determination to put a woman at the head of the Federal legal establishment."

Barely three weeks later, on January 14, 1993, the *Times* ran a page-one story on the nanny/driver employment facts, which quickly came to be known as the "Zoë Baird problem." The story led to one of the most bizarre confirmation sagas in history. By the date of the *Times* disclosure, Baird and her husband had paid nearly $16,000 in delinquent social security taxes and penalties, and they had also released documentation showing that they had relied on the advice of an immigration lawyer in handling the Peruvians' situation. Initial public reaction was relatively sub-

dued, with some in the press and Congress characterizing Baird's actions as an "honest mistake" or a technical violation. While Senator Joe Biden, chairman of
the Senate Judiciary Committee, privately stated some
concern about the nomination, not a single member
of the committee publicly voiced any opposition to
the Baird candidacy when the hearings opened during
inauguration week of January 1993.

Then Zoë Baird took center stage. She told the
committee and, via television, the nation the details of
her nanny situation, then responded to lengthy questioning from the members. The committee appeared
to receive the information with equanimity. The
nation did not. The nominee's style and situation trig-
gered some deep-seated anti-yuppie animosity that
brought Middle America to attention. Before the session was over, the office telephones of the senators
were ringing off their hooks. Letters and adverse newspaper commentary were not far behind. Opposition
in the Senate mounted, and no constituency group—
including, notably, no women's groups—rose to
mount a vigorous defense. At the conclusion of a second day of contentious hearings, it had become clear
that the Baird nomination was in terminal trouble.
The next day she asked the president to withdraw her
nomination.

As we all knew by the time this drama had played
out, the Zoë Baird problem was neither unique nor
could it logically be confined to just one nominee.
Whether a candidate had employed illegal aliens

and/or had failed to pay social security taxes for household help—a "Zoë Baird standard"—immediately became an important part of inquiries of prospective cabinet officers and others subject to Senate confirmation. The White House counsel's office struggled to develop practical rules for screening on these issues, but many potential candidates simply gave up rather than face the intense personal scrutiny.

The president's next choice for attorney general was U.S. district judge Kimba Wood of New York, but she was beset by her own variant of the Zoë Baird problem. Judge Wood had hired an illegal immigrant but at a time when it was not illegal for her to do so. Nevertheless, the White House concluded that another candidate was needed since Wood had not been forthcoming about her employee and because the West Wing had no stomach for drawing fine, technical distinctions between the Wood and Baird cases. So on February 5, Judge Wood withdrew. The White House quickly turned to Janet Reno, the district attorney of Dade County, Florida, who stepped up to the confirmation plate and was swiftly permitted to circle the bases by a relieved U.S. Senate.

The search for diversity produced some other awkward moments and disappointments. The choice of Federico Peña, a Hispanic-American, for secretary of transportation left the capable Bill Daley of Chicago, a highly valuable campaign supporter, an odd man out in a last-minute shuffle. Hazel O'Leary, an African-American and the executive vice president for corporate affairs at a Minneapolis power company, was chosen as energy secretary over former senator Tim Wirth of Colorado and a list of other highly qualified candidates. Despite our gains on the diversity front, the pressure from ethnic, racial, and gender interest groups for greater representation continued unabated. Indeed, women's groups pressured the president-elect so relentlessly for the appointment of more women to the cabinet that he uncharacteristically lost his cool in public, lashing out at what he called "bean counters" and "math games."

Notwithstanding the setbacks and aggravations, in retrospect we clearly accomplished a great deal. The symbolic and exemplary value of seeking a cabinet that "looked like America" outweighed whatever transient problems we encountered. Cabinet appointments had too long been a preserve of white males, and we showed that qualified appointees could be found among women and minority groups that had been seriously underrepresented in the past. Not only were the people chosen by the president equipped to do their jobs, they performed another vital service for the administration and the country: they were role models, inspiring and encouraging the next generation.

As strongly as I feel about diversity, I do not advocate arbitrarily consigning a cabinet position to a particular gender or minority group. Likewise, I believe that a president should not reach too far into amateur ranks simply to achieve diversity, as there will inevitably be a price paid in performance. The increasing diversity of state and local governments presages strong candidates in the future. I am confident that there are Americans of every race, ethnicity, and gender who are deserving and capable of performing at the highest levels of public service. It strengthens our nation to seek them out and give them a chance.

THE ECONOMIC TEAM

Consistent with the central theme of his campaign, Clinton placed high importance on assembling a strong economic team. Shortly after the election, we developed a formidable list of candidates for secretary of the treasury, including Lloyd Bentsen, Paul Volcker, Bob Rubin, Felix Rohatyn, Bob Hormats, Hugh McColl (a North Carolina banker), and John McCoy (an Ohio banker).

Though during cabinet selection we tried to avoid designating favorites until we had discussed all credible candidates, from the outset of our work Lloyd Bentsen was obviously at the top of the list. Tall, suave, and distinguished, Bentsen had been the Democratic vice presidential candidate in 1988. In his four terms in the Senate and as then-current chairman of the powerful Senate Finance Committee, he had earned a reputation in the government and business communities as able and solid. For this new and untried administration, Bentsen's appointment would send a strong message of experience and stability.

To ensure that my discussions with Bentsen got off on the right note, I decided to go to Houston to talk with him rather than asking him to travel to Little Rock. We met for dinner at a quiet table in the suburban Ritz-Carlton Hotel and were joined by his wife, B.A. (for Beryl Ann). Bentsen had thrown his support to Clinton only after the governor had locked up the nomination, and I was uncertain what his attitude would be about the president-elect. Rather than engaging in a full-blown formal interview, I told him that Clinton had admired him for many years and wanted us to talk about potential problems in naming him secretary of the treasury. Bentsen and his wife soon put me at ease, making it clear they were whole-hearted Clinton supporters and that they wanted to join the team.

Bentsen dealt forthrightly with whether his appointment would lead to the loss of a Texas senatorial seat for the Democrats. He cautioned that it would be difficult for any Democrat to win in Texas given the current political environment. Perhaps to make sure that our conversation didn't end right there, he added that, in any event, he might retire from the Senate in 1994. He said that if he resigned now to accept a cabinet appointment, the person whom Governor Ann Richards appointed to replace him would have at least as good a chance to win the seat outright in 1994 as a Democrat who won a primary nomination.

In Washington, Bentsen had functioned effectively as chairman of the Senate Finance Committee. A capable friend in such a key spot would be important to the Clinton administration, and the new president was concerned about the loss of Bentsen's leadership if he was brought into the cabinet. I asked Bentsen how we could minimize the impact of his departure. He counseled that the best approach would be to convince his likely successor to the chairmanship of the Senate Finance Committee, Senator Daniel Patrick Moynihan, that he was part of Clinton's inner circle. It was a good plan, but Clinton was never able to execute it. Notwithstanding the president's formidable personal skills, he simply couldn't establish a working rapport with the senior senator from New York. They were just not built to work in harmony.

In approaching appointments, one of Clinton's absolutes was that officials sharing responsibility in a given area be able to work as a team. In the economic sphere, he was mindful of the heavy cost to President Bush of the clashes between his treasury secretary, Nicholas Brady, and White House economic adviser Dick Darman. Clinton intended to avoid a repeat of that situation. Bentsen was reassuring on this point, expressing enthusiasm for other prospective members of the economic team. I returned to Little Rock the next morning and gave Clinton an upbeat report on my talk with Bentsen. From that point forward, the senator from Texas was firmly set as the Treasury nominee.

To speed up and sharpen decision-making on economic matters, Clinton decided to create a National Economic Council (NEC) with a mandate to coordinate the work of the economic departments and agencies. Because this was a significant, high-profile innovation for the new administration, Clinton took special care in selecting the NEC's first chairman. Bob Rubin's name quickly rose to the top of a talented list. As cochairman of the fabulously successful investment-banking firm Goldman Sachs, Rubin had a reputation for extracting the best from brilliant but iconoclastic individuals. In the process, he had ably served a host of Goldman Sachs clients, including our Treasury nominee-presumptive, Lloyd Bentsen. Though Bentsen had expressed some apprehension about our plan to create a White House economic coordinator, when he learned that we had Bob Rubin in mind for the job, he decided the arrangement would work.

When I finally tracked Rubin down to sound him out about the NEC job, I reached him at 3 A.M. local time in a Frankfurt, Germany, hotel. He seemed to come awake immediately, and said he would come to talk with the president-elect as soon as he returned to the States. He told me several times in later years, with varying degrees of appreciation, that he thought of our conversation as a moment that changed his life. He was immensely impressive in his interview with Clinton and, while in Little Rock, managed to negotiate a strong mandate for the new NEC.

Rubin's outstanding performance in Washington proved to be a major factor in sustaining our booming national economy. He will long be remembered for his consistent pressure for fiscal discipline, his steady nerves at the time of the Mexico bailout in 1995, and his successful opposition to the straitjacket of a balanced-budget constitutional amendment. When Lloyd Bentsen resigned as treasury secretary on December 6, 1994, Rubin was the clear choice to succeed him and thereafter became the most powerful member of the cabinet.

With Bentsen and Rubin penciled in, we turned to the job of director of the Office of Management and Budget. In Washington, the initials OMB are so commonly used that officials sometimes forget what the acronym stands for. The director is responsible not only for preparing the national budget but for reviewing legislative proposals from all departments for their possible budget impact—an awesome power in a town where initiatives rise or fall depending on their projected costs. In the current era, when balancing the budget has become a bipartisan fixation, the job of director has assumed a near-holy aura.

Our review process produced two excellent candidates for OMB director, who were invited to interview in Little Rock: Leon Panetta, later to become White House chief of staff, and Alice Rivlin, former director of the Congressional Budget Office. Panetta greatly impressed the president-elect with his vitality, good humor, and vast knowledge of the budget process

("Best interview yet!"). At the same time, the president-elect found Rivlin distinguished, knowledgeable, and smart. In a close call and lucky parlay, Clinton picked Panetta as director and was able to persuade Rivlin to become his deputy. Her loyalty and good judgment in taking the number two job paid off handsomely, as she was named to the director's job when Panetta became White House chief of staff in 1994.

In rounding out his core economic team, Clinton advanced the cause of both quality and gender diversity by choosing Professor Laura Tyson as chairman of the Council of Economic Advisers. A professor of economics at the University of California at Berkeley, she was the first woman to be named to the post. In interviews with Clinton, Tyson impressed him because she could articulate complex economic concepts in simple but noncondescending terms. From her first day on the team, she kept the president supplied with crisp, comprehensible summaries of economic events and facts that he often used in talking to the press and the public.

The selection for one of the key economic positions, U.S. trade representative, was in flux until the very end. Former Arizona governor Bruce Babbitt had been penciled in and wanted the job. At the last minute, Clinton decided to shift Babbitt to secretary of the interior, feeling that his experience and reputation would be more useful in dealing with the sensitive water and grazing issues of the West. Babbitt had come to Little Rock and, after meeting with the president-elect, waited for hours in a room at the Excelsior Hotel for word on his future. When I called to tell him Clinton wanted him to oversee Interior, he could scarcely conceal his disappointment. "That's great, Chris," he said, "but whatever happened to the trade representative job?"

The president-elect wanted Mickey Kantor as U.S. trade representative. Kantor, who had not yet been penciled in for any top job in the new administration, was an inspired choice. Though he lacked prior international trade experience, his toughness, savvy, and knowledge of domestic politics provided just the right tools for negotiating trade agreements between the United States and the rest of the world. When in 1998 the president found himself about to be engulfed in the Lewinsky tide, it was predictable that he would call upon the stalwart Kantor for counsel, and that Mickey would answer the call.

THE FOREIGN POLICY TEAM

The Republicans' twelve-year stranglehold on the executive branch had a special impact on the search for a secretary of defense. Qualified, Democratic-friendly candidates for the job were relatively scarce, and those with the requisite defense-related experience seemed mainly to be found in Congress.

Senator Sam Nunn, chairman of the Senate Armed Services Committee, was a front-runner because of his well-deserved national and international reputation as a defense expert. Clinton had long telephone conversations with Nunn and reported that the senator wasn't interested in the position. What I was *not* told about those conversations was that the job Senator Nunn said he really wanted was secretary of state. Despite Clinton's best efforts to turn Nunn's interest back to defense, he wouldn't budge.

With Nunn out of the field for defense secretary, the search focused on Les Aspin, chairman of the House Armed Services Committee, and on Oklahoma congressman Dave McCurdy. Aspin, known as one of the Defense Department "whiz kids" many years earlier, had been chosen to chair the House Armed Services Committee because of his expertise on defense matters, even though he was not the senior Democratic member. As a Democrat who supported the Persian Gulf War and the funding of the MX missile, he had good centrist credentials. McCurdy, a prominent member of the House Intelligence Committee, was a rising Democratic star with his own ambition to be president. Indeed, earlier in 1992, long before the cabinet selection began, Congressman McCurdy had invited me to a one-on-one breakfast at the Peninsula Hotel in Beverly Hills to tell me of his long-term presidential aspirations.

Once he knew he was under consideration for secretary of defense, McCurdy made a bad move. To advance his candidacy, he decided to play on the fact that Aspin's appointment would leave the House

Armed Services Committee in the hands of liberal California congressman Ron Dellums. McCurdy began circulating word that Aspin's departure from that committee, leaving Dellums in charge, would impair national security. When this suggestion reached the press and the source was identified, it was regarded as a hit below the belt. McCurdy also proved to be wrong. After Aspin was appointed secretary of defense, Dellums turned out to be a responsible, if eloquently liberal, chairman.

I invited Aspin to Little Rock for the usual interviews. Over lunch before his meeting with the president-elect, I found him a lively conversationalist and understood why the president had said he preferred discussing theoretical defense concepts with Aspin more than anyone else he knew. That afternoon, after the president-elect and Aspin had had a reassuring conversation, Clinton offered him the secretaryship and Aspin accepted on the spot.

Though we all had high hopes for Les Aspin's tenure as secretary of defense, looking back it is easy enough to identify the factors that led to his resignation only fourteen months after his appointment. He had developed his working habits in the relatively undisciplined atmosphere of the Congress and had no experience managing a multibillion-dollar organization of mostly tenured employees. He also had a testy relationship with the man who knew everything about the Pentagon, Joint Chiefs chairman Colin Powell, having jousted with him about military intervention in the Balkans. So, although Aspin's appointment was widely praised in the press and on Capitol Hill, his welcome at the Pentagon was not warm. Given how much an incoming cabinet member depends on the resident professionals, especially in the hierarchical and sometimes hidebound Pentagon, Aspin's stint at Defense may have been doomed from the start.

The United Nations ambassador was the next foreign policy post to be considered. Clinton had upped the importance of this job, announcing that he intended to elevate the position to cabinet status. One of the names on the list was Ron Brown, who sought me out to discuss the position when I flew to Washington with Clinton on December 7 for a postelection celebration and fund-raiser.

Brown asked me whether in the Clinton administration the U.N. ambassador could function as coequal to the secretary of state in the foreign policy establishment. Although the president had not yet chosen his secretary of state, I was pretty sure I knew how to answer Brown's question. With as much diplomacy as I could muster, I told Brown that while the U.N. ambassador would enjoy significant authority and autonomy, the secretary of state, as a matter of principle, had to be in charge of the foreign affairs policy-making apparatus. I could see from Brown's expression that he was disappointed, and following our exchange, he seemed to lose interest in the U.N. position. Brown later indicated he wanted a cabinet position that had not previously been held by an

African-American. The president obliged him by
naming him secretary of commerce, a post he filled
with energy and ability until April 3, 1996, when he
died in a plane crash while leading an economic delegation to the Balkans.

Madeleine Albright, whom I invited to Little Rock
to talk with the president-elect, had excellent credentials for the U.N. job. She had been a foreign policy
aide to Senator Ed Muskie, had served on the
National Security Council staff in the Carter administration, and had been a top adviser in the Mondale
and Dukakis presidential campaigns. After a good talk
with Clinton and aided by a strong push from
women's groups, Albright got the ambassador's job—
and a platform from which she would eventually rise
to become secretary of state.

On an afternoon in mid-December, our cabinet
selection focus moved to the State Department. After
discussing the department's mission at length, we
developed a strong list of candidates for secretary—a
list that included Colin Powell, Lee Hamilton, Bill
Bradley, Paul Sarbanes, George Mitchell, Tom Foley,
and David Boren. Consistent with my wishes, my
name was not on the list, at least not on the list that I
heard discussed that afternoon. From the outset of the
transition, I'd felt that I could not appropriately manage the transition process and also be a candidate for a
cabinet job. I'd said as much when I accepted the transition director position in November, and no one had
argued with me at the time.

As our meeting broke up, the president-elect asked me to stay behind. Standing alone with me in an ante-room, he told me he didn't want to waste any more time discussing the secretary of state position: I was his choice and, he said, the vice president–elect agreed.

The offer caught me off guard. Since the press had speculated about my being chosen for State, the thought of serving in the job had certainly crossed my mind. Still, I knew that Clinton was under pressure from his inner circle to avoid putting people in his cabinet who might be characterized as Carter adminis-tration "retreads." I also had no reason to foresee that the offer of what many feel is the most powerful appointed job in the world would be made as I stood leaning against the wall of someone's den. Gathering my composure, I told the president-elect that I was greatly complimented but needed a little time to pon-

December 22, 1992: At the announcement
of my nomination as secretary of state.

der the idea. We parted with the understanding that I would give him my answer shortly.

After several telephone calls with my family and a sleepless night, I met with Clinton the next morning and told him I wanted the job. In retrospect, I don't suppose there was any real probability that I would have turned it down. Clinton said he was pleased with my decision and agreed that once my appointment was made public, I should immediately begin preparing for my new duties as the sixty-third secretary of state.

People sometimes ask me how Bill Clinton came to pick me for the job of secretary of state. The answer is I don't really know. The president himself addressed that question at the unveiling of my State Department portrait in 1999: "People ask me all the time, how did you ever decide to make Warren Christopher your first secretary of state? And I say, you know, I don't know—it just sort of came to me in the transition process—which Warren Christopher *ran*."

◆

10

A NEW KIND OF LIFE

THE RHYTHMS OF A MOVE FROM PRIVATE TO public life were familiar to me by now: winding down and closing out old responsibilities, climbing steeply up the learning curve of the new. I also steeled myself for the predictable intrusion into my personal affairs. Friends, colleagues, and neighbors would be approached by somber government agents charged with asking, once again, whether I was a loyal American. My investments would be flyspecked, cataloged, and assessed for any possible conflicts of interest. Everything I had said or written publicly would be retrieved and analyzed in anticipation of questions from Congress or the international press.

At some level, I was prepared for all of this. I understood and was ready to pay the price for the extraordinary opportunity that the president-elect had handed me. But what I did not, could not, know until the moment was upon me was the nature of the life Marie and I would lead for the next four years. That life would be defined largely without reference to our established living habits or preferences. Instead, our surroundings and movements would be governed by an idea: how the secretary of state was expected to relate to the world and move across its surface. This meant that our freedom of movement and expression—indeed, most of the spontaneity in our lives—would be put on hold for the next four years.

SECURITY BUT NOT PRIVACY

It was January 20, 1993—inauguration day for William Jefferson Clinton. "I'll take Larry Eagleburger down to his home in Charlottesville, and then I'll pick you up," said Ron Mazer, head of the Diplomatic Security (DS) detail for the secretary of state. Today Mazer was "continuity man." Eagleburger, the Bush administration's last secretary of state, was his outgoing responsibility; I, the incoming. Mazer's task was to deliver one package safely back to private life and fetch its replacement—me.

The Diplomatic Security corps is to the secretary of state what the Secret Service is to the president. Wherever I was, DS was charged with knowing I was there, making sure I was safe, and if the need arose, taking me instantly to the State Department or to a telephone. Two agents, unfailingly pleasant and considerate, accompanied me whenever I left my home or office, and backup agents were always in the vicinity.

I accepted from the outset that the security surrounding the secretary of state was not merely for show. Still, at any given moment it was difficult to feel that one really needed so much protecting. I had never feared for my life. The few menacing situations I had faced in my prior public stints—the mob in Taiwan and the urban rioters in the United States—had left me with no residue of apprehension. Thus, when I found myself on January 20, 1993, surrounded by people whose job it was to stop bullets headed in my direction, I could not help feeling it was just a bit much. Their presence seemed not simply excessive but had the impact, as intended, of distancing me from people and drawing attention to my isolation. For some, this might have been a titillating manifestation of power. For me, it was disconcerting.

The impact of my security entourage extended beyond my immediate person or family. Events that had been simple in private life became complex and awkward. When friends invited Marie and me to dinner, we were preceded several hours in advance by agents who surveyed their balconies and crawled through their basements to get the feel of the place. When we booked a table for two at a restaurant, the establishment had to set aside a second table for two additional guests who would order only iced tea and spend the evening scanning the other patrons. When I asked one of our agents why he never ate on these occasions, he said, "If someone takes a pass at the secretary, I don't want to have a mouthful of calamari."

DS held sway over every aspect of our lives— including our choice of a home in Washington. Marie found a modern, four-story town house in Georgetown available for lease. DS let us know they regarded this as a marginal choice. The house, they noted, was only a few doors off busy Wisconsin Avenue and was not large enough to accommodate a security command post in addition to the Christophers. When we made it clear that we really did intend to sign a lease for the place, DS quickly adjusted and improvised. They rented space for their command center over a store on Wisconsin Avenue that looked straight down our street. They installed cameras and high-powered viewing devices that allowed them to monitor our home from all angles. They also stationed an agent in a car immediately outside our front door.

Not long after we moved in, DS demonstrated the utility of these arrangements. Several hours after we had gone to bed one night, I was awakened by a noise in the small yard that adjoined our house. No more than a few seconds later, I heard the voice of one of our agents commanding, "Lie flat on the ground— don't even think about moving!" When I looked outside, I saw two DS agents, guns drawn, standing over three young men who were spread-eagled on their stomachs. I later learned the three had randomly entered our backyard while running from a police patrol. To their misfortune, they'd happened upon a fortified encampment.

One habit that I insisted on maintaining while secretary was my daily run. I told DS to expect me at the door of my house (or hotel room, if on the road) for a thirty-minute jog at five-thirty every morning. When I appeared for my first morning's jog, I found an agent in sweat clothes waiting for me. As we began our run through Georgetown, a tail car moved in slowly behind us. Over four years, my jogging partners included agents who could run much faster and farther than I, as well as a few for whom I felt I served as a personal trainer.

To enable me to maintain my jogging routine when traveling abroad, DS agents who were sent ahead to check out hotel security, vehicle routes, and the like were also tasked to map out a suitable running route for me. These efforts produced some of the most memorable runs of my life: beside Lake Geneva in Switzerland; around the Emperor's Palace in Tokyo; and along the bay near the Sydney Opera House. In Jerusalem, because security was a special concern, the agents arranged for me to run at sunrise inside a deserted soccer stadium.

DOING BUSINESS

When my daily run ended, the real marathon began. By 6:45 A.M., I was usually en route to the department in the backseat of an armor-plated Cadillac, two DS agents in the front seat with powerful weapons at their feet. Tailing us was a black sports utility vehicle carrying more agents and more guns. We entered the department through an underground garage, another bow to security concerns. I was then ushered to a private elevator for the seven-floor ascent to my office.

My day at the office typically began with a light breakfast and a quick scan of the morning intelligence digests, as well as the *New York Times, Washington Post,* and *Wall Street Journal.* While I was still eating, my executive assistant would arrive to brief me on what the day held in store. Usually, the schedule promised the equivalent of twelve hours of meetings. I learned quickly that my aides—experienced Foreign Service officers—regarded it as their responsibility to accommodate all reasonable requests for my time. As a result, the schedules they handed me each morning were worthy of a credit dentist.

Controlling my schedule was only one of the new minor challenges I faced. Another was controlling the beginning and ending of my meetings. At my law firm, I'd made it my practice to go to the offices of other lawyers for meetings, partly out of courtesy and partly to enable me to bring a discussion to an end by exiting the room. But at the Department of State, things did not work that way. The secretary rarely visited anyone in the building and seldom visited people elsewhere in Washington unless that someone ranked as the secretary's equivalent or superior. I could not countermand that practice, in large part because the Foreign Service believed that their own status in Washington turned on the respect and deference accorded their secretary.

The hobbling of my control over how and where I worked was exacerbated by diplomatic protocol. Whenever a foreign minister chose to come to Washington and I was in the city, I was expected to receive him or her, as well as the inevitable trailing delegation. Whatever else might be on my calendar, these largely ceremonial moments were sacrosanct. To refuse such encounters was to risk damaging our international relationships. And so, at least once a week whenever I was in Washington, I stood at the door of my ceremonial office; smiled as a throng of faces filed past me; smiled yet again as we posed for photographs; then sat and drank coffee with the group until they left.

One meeting place outside the department that is regarded as an appropriate destination for the secretary of state is the White House. Contrary to popular impression, many of the most important meetings that take place at 1600 Pennsylvania Avenue are not scheduled for the Oval Office. Rather, they occur in a drab, windowless, relatively small space in the basement of the West Wing known as the Situation Room. There, twelve leather chairs are squeezed around an oblong table. These chairs are reserved for "principals," the ranking people in attendance. Behind each of the principals' chairs is another chair, intended for an aide. The room, heavily secured against outside eavesdropping, is equipped for audiovisual presentations and for secure videoconferences with other agencies and overseas posts.

The precise composition of the group attending my meetings in the Situation Room would vary. Usually Tony Lake, the national security adviser, would sit at one end of the conference table, with the secretary of defense on his immediate right and me on his left. When the president attended, he generally sat at the other end of the table. The meetings—convened to discuss and resolve the toughest diplomatic, security, and defense issues—could last for a few minutes or for many hours.

While the president or national security adviser would sometimes designate a Situation Room meeting as "principals only"—meaning that I was to come alone—more often our meetings were slated for "principals plus one" or two. When I was presented with such an option, I was obliged to weigh carefully who would join me. No bureaucratic decision in the government is more delicate or is accorded more importance by career civil servants than who is chosen to join a cabinet secretary in a meeting at the White House. In selecting who would sit in the chair behind me in the Situation Room, I had to consider not only the substantive skills I required, but the consequences of my choice for the one chosen and the ones left behind. During my four years I received more reclamas (requests for reconsideration) on the subject of who would be my "plus one" than on any policy matter I can recall.

Before leaving for a Situation Room session, I would hold a "prebrief" in my office study to discuss what I intended to say at the meeting. The attendees would be representatives of all the bureaus and offices in the department with an interest in the subject matter. These sessions were often more spirited than the ones that followed at the White House. Seldom were all corners of the department in accord on an important issue. I might hear one position ardently advocated by a geographical bureau (e.g., Europe), a different one from a functional bureau (e.g., political-military), and a third from the undersecretary for global affairs. I would listen to all, announce my decision, then depart for the White House. Sometimes an earnest advocate of a losing position would follow me out of my office into my elevator, down to my car, arguing all the way for a reversal.

THE OVAL OFFICE

Just as I was obliged to receive foreign ministers visiting Washington, the president was expected to welcome visiting foreign leaders to the Oval Office. For the head of a foreign government to come to Washington without seeing the president, even briefly, would be viewed by many in the diplomatic world as evidence of a failed journey. With more than 170 countries having representatives in Washington, the number of requests for such appointments was staggering. I maintained a constant dialogue with the National Security Council and the White House schedulers to achieve at least a modicum of balance in Oval Office invitations to leaders of developing countries and to those from the industrialized countries of Europe and Asia.

The drill for a presidential meeting with a foreign leader was roughly as follows: I would send the president a memorandum about the visit and the visitor. Tony Lake would weigh in with his observations and thoughts. Just before the visitor arrived, I would join Lake, other cabinet members, and senior aides in a parade into the Oval Office to deliver an oral briefing to the president. The half dozen or so of us would crowd around the president's huge desk, where he sat awaiting our arrival. One of our number would begin by describing what the United States wanted to achieve in the coming meeting and by trying to predict what issues the foreign leader would raise. Typically this information would be delivered at machine-gun speed because too little time had been allotted for our briefing and because the president was behind in his schedule.

When the opening briefer finished, others in our circle would chime in with independent perspectives,

Briefing the president before a foreign visitor
is ushered in to meet with him.

frequently talking over one another. The president, often working on a crossword puzzle as everyone spoke, took it all in. Early in our relationship, I was disabused of the idea that he resorted to doing crossword puzzles out of boredom. He just seemed to need to do two things at once. His questions, inevitably penetrating to the heart of the matter under discussion, made it clear that he was fully engaged in and processing the conversation around him.

After the briefing on substance ended, a briefing on the press would begin. Because reporters and still photographers are traditionally ushered into the Oval Office just after a foreign leader has entered, the president has to get ready for questions from the media. While common sense and common courtesy might suggest that reporters' inquiries should relate to the visitor or his country, I soon learned that neither constraint applied in this situation. Reporters used such occasions to engage the president on the hot topic of the day, frequently ignoring his foreign visitor. Thus, just before his appearance, the president would huddle with his press secretary and one or two key advisers to try to anticipate reporters' questions and formulate possible answers.

When the press had finally been hustled out, the foreign guest was usually invited to speak first. This courtesy sometimes produced disaster for the invitee. Given the president of the United States as a captive audience, sometimes a foreign leader—particularly one who had waited months or years for the moment—felt compelled to deliver a soliloquy on his country's history, achievements, hopes, aspirations, and longitudes. One foreign leader used forty-four minutes of his scheduled forty-five-minute meeting to serve up such a monologue. When the speech finally sputtered to an end, I informed the visitor's shocked ambassador that the meeting with the president was over. Our guest looked in Clinton's direction as if to appeal, but the president just smiled, stood up, and bid the visitor adieu.

Despite the typically chaotic circumstances surrounding these events, the president never failed to deliver. When the moment came to perform, he accurately reproduced the useful kernels from his briefing, embellished with imaginative insights of his own. His celebrated ability to connect in one-on-one situations was displayed to its best advantage at these moments. He instinctively understood and related to his foreign visitors, both as dignitaries and political figures. I personally witnessed his meetings with scores of world leaders and saw him establish a quick rapport with the large majority of them. With his gift for empathy, he managed to become a close and trusted confidant of personalities as diverse as Yitzhak Rabin, Nelson Mandela, Jean-Bertrand Aristide, and Yassir Arafat.

After a foreign leader and his entourage had left the Oval Office, the president sometimes asked me to stay for a brief, one-on-one discussion of what had just occurred, then turned to a quick review of key pending and potential foreign policy issues. These personal, unstructured exchanges were extremely valuable. They gave me an undistorted view into the president's thinking and he into mine. In an environment where policy tends to be communicated through aides or carefully crafted memoranda, such moments are gold.

Before a farewell dinner.

WATCHING MY WORDS

While I had dealt with journalists before, I had never experienced anything like the scrutiny accorded my actions and words by the score of reporters who, full-time, cover the State Department. This formidable crew includes dozens of Washington-based columnists who write or broadcast comment principally on foreign affairs, as well as a huge foreign press contingent, poised to cover any subject affecting their countries or regions.

It didn't take me long to recognize that my reputation, and that of the department, would depend heavily on how this large and talented group characterized and interpreted what I said and did. It also became readily apparent that there was no respite from their scrutiny. Fortunately, I had superb help.

Hiring Mike McCurry as State Department spokesman was one of the best personnel decisions I've ever made. His mastery of the states of play and our policy in every part of the world, coupled with a winning, often self-deprecating humor, gained him credibility and admirers from his first day on the job. Unfortunately for me, McCurry's talents came to be known too widely. In late 1994, the president plucked him from State and placed him in the toughest press relations job in the world—White House press secretary. During his nearly two years with me, however, Mike saved our bacon and assorted other parts of the department's menu on occasions too numerous to mention.

My second, less visible help with the press came from Tom Donilon, my chief of staff. Though only thirty-eight, Donilon had dealt with the major league press for nearly fifteen years, beginning as an assistant in the Carter White House. On an average day at the State Department, Donilon took more than a dozen calls from reporters, providing information, clarification, and argument as the situation required. With his highly developed insider network, uncanny political instincts, and ability to charm snakes from trees, Tom kept us out of trouble and, when he couldn't, helped to extricate us.

Discussions with Donilon and McCurry (or his able successor, Nick Burns) preceded every encounter I had with the press. They made sure I was up-to-date on developments in every relevant locale and also that I understood the background and perspective of the reporters with whom I would deal. Even with the expert help they provided, I give myself a middling grade in press relations. I was not what reporters were looking for—a colorful talker who dispensed quotable tidbits as he went. Perhaps because of my background as a lawyer, I am hyperconscious of the ease with which words can be misunderstood or distorted. As a result, I use them deliberately and sparingly. This is not, and was not, grist for inspired prose or punditry.

Another hangover from my legal training was the obsession with preparation. I knew that whatever I said to a member of the press would be examined not simply for some new fact or position, but for something even slightly wrong or out of sync with what others in the administration were saying on the same topic. Consequently, my run-up to any press encounter was a self-imposed stress test. To get ready for a Sunday TV appearance, for example, late on Saturday morning I would receive a briefing from department specialists on the geographic or subject area likely to be the focus of questioning, then spend much of Saturday afternoon in question-and-answer sessions with my staff. Saturday night I would look over my notes and try, often unsuccessfully, to go to sleep.

I would awaken at about 5 A.M. on Sunday morning, check overnight developments, and skim the Sunday papers. The Sunday front pages and opinion sections, I came to learn, were often the source of questions from the reporters who appeared on these programs. By 9 A.M. I had participated in a conference call with other administration officials who were scheduled to appear on Sunday interview shows. Generally speaking, our goal was to sound as if we were singing from the same hymnal. Occasionally, we succeeded. In addition, these Sunday-morning calls sometimes produced substantive policy results, as we struggled to agree on definitions or descriptions of positions on matters that had developed overnight.

Of my various forays into the press maw, the ones I found consistently most satisfying were my appearances with Jim Lehrer on the PBS *NewsHour*. My relative comfort derived both from the format of the program, permitting full answers and follow-up discussion, and from Lehrer's approach to his job. He is not a "gotcha" journalist, someone out to prove a point or make a reputation on the basis of rapid-fire exchanges with a notable guest. Rather, he seems genuinely interested in getting to the heart of things and in taking and giving the time necessary to do so. His style, particularly when paired with my own, may not have made for compelling television, but it certainly produced a deeper and clearer discussion of key issues than one found in the vast majority of competing shows.

The press's intense focus on what I had to say about world events was not a surprise. However, it was beyond my imagination that their interest extended to what car I drove, movies I saw, clothes I wore, and wine I drank. For example, a few weeks after we set up housekeeping in Washington, the *Wall Street Journal* reported that my wife had arrived at a luncheon driving a foreign-made car. The story had the make of the car wrong, failing to reveal that it had been made by an American-owned manufacturer. More to the point, however, was the question that came to Marie's lips and mine simultaneously upon reading the *Journal* piece: "Who in the world could possibly care?"

Though we never got a satisfactory answer to our question, it quickly became apparent that reporters felt that someone, somewhere, wanted to read or hear about what we were doing that day. When we went to see *Babe,* the charming movie about a pig that learns to perform as a Border collie, stories in the press speculated that the pressures of my work had caused me to revert to my childhood. When the Strobe Talbotts and the Warren Christophers went to see *Fargo* late one Saturday afternoon, the press featured our outing as a dereliction of duty, failing to note that we would spend all the rest of the weekend at our desks. It was enough to tempt me to rent videos for the duration.

For some, I suppose, the attention and celebrity that came with my new job might have been seen as an added benefit. For me, it was the opposite. My career, reputation, and effectiveness had derived from, and depended upon, my being a private, discreet, reserved, and sometimes modest person. To try to change, to attempt to become someone else, would lessen my ability to do what I had come to Washington to do. I decided that even if my style wasn't what the press was looking for, I had to remain who and what I was.

FROM HERE TO THERE

I have never aspired to own a plane. This is not to say that I have never fantasized about having absolute control over when and how I travel. Anyone who has drawn the middle seat in coach, or who has learned that a "minor mechanical problem" will delay a departure for anywhere between twenty minutes and ten hours, has undoubtedly experienced his or her own version of this fantasy. Still, prior to January 1993, I had never seriously considered what travel arrangements focused exclusively on *my* schedule and *my* destination would be like.

The first exposure I had to secretarial travel came less than a month after I was sworn in. On the evening of February 17, 1993, I attended the president's State of the Union address. As the last round of applause died out, my security team ushered me to my car and on to Andrews Air Force Base for my initial official trip abroad—to the Middle East.

The first unusual thing I noticed was that upon reaching the airport my car did not stop in the parking lot or even in front of the terminal. Instead, we drove onto the tarmac and speeded toward a four-engine aircraft, bathed in floodlights, with the UNITED STATES OF AMERICA printed on the fuselage, set off by the American flag. This was heady stuff—so exciting, in fact, that I barely noticed that the plane was a thirty-year-old Boeing 707, one of several such artifacts from the dawn of the jet age that had been reserved for my use. One of those, the aircraft that bore President Kennedy's body from Dallas to Washington on November 22, 1963, is now in the collection of the Smithsonian Institution.

The aides who would travel with me, as well as their baggage, were already aboard the plane when we approached. The standing instruction to all in the party was that they were to be in their places before I climbed the stairs to the plane. As a result, when I entered the cabin, the door closed behind me and the engines revved. We were airborne in a few minutes.

Once aloft, I worked my way from front to back to familiarize myself with this new environment. Immediately behind the cockpit and entry door was a panel of lights and switches before which sat two air force communications experts. While I never gained any real sense of how their gadgetry operated, I learned quickly that they could put me in touch almost instantly with anyone, anywhere in the world. Unfortunately, the system was bidirectional. Even worse, when I was aloft, it was not possible, or at least not credible, for someone to put off a caller by saying that I'd stepped out for a few minutes. As a consequence, though I'd thought that my isolated traveling hours might be spent in preparation or even in catching a nap, the reality was that I was often on the phone.

Behind the communications panel were several rows of seats occupied by a backup flight crew and by

My trusty chariot:
a thirty-year-old Boeing 707.

my Diplomatic Security agents. Next came my compartment, spacious enough for meetings with as many
as five staff members, and versatile enough to double
as a flying hotel room, complete with convertible sofa
bed and bathroom. Behind my compartment was a
small conference area that housed my senior staff.
Behind them was an area occupied by assistant secretaries, Foreign Service officers, secretaries, technicians,
and sufficient office machinery, including computers,
a fax, and a full-size copier, to keep a flood of paper
churning out (and in) while we moved across the
world.

Behind all the rest was the press section, capable of
accommodating as many as twenty people. By custom, and at the direction of my advisers Donilon and
McCurry, I appeared before the traveling press only
when I had a mission—something to say or do that
had been planned in advance. Free-form discussions
with the traveling press were, they believed, a recipe
for trouble.

Because of the 707's limited range, I learned quickly
that there was no such thing as a nonstop flight from
Washington to the Middle East or even to many European capitals. My first trip eastward from Washington,
like most of those that followed, featured a refueling
stop at Shannon, Ireland, a six-hour flight from Washington. At Shannon, most of us got off to stretch our
legs, to browse the usually empty duty-free store, or to
saunter over to the stand-up bar in the middle of the
transit lounge. On our first Shannon stopover, a num-

ber of my companions found that the bar offered a superb Irish coffee and urged me to join them. Thinking about the day that awaited me in the Mideast, I agreed, but asked the bartender to leave out the whiskey and to make the coffee decaf. He gave me a withering look, then silently filled my order. The next time we stopped in Shannon, I stepped up to the bar and a cup of steaming something with whipped cream on top was placed in front of me. I asked the bartender what was in the cup and he replied, "It's a 'Christopher'—an Irish coffee with no Irish and no coffee."

From Shannon, we flew five hours to Cairo. As it was now daylight, everyone was up and working, expecting me to do the same. First came my executive assistant with the daily intelligence report and a briefing on overnight developments around the world. Then came a raft of paper containing every possible item of information I might require when we hit the ground. Behind the paper came Ed Djerejian, Dennis Ross, and other officers from the department's Near Eastern Bureau, who crowded into my cabin and delivered summaries of what lay ahead. As this would be my first face-to-face meeting with top leaders in the region, everyone was anxious to see that I did my best. I was engulfed by paper, trying to avoid drowning.

While I was immersed in all of this briefing material, Mike McCurry rapped on my compartment door to announce that it was "show time." The moment had come for me to walk to the rear of the aircraft, enter the press lair, and say something secretarial. On this occasion, I was to give a modest preview of what I had in mind for my meetings in Cairo and Amman. Because the noise of the 707's engines drowned out even basso profundo voices, McCurry said I would have to stand at the front of the press compartment with a portable mike and headphones so the reporters and I could hear and speak to one another. As I stood, microphone in hand, looking at the small group in the press compartment, I felt like a nightclub singer who had failed to draw a crowd on opening night. And like any other new act, I was going to have to wait for the morning papers to find out how I had done.

We landed just before 7 P.M. local time. I descended the steps of the plane and read a statement that I had prepared en route, the principal purpose of which was to give the local press something to use immediately. Then I climbed into a limousine that looked very much like the one I had exited at Andrews Air Force Base nearly fifteen hours earlier, and we took off at breakneck speed, coming to rest in short order before the Semiramis Hotel. I was ushered out and up to a floor of the hotel that had been set aside for the secretary of state and his entourage. Armed guards sat at the elevator doors, and more stood at the ready down each hall. A stand-alone telephone system, with instruments in each room on our floor, enabled us to speak instantly to various offices in Washington and to one another. A portion of the floor had been converted to offices, replete with computers, copiers, and fax machines. We were a self-contained community, one that would disappear with my departure and be replicated at each foreign stop I would make until I left office.

Over the next four days I traveled to eight countries, met the kings, presidents, and/or prime ministers of each, and checked into and out of seven hotels. Over the next four years I traveled almost eight hundred thousand miles and occupied more hotel suites than I can remember. I've been asked about my travel fatigue. Though the question is usually put with delicacy, the subtext is pretty clear: How did I manage a few times, in full view of the TV cameras, to fall asleep in public and keep my job? One answer is that you just can't help getting tired at the wrong time of day when you're in someone else's time zone. Another answer is that not everyone whose eyes are closed is sleeping. I leave it at that.

While the novelty of my travel arrangements faded quickly, the excitement and exhilaration that attached to my arrivals in distant capitals never abated. As I exited the door of my 707, emblazoned with my country's name and flag, I felt that the waiting crowds saw something more than an aging lawyer with a temporary lease on his own airplane. America had found a way to deliver up a feeling, as well as a person, to the rest of the world. The aura of our country and of the highest-ranking cabinet member within its government hovered around and above me.

Such was the life into which I transitioned in January 1993, an environment having less to do with who I was than what I represented. Whether I needed or wanted the security, attention, or comfort was beside the point. I now wore the mantle on which these perquisites were embroidered.

11

◆

THE PROMISE OF PEACE

THE ITINERARY AND SUBSTANCE OF MY FIRST trip abroad as secretary were dictated by the state of the Middle East "game board." As of early 1993, Israel was encircled by antagonists, just as it had been for the preceding four decades. With Syria and Lebanon to the north, Jordan to the east, and the Palestinians contesting every inch of the West Bank and Gaza, the Jewish state was an island in a hostile sea. The Israeli-Egyptian agreement negotiated at Camp David during the Carter administration had produced only a cold peace. In more than a decade, President Mubarak of Egypt had never once traveled to Israel.

After the Gulf War with Iraq, the Bush administration had made a determined effort to jump-start the peace process. The immediate goal was to find a format and terms of reference acceptable to the Likud government in Israel and to the principal Arab leaders. Reflecting the deep hostility between the parties, it took nine trips to the Middle East by Secretary James Baker to persuade both sides to attend peace talks in Madrid in October 1991.

The Madrid Conference launched four tracks of bilateral negotiations between Israel on the one hand, and Lebanon, Syria, Jordan, and the Palestinians on the other. But almost as soon as the talks began, they slowed to a crawl. None of the Arab parties wanted to commit to anything of substance until after the June 23, 1992, elections in Israel, in which the Labor Party's Yitzhak Rabin was challenging Likud's Yitzhak Shamir.

When Rabin defeated Shamir, it seemed that the moment was finally at hand for the restart of serious substantive talks. This time, however, a development in the United States complicated the process. In August, Jim Baker announced he would leave the State Department to manage President Bush's 1992 reelection campaign. His departure meant that the peace talks would remain on hold until after the American presidential election. When, on November 3, the American people decided that Bill Clinton would lead the country for the next four years, hopes for movement in the peace process rose once again. The optimism, however, was short-lived.

In December 1992, before the Clinton administration even took office, Israel deported four hundred Palestinians to a no-man's-land in the mountains of Lebanon. The Israelis acted without semblance of due process, and the United Nations Security Council adopted a resolution denouncing the deportations as a violation of international law. Until this issue was resolved, there would plainly be no movement on any of the four negotiating tracks established at Madrid. Changing this picture was to be my maiden challenge in the thorny world of Middle East diplomacy.

FIRST PROBLEM— FIRST IMPRESSIONS

The key to resolving the problem was held by Yitzhak Rabin, who had ordered the deportations as a reprisal for an outburst of killings in the occupied territories. He wanted to restart the peace process, but politics and principle made it impossible for him to permit the immediate return of all the deportees.

I would have much preferred that my first official communication with Rabin come in a face-to-face meeting, but the need to resolve the deportee issue was too urgent to await ideal circumstances. So, at the end of my first week in office, I initiated telephone calls to Rabin to probe for an opening. Not wanting to take him by surprise, I asked Dennis Ross, the special Middle East coordinator, to lay the groundwork for my call by contacting Rabin's military aide, Danny Yatom.

Through Ross, the message came back that Rabin was waiting to hear from me.

In our first telephone conversation, as in person, Rabin was formal and gruff. Yet I was immediately taken by his candor. He stated plainly what he was willing to do and what he would not do. He was not open to debate, he said, on what he regarded as matters of Israel's security. After some gentle prodding, however, he said what he would do: return one hundred of the four hundred deportees and reduce the deportation terms of the remaining three hundred, meaning that all four hundred would be back in Israel by the end of 1993.

I thought Rabin's proposal should and would fly with the Arab leaders, and I mounted a telephone campaign to test the waters. By early February 1993, I was sufficiently confident that the Arabs would be placated by Rabin's actions that I directed my staff to begin planning my inaugural trip abroad, the ten-day visit to eight Middle Eastern cities that began on the evening of the president's State of the Union address. The goal of the trip was twofold: to make my first direct contact with the key players and to push each of them to restart the four negotiating tracks defined at Madrid.

As I began to immerse myself in the backgrounds of the Arab leaders I was to meet, I was struck by a characteristic they shared. Despite the uncertain, treacherous conditions that had prevailed in the region for many years, virtually every figure of authority I would encounter had been in place for more than a decade. All had attended the Madrid Conference in 1991, and all had participated in the twists and turns that marked the contemporary peace process. I felt that each would understand that the advent of new administrations in Tel Aviv and Washington created a unique opportunity for progress, perhaps a breakthrough, in the peace process.

In Cairo, our first stop after leaving Washington on February 18, 1993, I met with Hosni Mubarak, Egypt's president since the assassination of Anwar Sadat in October 1981. Perhaps because he had assumed office suddenly, Mubarak was widely underestimated and, for a time, was overshadowed by the legacy and memory of his predecessor. After several years, however, it became clear that Mubarak was more than just a transitional leader, and as he consolidated his power, he began to emerge as a real force in the region.

Simply shaking Mubarak's hand confirmed one detail of the background I'd been provided by my staff: he is a physically powerful man. Regular exercise, including vigorous handball matches, had produced a superbly conditioned sixty-four-year-old. Mubarak was impeccably groomed and meticulous. He kept a box of wash-and-dry towels on his coffee table, which he used freely.

Mubarak professed great interest in assisting the peace process and, given his close relationship with Yassir Arafat, was an important figure in determining whether the parties would in fact resume negotiations. On this visit as in subsequent ones, I found it difficult to get him to engage. My impression was that he came to meetings wanting to convey a single thought and, once he'd transmitted his message, had little interest in going beyond it or in discussing any other subject. On this occasion, the one and only message he wanted to deliver was that I should press Rabin to "hurry up" in carrying out his plan for the return of the Palestinian deportees.

As I traveled to the other key Arab countries—Jordan, Syria, Saudi Arabia, Kuwait, and Lebanon—I found a consensus of sorts. There was grudging acquiescence to Rabin's plan for defusing the deportee issue and genuine enthusiasm for restarting the peace process. The timing of the trip shortly after the inauguration had proven fortuitous. All of the leaders I met plainly wanted to be seen as cooperating with a new U.S. administration.

I deliberately made Israel the last Middle East stop on the trip so I could give Rabin a firsthand account of the reactions of his Arab neighbors. After a day of traveling to Saudi Arabia, Kuwait, Cyprus, and Lebanon, my plane touched down in Tel Aviv on February 22, 1993. Foreign Minister Shimon Peres was on hand to greet and escort me from the bustling, secular environment of Tel Aviv to the Orthodox enclave of Jerusalem. I was to take this trip dozens of times over the next four years, but Peres's eloquent commentary as we passed sites of heroic battles by Israeli soldiers in wars past made the first journey especially memorable.

The next night Rabin invited me to a late supper at his official residence in Jerusalem (his private home was in Tel Aviv). I learned over time that Rabin liked these late-dinner meetings, both as a means of packing more work into his day, and, I surmised, to move into a less formal atmosphere, away from the curious eyes and ears at the prime minister's headquarters. We usually were joined by just one aide apiece—Rabin by the Israeli ambassador to the United States, Itamar Rabinovich, and I by Dennis Ross. After a long day, we generally unwound with a glass of wine or Scotch and a nosh from a tray of cheeses, hard rolls, and tomatoes. I came to regard these supper invitations as acts of personal courtesy that greatly softened the impact of Rabin's somewhat forbidding persona. On this first occasion, Rabin listened intently to my report of the mood in Arab capitals, then simply said that he would prepare for a resumption of negotiations.

In the months following my initial trip, Rabin did what he said he would do regarding the Palestinian deportees. As a result, negotiations with Israel restarted on all four tracks—Syria, Jordan, Lebanon, and the Palestinians. Negotiating sessions took place in both Washington and the region. Rabin gave priority to the Syrian track until August 1993, when the focus shifted suddenly and unexpectedly to the Palestinians.

POINT MUGU

On August 26, 1993, the telephone rang at our beach house near Santa Barbara where Marie and I were vacationing. The State Department Operations Center said that Yitzhak Rabin was calling. As I had seen Rabin in Israel earlier that month, I figured that something extraordinary had happened to prompt the call.

Rabin came on the line and, with his usual no-frills style, got immediately to the point. He said a breakthrough had occurred in the negotiations in Oslo between the Israelis and the Palestinians and asked if his foreign minister, Shimon Peres, could come to see me in California. "I'd like to know what you think about this," Rabin said. One would not say no to this sort of request, and I didn't. I suggested Peres fly to Point Mugu, California, a nearby naval air station poised on the edge of the Pacific Ocean, and that he brief me there.

Twenty-four hours later I stood on the Point Mugu tarmac, waiting for Peres's plane to touch down. As I waited, I consulted my mental file on the personality I was about to encounter and mulled over the contrasts between him and Yitzhak Rabin. Where Rabin was taciturn and practical, Peres was expansive, even visionary. Longtime rivals in Israel's Labor Party, the two had been brought together in a new cabinet after the party's victory in 1992, but they were still highly suspicious of one another. Rabin had quietly indicated to me that my dealings on matters of substance should be with him, and that he, in turn, would brief Peres. The developments in Oslo had apparently created a new dynamic.

As Peres's plane descended, I truly didn't know what news he was carrying. I'd been aware of the secret discussions between the Israelis and the Palestinians in Oslo, but because of Rabin's open skepticism, had never thought much would come of them. Peres descended the portable steps, shook my hand, and walked with me to a conference room at the Point Mugu Officers' Club. We were joined by Dennis Ross, who had flown out from Washington, and Norwegian foreign minister Johan Holst, who had played a valuable role at Oslo and had accompanied Peres on his flight to California.

As soon as we reached a conference room, Peres told me that Israel and the PLO had reached agreement on a declaration of principles for the future of the West Bank and the Gaza Strip. I was surprised both by the message and by the absence of leaks. Peres agreed that the accomplishment was unprecedented: "Keeping secrets is not usually one of our national characteristics."

Peres then spent an hour leading Dennis Ross and me through the details of the agreement. When he finished, I told him he had done a tremendous job. While the agreement was very general and, most notably, was silent on the specific steps needed to accomplish its broad goals, it plainly marked a change in the dynamic of the peace process.

I thought we should drink a celebratory glass of

wine. As we drank, Peres casually made an offer that startled me. He was so eager to win unqualified U.S. support for the new accord that he was willing to have its authorship attributed to the Clinton administration. I immediately declined, saying we could not even consider such a deception. His next offer, however, was one I could accept. He asked if the United States would host the signing ceremony. I immediately agreed.

THE BLUE ROOM

Two weeks later, about forty diplomats and functionaries milled about the Blue Room of the White House on an unseasonably hot morning, mentally rehearsing their roles in the imminent ceremony. Waiting outside on the South Lawn were three thousand invited guests, who had come to witness a moment that would formally end more than four decades of hostilities between the Israelis and the Palestinians. Among the crowd was the entire diplomatic corps, including Arab ambassadors who usually avoided events involving Israeli participants. Longtime enemies sat side by side, joining diplomats who couldn't quite believe that this ceremony was actually happening.

The U.S. contingent from outside the current administration was led by former presidents Jimmy Carter and George Bush, who had spent the preceding night in the White House as the president's guests. On hand also were eight former secretaries of state—William Rogers, Henry Kissinger, Alexander Haig, George Shultz, Cyrus Vance, Edmund Muskie, Jim Baker, and Larry Eagleburger. I would have loved an hour to reminisce with each of them about their experiences in the Middle East, but my time this day was claimed by resolving last-minute snags, juggling the egos of foreign leaders, and making brief appearances at a series of official events. Joining the luminaries in the audience were hundreds of less prominent Americans, public and private, who had spent years working for peace in the Middle East.

President Clinton was to be the host and master of ceremonies at the morning's events. In a half century of close-up observation of political leaders, I have never seen a cooler customer than Bill Clinton on the cusp of a historic moment. He seems to thrive on the pressure that builds before a major public appearance. Indeed, he consciously adds to that pressure, rewriting his speeches up to and often through the last minute, sometimes making changes en route to an event. Though his habits drive aides and TelePrompTer operators to distraction, the turmoil seldom shows in the result.

On this occasion, however, the first international ceremony of his new administration, Clinton was obviously nervous. He said he had awakened at 3 A.M., read the entire biblical Book of Joshua, worked on his speech, and walked through every step of the ceremony. Recalling the trumpets of Jericho in the Book of Joshua, he had chosen a tie with gold trumpets on a blue background. In the Blue Room, he moved from delegation to delegation, making introductions and putting people at ease.

Yassir Arafat was present, as we believed he had to be. Because he was the undisputed leader of the Palestinians, we wanted him there in the flesh to manifest his personal commitment to the agreement that had been negotiated in Oslo by his lieutenants. With the PLO close to bankruptcy, Arafat had grasped the Oslo accord as a means of gaining land (Gaza and Jericho), as well as early recognition of his authority in sectors of the West Bank. As he huddled with his advisers and greeted other participants, I sensed that his lifetime of living at the periphery of diplomatic society had put him slightly off-balance when he was called upon to appear front and center on the world stage.

Arafat wore an olive green uniform, garnished with his trademark black-and-white kaffiyeh headdress. For many years, his distinctive garb had managed to turn a rather homely man into a colorful figure and had served as an emblem for his supporters. He'd often added a pistol to his belt to complete the picture. I noted with relief that on this day he had left the pistol at home.

Yitzhak Rabin was visibly tense, and with good reason. Since his foreign minister, Shimon Peres, had led the Oslo negotiations, Rabin's appearance as head of the Israeli delegation was likely to abrade an already competitive relationship. But once Arafat had signaled his willingness to attend, the die was cast. If the leader of the Palestinians was to be present, Israel's top representative had to be there as well. When I called Rabin to tell him that the president personally wanted him to attend, he responded in a gruffer than usual tone, "I will come; I have no choice."

Rabin was also uncomfortable, I realized, about having to appear in physical proximity to Arafat. For years, he had regarded the Palestinian leader as Israel's mortal enemy. Today they would be visually welded together before the world in a risky partnership. In the minutes before the ceremony, I watched Rabin circle the Blue Room to avoid having to shake hands with Arafat. Arafat did not seem to notice. When Rabin was asked what he intended to do or say when the documents were signed on the White House lawn, he remarked only, "I will do what I have to do."

Despite his official ranking as second to Rabin, Shimon Peres was a prominent figure at the ceremony. His foreign ministry had been the architect of the Oslo agreement. In contrast to Rabin, Peres was seldom uncomfortable in a public setting. He had dealt with the Palestinians in Oslo, and for him, the Blue Room provided an opportunity to renew acquaintances and a stage for celebrating the triumph. While in our previous encounters I'd felt or imagined a strain in my relations with Peres, on this occasion he was open and friendly.

The Russians made it clear that they also felt entitled to marquee billing because they had cochaired the 1991 Madrid Conference. Their representative was Foreign Minister Andrei Kozyrev, whose boyish good looks and fluent English made him an attractive television personality. Kozyrev was also an unabashed advocate of "Westernizing" Russia, hoping to integrate it as quickly as possible into the institutions of the West. This was an opportunity to stand shoulder to shoulder with America in a moment of triumph. Kozyrev's personal involvement in the Middle East peace process, however, was limited, and his arrival only minutes before the ceremony added to the impression that he was crashing someone else's party.

The least-known visitor with a speaking role at the ceremony was Arafat's diplomatic adviser, Mahmoud Abbas. A shadowy, intriguing figure, best known by his nom de guerre, Abu Mazen, he had been in charge of the PLO's secret contacts with the Israelis. His bronzed face, silver hair, and pleasant manner made him look more like a successful foreign banker than a feared guerrilla leader.

Having agreed with Peres at Point Mugu that the United States would be the host of the signing ceremony, I paced anxiously around the Blue Room wondering if I'd made a mistake. Would Arafat balk at the last moment? Would Rabin, the old tank commander, speak too harshly? As events transpired, the only noteworthy presigning deviation from our plans was a successful last-minute plea by the Palestinians that the previously taboo initials PLO (Palestinian Liberation Organization) be used in the signing documents.

As the names of the participants were announced on the White House lawn, we walked into the bright sunlight and took our places on the speakers' platform. Clinton's poignant opening remarks, emphasizing the history of the region and the contributions of those who had preceded him, set exactly the right tone. He was followed by Rabin, who made the speech of the day—probably the speech of his life. In a deep, gravelly voice, obviously struggling to control his emotions, he began, "This signing . . . today . . . it's not so easy, neither for myself as a soldier in Israel's war, nor for the people of Israel." Steadying himself, he hit his stride. "Let me say to you, the Palestinians, we are destined to live together on the same soil in the same land . . . we who've fought against you, the Pales-

September 13, 1993: The signing of the
Israeli-Palestinian peace accord.

tinians, we say to you in a loud and clear voice, enough of blood and tears. Enough!" He continued, "We, like you, are people—people who want to build a home, to plant a tree, to love, to live side by side with you in dignity, in empathy, as human beings, as free men."

In the speeches that followed, none of us—not Arafat, Peres, Abu Mazen, Kozyrev, nor I—could match Rabin's impact. Perhaps the best that can be said is that none of us broke the spell he cast. When the ceremony concluded, Clinton turned, shook hands with Arafat, turned the other way to shake hands with Rabin, then moved back a step and spread his arms to encircle and draw the two together for their historic handshake—the picture of the decade.

While Rabin stayed for a private lunch with President Clinton, Arafat and other dignitaries adjourned to the State Department to lunch with me. As I rode back to the department to greet them, I could only marvel at what had just happened and how quickly the world had changed. Until the 1990s, Arafat had been feared and reviled as a terrorist, a hated symbol in Israel and persona non grata in the United States. On September 13, 1993, he'd appeared as an honored, invited guest at a White House ceremony signaling that the Palestinians, Israel, and the United States had become mutually dependent partners. Anything, *everything,* seemed possible.

PURSUING THE DETAILS

The most obvious and pressing problem that presented itself after the signing was economic. Vast resources would be necessary to turn the promise of peace into reality for the impoverished Palestinians. In response to that need, I organized the first donors' conference at the State Department. Less than a month after the accord was signed, representatives of forty-six nations appeared in Washington and pledged more than $2.5 billion in development aid for the Palestinians over the next three years. Collecting on the pledges reminded me of a lesson I had learned when I had a newspaper route at age fourteen: the wealthiest are often the slowest to pay. A year later, we were still reminding Saudi Arabia of its $100 million commitment.

On October 6, 1993, only three weeks after the signing ceremony, Rabin and Arafat met in Cairo to begin negotiations to implement their agreement. The United States was to play the role of honest broker. The goal was an agreement that would give the Palestinians limited governing authority in the West Bank and self-rule in the city of Jericho and in the Gaza Strip. It proved to be no easy assignment. Bickering went on month after month, from October to April, in a number of cities across the Middle East and Europe. When agreement finally seemed at hand, Egypt's President Mubarak invited me to join him in pressing Rabin and Arafat to close the remaining gaps, key among them being settling the boundaries of Jericho and defining the areas within Gaza that would remain under Israeli control.

We met at one of Mubarak's Cairo palaces on May 3, 1994. After initial exchanges between Rabin and Arafat, Mubarak put them and their aides in a conference room beside his office with instructions to conclude the remaining issues. It was a variation on a technique I had seen effectively used by judges in settling civil litigation. The principal difference in this case was that, unlike a judge, Mubarak could not force the parties to remain in the room until they reached agreement. Mubarak and I did keep things moving, however, functioning as a kind of tag team mediating between the adversaries.

As the hours passed without agreement, Mubarak ordered in stacks of pita-and-hummus sandwiches from a sidewalk vendor, directing everyone to join him in his birthday celebration. Picking up a hummus sandwich would have violated my rule about surviving in the Middle East. That rule is to eat nothing—or, if pressed, next to nothing—that is not canned, bottled, or cooked to death. Hummus sandwiches did not qualify. Accordingly, as others in the room dived for the food, I held back. Arafat also stayed away from the platter, so I felt my judgment vindicated. Then I noticed that Mubarak was watching me, his sandwich in hand, plainly waiting for me to act. Trapped, I decided to revert to the "next to nothing" alternative. Picking up a hummus sandwich,

I took a few bites—and survived to tell the tale.

Sometime after midnight, Mubarak and I decided it was time to bring the negotiations to a close. We found Rabin and Arafat poring over giant maps of Jericho and Gaza, quibbling over minutiae. At one point, Arafat made an expansive claim concerning the Jericho city limits, prompting some of Rabin's aides to snicker. Arafat stopped, glared at them, and in a deeply wounded voice said, "You are laughing at me. You think I am a clown—I know it!" Rabin, immediately sensing that his staff had seriously erred, said in his deepest and gravest voice, "No, Mr. Chairman, we take you very seriously." The negotiations proceeded, and by shortly after 2 A.M., the details had been settled. Success seemed finally in hand.

Mubarak immediately set about planning an elaborate ceremony to mark the signing of the agreement transferring control of Gaza and Jericho to the Palestinians. The next afternoon, despite the short notice, a large audience, including a significant contingent of the print and television media, gathered for the event. Arafat was to sign for the Palestinians, Rabin for Israel, and Mubarak and I would sign as witnesses. But when the moment came for Arafat to initial the critical maps appended to the agreement, he bent over, squinted at the documents, then backed away, saying he wouldn't sign. He said the maps didn't accurately delineate the territory to be transferred to the Palestinians.

The following minutes were among the most

May 4, 1994: Chaos in Cairo.
Arafat balks at signing maps.

bizarre I have spent in public life. In full view of an audience of hundreds, and more importantly, before the world's press and a score of TV cameras, one person after another tried to reason with Arafat. He wouldn't budge. Rabin reminded him that they had shaken hands on the deal the night before. Mubarak told Arafat that, as host, he was personally offended and embarrassed.

After several of these unsuccessful gambits, I decided we needed to get the ensemble off the stage and out of the glare of television lights. I suggested we repair to an anteroom just behind the stage. There, after another half hour of wrangling, Arafat was finally persuaded to sign, subject to verifying later the accuracy of the maps. The storm had passed, but Arafat's maneuver had left me queasy about the future, a feeling doubtlessly enhanced by a hummus sandwich.

LOSING A FRIEND

It took the parties, with U.S. help, another year to reach the next landmark agreement, known as the Interim Agreement or Oslo II. This October 1995 accord was signed in Washington and provided for the withdrawal of the Israeli army from the nine most populous cities of the West Bank. It also gave the Palestinian Authority control over the vast majority of Palestinians in the area. Although the journey from the Declaration of Principles to a fully implemented Israeli-Palestinian agreement was taking longer than we had hoped—it was now more than two years since the ceremony on the White House lawn—the steady progress gave us a sense that it was only a matter of time. Then came something we hadn't planned for: fate.

I was alone with President Clinton in the Oval Office on November 4, 1995, when we received word that Yitzhak Rabin had been assassinated by a twenty-seven-year-old right-wing Jew. I had never before seen any news affect Clinton so profoundly. He was quiet for a long minute, and his silence made me feel almost as if I were inside his mind. His friend, a leader like himself, had met a violent end. In his silence, I think the president was reflecting on his own mortality, con-

With Rabin in the White House Cabinet Room.

templating what lay ahead for him and perhaps thinking of the price he himself had committed to pay for
assuming leadership of our country. When he finally
spoke, he quietly told me he wanted to go to Rabin's
funeral, halfway around the world.

I flew with the president and a large bipartisan delegation to represent the United States at Rabin's funeral. This sad event brought an unprecedented group of Arab leaders to Jerusalem, the city conquered by Israel in 1967. For Egypt's Mubarak, it was the first visit ever; for King Hussein, the first in twenty-eight years. They were joined by ministers from Oman and Qatar, white robes in a sea of dark suits. Their presence served as mute testimony that the man who lay in state before them had succeeded in ending Israel's long isolation.

I sat in the row behind the heads of state and watched as they slowly made their way to the podium to say a few words. No one matched the eloquence and historical reach of King Hussein. Wearing a red-and-white-checkered headdress, he evoked the memory of his grandfather, who was assassinated in his presence by Muslim extremists in Jerusalem in 1951: "We are . . . determined to continue the legacy for which my friend fell, as did my grandfather in this very city when I was with him and but a boy."

President Clinton spoke briefly and somberly, ending his remarks with the Hebrew words for "Goodbye, friend." The next day, those same words appeared on billboards all over Jerusalem, the Israeli people adopting Clinton's phrase as their own words of farewell.

Others spoke movingly, but none as poignantly as seventeen-year-old Noa Ben-Artzi Philosof, Rabin's granddaughter. A few months before, I had met Noa when I visited Rabin in his Tel Aviv office and had seen his soldier's face break suddenly into a warm smile when the beautiful young girl had stopped in to say hello. On the day of his funeral, Noa, unlike those who preceded her to the podium, spoke to, not of, her grandfather: "Others greater than I have already eulogized you, but none of them ever had the pleasure I had to feel the caresses of your warm, soft hands, to merit your warm embrace that was reserved only for us, to see your half smile that always told me so much, that same smile which is no longer, frozen in the grave with you."

As I made the long return flight to the United States aboard *Air Force One,* it was difficult not to feel that we had suffered two tragedies: the loss of Rabin, a friend and ally of great sense, wisdom, and authority—and the slipping away of the promise of peace just as we seemed to stand on its threshold.

12

MIDDLE EAST ANTIPODES

THE NOVEMBER 6, 1995, FUNERAL SERVICE FOR Yitzhak Rabin provided more than a chance for collective reflection on the life of someone who had brought the Middle East to the brink of peace. It was also an opportunity to consider which of the Mideast players had, and had not, made the most of Rabin's presence in the peace process. Among those who had seized the moment was Jordan's King Hussein, who had the courage and confidence to grasp the opportunity that Rabin's strength had presented. On the other end of the spectrum was President Hafiz Assad of Syria, whose absence from the group of official mourners was a reminder of the mistrust and suspicion that had disabled him from seizing a unique chance for peace.

These two—Hussein and Assad—bracketed the extremes of the Middle East peace process as I came to know it. The striking differences in their personalities and styles became, for me, markers of the unpredictable, often harsh political terrain that I traveled in the region during my years as secretary.

KING HUSSEIN

When I first visited the king of Jordan in February 1993, he was fifty-eight years old and had held the throne for four decades. In those forty years, he had survived several assassination attempts and seismic shifts in the political alignment of the Middle East. Balding but still handsome, fighting cancer and his weight, he rationed himself to a few cigarettes a day and tried to ignore the tray of cashews placed before us.

At the time of my first visit, the United States had not officially forgiven the king's opposition to us and our allies in the Gulf War against Iraq. I was therefore primed to start our relationship cautiously. After a few exchanges, however, my reserve slipped away. One could not spend more than a few minutes in this man's presence without being drawn in by his warmth and sensitivity.

A stop to see the king of Jordan became a fixture of nearly every one of my subsequent trips to the Middle East. Typically, he would greet me at the entrance of his palace and ask if the two of us could spend a few

December 6, 1993: With King Hussein
in front of Raghadan Palace, Amman.

minutes alone. We would then repair to his paneled
study to talk over the real business of my trip, candidly
reviewing current attitudes and obstacles. When he
and I finished, we would adjourn for an elaborate
ensemble lunch, the king joined by Crown Prince
Hassan and the members of his cabinet, and I by my
staff. While we would review the status of the peace
process in this larger group, the conversation was typically general and rarely broke new ground.

Jordan had handicaps that not even charismatic
leadership could overcome. With no oil and few natural resources, the country was dependent on its oil-

rich neighbors for trade and aid. About half its population was impoverished Palestinians, who were a
drain on the economy and a constant source of fer-
ment. In 1970, the PLO had tried to depose the
young king, but he had beaten back that effort,
notwithstanding the significant help that Syria had
given his Palestinian opponents.

The September 1993 Oslo agreement promised to
create a new set of facts on the ground for all of Israel's
neighbors, but none more so than Jordan. For Jordan,
the agreement foreshadowed that a Palestinian state
might someday sit on the country's western border.
Given the history of troubled relations between King
Hussein and the Palestinians, this was not good news.
That the king had been kept in the dark about the
Oslo negotiations until they had ripened into agreement only heightened his sense of concern and mistrust, directed mostly at Yassir Arafat.

Faced with the new reality created by the Oslo
agreement, King Hussein had the option of reacting
cautiously, with silence or even hostility, or seizing the
moment to do something bold. To his credit, he chose
the latter.

For two decades, during years of official outward
enmity between Israel and Jordan, Hussein had held a
series of secret meetings with Israel's prime ministers,
usually focusing on security issues. After the 1992
elections in Israel, Yitzhak Rabin had attended these
meetings for Israel. By the time of the Oslo agreement
in the fall of 1993, Rabin and the king had developed

genuine affection and respect for one another. On October 6, 1993, less than a month after the White House signing ceremony, Rabin had traveled to Jordan to talk secretly with King Hussein about a change in Israeli-Jordanian relations that would parallel the recent sea change in Israeli-Palestinian relations.

Although I was not present for the Rabin-Hussein meeting, a report I received from our ambassador in Amman immediately afterward gave me reason for optimism. The king had recognized that the Oslo agreement had changed the landscape of regional politics. Palestinian self-rule was going to be established on the West Bank, and Jordan needed a stronger relationship with Israel to deal with that change on the ground. Four weeks later, Israel's Foreign Minister Shimon Peres held a follow-up meeting with the king, and together they hammered out the outlines of an Israeli-Jordanian peace treaty. A key missing piece in the picture was something the king wanted but Israel could not itself supply: the moral, political, and financial support of Washington.

Just as these encouraging developments were taking place, events intervened to stall a Jordanian-Israeli peace. News of Peres's trip to talk with King Hussein leaked to the press, and the king, unsettled by the publicity, put negotiations with Israel on the back burner. Six months passed before he was confident enough to consider resuming the dialogue.

On April 26, 1994, I met with King Hussein at his home in London and urged him to renew his discussions with Israel. He told me he wanted to proceed but was preoccupied with concern over the solvency of the Jordanian government. Reserves for foreign exchange had fallen to $400 million and threatened to dip further. I told him an Israel-Jordan peace treaty could open the way for forgiveness of Jordanian debt to the United States and could prompt U.S. support for modernizing Jordan's armed forces as well. I did not need to point out that in addition to these significant benefits, a treaty could also establish a mechanism to define the ambiguous border between the two countries and provide a basis for dealing with Jordan's water shortage. By the conclusion of the meeting, I sensed that the king felt that the moment was again at hand to address peace with Israel.

In June 1994, Yitzhak Rabin and King Hussein had another of their unpublicized meetings, this one in London. They established secret working groups to refine the details of a treaty. On July 25, 1994, having reached agreement in principle, the two leaders appeared in Washington to sign a declaration ending the state of belligerency that had existed between Israel and Jordan for four decades. In anticipation of that moment, I had worked out an agreement in Washington with the Treasury Department and the White House on a package for Jordan of $700 million in debt forgiveness and $200 million in military equipment.

The document signed in July 1994 was a preliminary to a full-blown peace agreement. During the remainder of the summer and early fall, Israeli and Jordanian working groups met repeatedly to resolve the disputed border and water-access issues that were key to a final peace. By mid-October, those details had been settled, and the parties were ready to sign an agreement. They scheduled a ceremony for October 27 at the Arava crossing on the remote border between Israel and Jordan, near the northernmost point of the Gulf of Aqaba. In recognition of the U.S. role in making the event possible, they invited the president and me to join in the ceremony.

On the appointed day, more than four thousand guests from Israel, Jordan, and neighboring countries gathered under the blazing desert sun of Arava. A huge black tent provided some shade, but it was even hotter inside the tent than in the open air. As we took our places on a makeshift platform looking out over the crowd, the scene was distorted by waves of heat moving over everything and everyone. The physical discomfort did not diminish the moment, at least not for me. Neighbors who had known only hostility in the half century since Israel had come into existence were about to embark on a new relationship, and the United States had helped to make it happen.

Before the speeches began, senior military officers who had for years studied each other's biography and habits from opposing trenches mingled in the heat, talking to each other and trading war stories. Rabin, the crusty tank commander, was wearing a heavy wool suit but seemed oblivious to the temperature.

King Hussein, in high spirits, had motorcycled the 170 miles from Amman on his Harley-Davidson. For him, the ceremony meant not only peace with a formidable adversary, but a return to the good graces of the United States. In his remarks, he called the agreement a "peace with dignity," noting there was no need for foreign monitors, such as those who still watched over the border between Israel and Egypt, years after their peace agreement. When the ceremony concluded, President Clinton and I joined the king on his royal yacht for a tour of the adjacent waters of the Gulf. Hussein was at the wheel and responded to the shouts and cheers of spectators on shore with repeated blasts of the yacht's whistle.

Having publicly embraced peace between Israel and Jordan, King Hussein became perhaps the most outspoken Arab proponent of a global Mideast peace. I told him in Amman in October 1995 that he had done more in one year to bring about peace with Israel than the Egyptians had in seventeen. His willingness to take political risks—perhaps spurred by his sense that his cancer was rapidly consuming him—grew noticeably after the desert ceremony.

At the Amman Economic Summit in late October 1995, just six days before Rabin's assassination, Egypt's Foreign Minister Amre Moussa launched a harsh and unexpected diatribe against unnamed Arab countries that were, he said, moving with unseemly haste to make peace with Israel. The comments were a thinly disguised attack on Hussein. The king, calm and focused as always, gave an extemporaneous and devastatingly effective reply. He said that if peace meant a better life for his people, "we are not just rushing, but running." The response was so powerful that Moussa was put on the defensive. I watched as he quickly made the rounds of the key Arab politicians and businessmen who had heard his remarks, pleading that he had been misunderstood.

Though in February 1999 King Hussein lost his battle with cancer, he had established himself as a figure of historic importance in the Mideast. His courage and foresight enabled him to leave his eldest son and successor, Abdullah, an invaluable gift—peace and the promise of prosperity.

Hafiz Assad

Assad's rise to power began with his membership in a secret group that staged a coup in 1963, bringing the Ba'th party to the fore. In 1970, ruthlessly outmaneuvering his Ba'th colleagues, he took sole control of the Syrian government. Thereafter, moving coolly and deliberately, he strengthened Syria's position among Arab states, with help from the Soviet Union. American diplomats who saw him during this period, from Henry Kissinger to Jim Baker, described him as masking his penchant for the brutal use of power with humor and a curious sort of charm. Based upon more than twenty meetings in Damascus with Assad during my four years as secretary, I saw that side of him, and more.

My visits to Syria had a fixed routine. Landing at the sleepy Damascus airport, I would be met by Farouk Shara, Syria's foreign minister, and a cadre of Assad's security men. Without ceremony, Shara and I would immediately depart for Damascus in the backseat of his ancient, armored limousine. Inside, lace antimacassars prevented our heads from soiling the already soiled cloth headrests. The hour's ride to the city was consumed by a cat-and-mouse game in which Shara tried to find out what I was bringing to Assad, and I tried to be elusive. We kept up this game until the sound of the driver's downshifting signaled that we were beginning the winding climb to Assad's mammoth new palace, perched on a mountain overlooking the city.

At the palace, an aide would be waiting to escort me through a vast carpeted entrance hall to the door of a hundred-foot-long room overlooking Damascus. Entering the hall, I'd see Assad's silhouette in the doorway, framed by floor-to-ceiling windows behind him.

After greeting me with a bemused smile, Assad would lead the way to a pair of large chairs, placed in parallel, both facing the opposite end of the huge room. After a few photos by his controlled press, we'd begin to talk. After half an hour, we would be served a round of sweet orange drinks. Then we'd talk some more, usually three to four hours more, interrupted

July 19, 1994: With Assad in Damascus.

only by the serving of thick, black coffee at around the two-hour mark.

From meeting to meeting, there were virtually no deviations in this routine, and no surprises, pleasant or otherwise. The structure of our encounters was so fixed and familiar that when, after two years of these meetings, Assad decided I should sit in his customary chair and he in mine, he explained through his translator that he'd been having neck pains and his doctor thought they might be caused by his having to turn in the same direction every time he addressed me.

The neck problem was the only reference Assad ever made to his health, a subject of major interest to all of the world's intelligence services. But despite recurring rumors of a heart attack and blood disease, his performance in our meetings was dogged and incisive. Even when he appeared less energetic than usual, he was still a formidable negotiator, examining every word from every angle.

PURSUING THE PEACE

The focus of my sessions with Assad, like their format, was also the same from meeting to meeting, a search for some basis, some opening, for a peace agreement between Israel and Syria. For the United States, an Israel-Syria agreement would not only remove a major threat to Israel, but would improve the American strategic position in the region as well. On taking office, I had approved a dual-containment policy as to Iran and Iraq, but hoped to find a way to improve relations with Syria, the third country in the northern tier of Arab states. Nothing would have furthered that goal better than reconciliation between Israel and Syria. Accordingly, shortly after President Clinton's inauguration, with Prime Minister Rabin's blessing I sought to produce some movement on the Israeli-Syria track by talking directly to Assad, the only man in Syria who mattered.

My first meeting with the Syrian dictator came on February 20, 1993. Nearly before I was seated, Assad launched into an extended monologue on Syrian history, a diversion that was to become a staple of our sessions. Filled with unfamiliar names, places, and dates, the Arabic words spilled ceaselessly from his mouth, and just as ceaselessly, his longtime interpreter, Buethina Sha'ban, a prominent local feminist, spilled out the English equivalents. My colleagues and I came to refer to these lectures as "putting on the cassette." I would fidget and squirm until the performance was over, often in no less than thirty minutes, and try to figure out the point he was trying to make.

When he chose to talk substance, Assad's message— delivered, repeated, and reinforced—was clear. He wasn't going to begin negotiating until Rabin committed to full Israeli withdrawal from the Golan Heights, which had been captured by Israel in the 1967 war. His argument was neither artful nor coy; it was all muscle. He was telling us the Israelis would have no secure peace, prosperity, or existence unless they met his nonnegotiable demand.

On leaving my first meeting with Assad, I flew directly to Jerusalem, where I reported Assad's principal demand to Rabin and waited for his response. After a slight pause, Rabin looked at me and gave the weary shrug of a fighter who knew the moves his opponent would make before he made them. Rabin fully understood that reaching an agreement with Assad was going to be the challenge of his life, and that the result would be in doubt until the final stroke of his adversary's pen on a settlement document.

In the late spring of 1993, another problem threatened to derail the dialogue yet again, the Hezbollah militia in southern Lebanon. The group, nominally controlled by Iran, is heavily dependent on Syria's good offices and approval for maintaining its presence in Lebanon. For example, Iranian aircraft bringing supplies to Hezbollah in Lebanon must refuel in Damascus. Hezbollah frequently conducts sporadic terrorist operations against Israeli-backed forces in the ten-mile security zone in southern Lebanon. In June of 1993, however, the Hezbollah exceeded the usual scope of its hostile actions, lobbing Katyusha rockets into Israel proper and endangering Israeli farmers near the Lebanese border.

Israel responded with Operation Accountability—air raids on Syrian artillery positions in Lebanon's Bekaa Valley and expulsion of thousands of Lebanese civilians from the southern part of their country. Television pictures of the mass movement northward of frightened, exhausted, and homeless Lebanese drew sharp criticism in the United States and Western Europe.

At this point, I received a message from Rabin asking me to use my relationship in Damascus to bring an end to the wider hostilities. I wasn't sure that I could help, but I knew that if the fighting escalated, there was no chance for useful dialogue. I awakened Syria's foreign minister at 4 A.M. Damascus time and asked him to stop the Hezbollah from firing the Katyusha rockets into Israel. Predictably, he said the Katyushas were a response to Israeli shelling of Arab villages north of the security zone. I told him that there was no time to apportion blame and implored him to stop the attacks.

After a long night of telephone calls to Damascus, Jerusalem, and Beirut, I brokered an oral agreement that the Hezbollah would stop firing rockets into northern Israel, and the Israelis would, in turn, end Operation Accountability. The formal parties to the oral agreement were Israel and Lebanon, but I looked to Syria to ensure that the Hezbollah went along. The agreement held, with minor deviations, for several years.

GOLAN: BREAKTHROUGH IN SIGHT

With the Katyusha attacks on northern Israel abated, at least for the time being, I could turn again to the broader goal of an Israeli-Syrian peace. When I arrived for my second visit to Jerusalem on the morning of August 3, 1993, Rabin was prepared to make a major move. He invited me into his small private office, with only U.S. ambassador Dennis Ross and Israeli ambassador Itamar Rabinovich present. As we drank coffee, Rabin came right to the point. He wanted me to pose a hypothetical question to Assad: What was Syria willing to do in exchange for Israel's full withdrawal from the territory in the Golan Heights seized by Israel in the 1967 war? More specifically, was Assad willing to (a) sign a stand-alone treaty with Israel, i.e., one without linkage to the Jordanian and the Palestinian negotiating tracks; (b) join in personal, public diplomacy to reassure the Israeli public of Syria's commitment to peace, including a meeting with Rabin; and (c) agree to a five-year timetable for Israel's full withdrawal from the Golan, with incremental normalization of relations between the two countries, such as the exchange of diplomats, as the withdrawal progressed? I was more than a little surprised. Rabin was entrusting me with what should have been the ultimate winning hand on the Syrian track: Israel's departure from the Golan Heights.

As Dennis Ross and I flew to Damascus the next day, I was barely able to contain my usually very containable self. Rabin had put in my pocket the promise that Assad had been demanding for years. My excitement and impatience made the tedious ride from the Damascus airport and the usual game en route with the Syrian foreign minister just a little harder to take. Finally we reached the palace, and there, as always, was Assad in profile, awaiting me in the doorway of the large, long room overlooking Damascus.

After the opening pleasantries were behind us, we sat down with only our translators and key aides present. I posed the hypothetical questions that Rabin had asked me to deliver. I thought I detected a thin smile on Assad's face, but his only verbal response was a series of nitpicking questions and contentious pronouncements that I tried to answer without displaying my irritation.

Assad said that public diplomacy should come only after a peace agreement, and that he could never meet with Rabin until the Golan had been returned to

Syria. While he would not resist a separate peace agreement with Israel, he said he could not agree to early normalization as withdrawal proceeded. Finally, he insisted that Israel's withdrawal be accomplished in six months, not five years, despite the need to dismantle the Israeli settlements in the Golan and find new homes in Israel for the settlers.

After four hours of discussion, Yitzhak Rabin's risky, visionary step had not found reciprocity in Damascus. Our meeting ended with Assad having given me little of consequence to bring to Rabin, apart from a willingness to talk further. Assad had responded to the hypothetical questions, implying an Israeli concession of enormous importance to Syria, as if he were playing an interesting but not very important board game.

When I met with Rabin the next day, I tried to put the best face on my session with Assad. I said he had accepted the basic concept that withdrawal and normalization should be sequenced and was willing to proceed without waiting for the Palestinian and Jordanian tracks. To maintain my credibility with Rabin, I also had to confess that Assad had not been forthcoming. Rabin was plainly disappointed that his initiative had drawn such an unimaginative and unyielding response from Damascus.

In the days that followed, I learned just how deeply disappointed Rabin was with Assad's reply. Though I did not know it at the time of our meeting, the discussions between the Israelis and the Palestinians in Oslo had reached a critical final stage. Rabin knew that if he gave the go-ahead for an Oslo pact, progress on all other tracks, including the Syrian, would be slowed for the foreseeable future. Accordingly, Rabin had held off giving his go-ahead to complete the Oslo agreement until he heard Assad's reaction. I later learned that in mid-August Rabin met with Foreign Minister Peres and authorized him to finalize the Oslo accord.

Israel and the Palestinians signed the Oslo agreement's Declaration of Principles on September 13, 1993. Not until April 1994 did Rabin feel sufficiently comfortable about the Palestinian track to authorize me to travel to the region to resume negotiations with the Syrians. Assad, having had more than six months to consider our prior discussion, seized the moment not to make a conciliatory gesture but to inject a new, highly controversial demand. He told me to tell Rabin that Israel's hypothetical full withdrawal from the Golan Heights had to go beyond the international border between the two countries. He wanted Syrian territory to extend to the line between Israel and Syria that existed before the 1967 war. A conversation that had ended badly in the summer of 1993 continued its downward spiral in the spring of 1994.

Before Rabin's death in November 1995, Assad had other chances to make progress toward a Syrian-Israeli peace. On each of those occasions, however, he failed to rise to the challenge. Of all the missed opportunities, none was more frustrating than that presented by President Clinton's visit to Syria on October 27, 1994.

Despite sharp controversy within the administration, the president decided to accept my recommendation that he stop in Syria after the signing of the Israel-Jordan peace treaty. This was not an easy call. Syria remained on the administration's list of countries that supported terrorism and refused to cooperate on anti-drug-trafficking efforts. As a result, the president had to weather criticism from several quarters for making the stop. Still, because we felt that the president's visit would give Assad a strong incentive and forum for publicly embracing the peace process and reassuring the Israeli public of his constructive intentions, Clinton decided to take the chance.

Assad did not merely miss a golden opportunity; he made us regret that we had presented it to him. In the press conference after meeting with the president, Assad failed to keep a commitment to denounce terrorism and fumbled the chance to make a gesture for peace. He even failed to express regret over the terrorist bombing of a Tel Aviv bus a week earlier. His performance was beyond disappointing; it was tragic. The only explanation I could muster was that Assad was immobilized by his ingrained mistrust of Israel.

As I struggled throughout 1995 to find mechanisms to keep the Israeli-Syrian negotiations going, the essence of what I'd concluded about Assad was reaffirmed. With an apparent obsession to do better for Syria than Sadat had done for Egypt, Assad preferred to fight over words and commas rather than act boldly. Rabin had shown himself a visionary by allowing me to present Assad with the possibility of a full Israeli withdrawal from the Golan. Assad, however, appeared paralyzed in the face of this historic opportunity.

On October 30, 1995, I was making another of my many visits to Assad. We had just concluded another long and unproductive discussion when I deviated from my usual farewell script to say, "Mr. President, have you considered that time might not be on your side?" Assad paused, looking puzzled by my comment. I elaborated, pointing out that Syria's per capita income was less than one-tenth that of Israel and the difference between the two countries was increasing. His expression suggested to me that my remark hit home. Perhaps waiting out events—a strategy that had worked for him for so many years—was no longer viable.

In subsequent meetings with Assad during 1996, though he repeated back to me my remark about Israel's growing economic advantage over Syria, he showed no sign that he appreciated its relevance to the Israeli-Syrian peace negotiations. When Yitzhak Rabin died on November 3, 1995, the Syrian dictator was still talking of preconditions and technicalities rather than the heart of the peace problem. I will always believe that with Rabin's death, Assad was forced to realize that he had missed an extraordinary opportunity for his country and his people—and for peace.

(On June 10, 2000, Hafiz Assad died of a heart attack in Damascus without having regained the Golan Heights. His son Bashar succeeded him.)

13

THE GLOBALIZATION OF TERROR

I WAS STANDING AT THE EDGE OF A HUGE CRATER. In front of me was an eight-story structure that had been ripped open from bottom to top. Just hours before, a truck filled with explosives had been parked here, then detonated. Electrical wires, plaster, pieces of carpet, pipes, and bits of clothing dangled from layers of ragged concrete flooring that jutted out at random angles and lengths. The smell in the air reminded me of being on a navy ship after its big guns were fired. The devastated structure was all that remained of Building 131 of the Khobar Towers complex, which had been used as a U.S. military barracks in the Saudi Arabian city of Dhahran.

After a minute or two, the shock gave way to questions: Who did this? Why? And, of course: Is this somehow connected to Oklahoma City? "Oklahoma City" had by this time become our national shorthand for the bombing of the Alfred P. Murrah Federal Building on April 19, 1995. Like every other American who read newspapers or watched television, I carried in my head a variety of images that the coverage had imprinted on me: the blackened, crippled hulk of the Murrah building; the treacherous obstacles to the search for survivors and victims; the pursuit and capture of those believed to be responsible. All of those pictures came back at this moment, more than a year later, as I gazed up at the destruction.

The news of the bombing at Khobar Towers, a place where hundreds of U.S. soldiers had lived while on assignment in Saudi Arabia, reached me at the Laromme Hotel in Jerusalem in the early hours of Wednesday, June 26, 1996. State Ops, the State Department Operations Center in Washington, called to report that at 10 P.M. the night before, nineteen American air force men had been killed and hundreds of service personnel and civilians wounded by the truck bomb. The perpetrator or perpetrators were unknown.

As I showered and shaved before dawn, preparing for another day of Middle East shuttling, my heart and head were in Saudi Arabia. We had stationed five thousand U.S. Air Force men and women there immediately after the 1991 Gulf War. Their job was to monitor Iraq's compliance with U.N. resolutions and to enforce the no-fly zone over southern Iraq. In the five years since the Gulf War, their mission had become routinized and their presence in Saudi Arabia a fact of life. Perhaps, I thought, we had allowed the seeming stability of the situation to lull us into a false sense of security.

As I was the highest-ranking American official in the region, and with members of the world press traveling on my plane, Tom Donilon and Nick Burns advised that I should say something about the bomb attack before beginning my scheduled official meetings. After checking on the latest developments from Dhahran and framing a statement of concern and condolence, I appeared in the hotel lobby at 7:25 A.M. to face the reporters. When I concluded, there were several questions, but we knew so few of the facts that I could not do much more than decline to speculate.

In the month preceding this trip, the Middle East peace process had sustained a body blow—the election of Bibi Netanyahu as Israel's new prime minister. Netanyahu, who had campaigned against the Oslo agreement, was seen by the Arab world as intransigent and belligerent. My job on this trip to the Middle East was to urge patience and resolve. After a breakfast meeting with Ezer Weizman, Israel's president, I flew to Cairo to meet with Egyptian president Hozni Mubarak and Palestinian leader Yassir Arafat. I went through the motions of my scheduled meetings, urging each leader to stay the course, but I was not in the moment. Repeatedly, I found myself returning to thoughts of the Dhahran bombing, its impact at home, and its meaning to our work. Between meetings in Cairo, I told Donilon that I wanted to go to Saudi Arabia—to see for myself what had happened and to do what I could to bring comfort to the survivors.

My schedule had called for me to fly from Cairo to Lyons, France, where President Clinton was attending the annual conference of leaders from the key industrialized nations. Changing the itinerary was no trivial matter. A U.S. transport aircraft carrying one hundred people had to be diverted for an unexpected four-hour stop in a badly shaken foreign country. Tom Donilon worked feverishly to make the arrangements—from getting permission for the visit from Saudi officials to making sure that our party was accorded full security—and at 3:40 P.M. we embarked on our two-hour-forty-minute flight to Dhahran.

The chargé d'affaires of the American embassy in Riyadh, Ted Kattouf, who had hurried the two hundred miles to Dhahran shortly after the explosion, met me at the airport and briefed me during the fifteen-minute drive to Khobar Towers. We arrived at the site of the bombing at dusk. Floodlights illuminated the crater and the shattered building, adding to the air of unreality. Having lived in a city where movie studios often do location shooting in the streets at night, I had to shake off the instinct that this was a film set; the devastation was simply too great to absorb immediately.

June 26, 1996: The scene at Khobar
Towers in Dhahran, Saudi Arabia.

It had been a sophisticated, well-organized attack. A
fuel truck, filled with explosives, had been driven to an
unguarded parking lot next to the apartment building.
The truck driver had set the fuse, then jumped into a
waiting car and sped off before the detonation. He
and his accomplices were presumed to have fled the
country. Based upon the magnitude of the explosion,
security officials believed that the truck had carried
five thousand pounds of explosive material, a quantity
that probably meant the components of this rolling
bomb had been smuggled across the border from a
neighboring country.

An air force sergeant, Alfredo Guerrero, may have
been the only one to catch a glimpse of the crime in
progress. He was patrolling the roof of Building 131
when he noted someone on the ground running from
the truck, shortly after it was parked. He immediately

concluded that the apartment house and its occupants were in imminent danger and ran down the stairs to alert people in the rooms below. Rushing through the corridor of the eighth floor, he pounded on doors, urging the occupants to move to the streets. Then he sped to the seventh floor and repeated the drill until the moment of the explosion. Suddenly, he was thrown to the corridor floor and immobilized as debris fell all around him. When the motion stopped, he had suffered deep cuts and bruises, but he was alive.

Saudi foreign minister Prince Saud al Faisal met me at the bomb site, joining me and the base commander, Brigadier General Terry Schwalier, in a tour of the devastation. Saud, fifty-five, had held his post longer than the foreign minister of any other major country and, while not in the Saudi line of succession, was an internationally recognized insider on Middle East foreign policy issues. We walked slowly through the rubble on the edge of the bomb crater until we reached the base of what was left of Building 131. Looking straight up at the shattered hulk, it seemed a miracle that more people had not been killed.

I next met alone with the FBI investigative team that had traveled to the scene from the U.S. embassy in Riyadh. When I rejoined Saud, he told me that the FBI would have the full cooperation of the Saudi government. It was a reassuring but ultimately empty promise.

From the bomb site, I went to a nearby Saudi military hospital where those most seriously wounded in the explosion had been taken. Less than twenty-four hours had passed since the blast, and the hospital was still struggling to cope with the massive surge of wounded. Fortunately for the survivors, the facility was as fully equipped as any to be found in a medium-sized American city.

The senior U.S. air force doctor, who had rushed to the bomb site shortly after the explosion, painted a horrifying picture of what he had found. The wounded lay all around, many bleeding profusely. Doctors at the scene identified and treated the most serious cases first, then sent them off by ambulance to the nearby hospitals. In all, 259 Americans, 147 Saudis, and 118 Bangladeshi workers had been killed or hurt. Most of the badly injured had been deeply cut by flying glass and required tourniquets to keep them from bleeding to death. The 19 American airmen who died, the doctor told me, were probably killed instantly by the explosive force of the blast.

When we moved from the doctor's office to one of the hospital wards, I was drawn to the bedside of an air force sergeant from New Hampshire, who had bandages wrapped around his torso and arms and tur-ban-style around his head. He said he had been work-ing at a computer in his apartment when he suddenly felt himself flying across the room. "It got dark. I hit the wall and glass came down all over," he said. According to his nurse, despite his serious injuries he went to the aid of others in the building until he was ordered to leave and get treatment.

In a makeshift children's ward, I visited with several Saudi children who had been living in apartment buildings near Khobar Towers. Though some of them lived blocks away from where the bomb had detonated, they had suffered serious injuries from shattered apartment windows. Notwithstanding what they had been through, the children displayed a wonderful resiliency. Once their wounds were dressed and their fears of further harm allayed, they turned their attention to the really important things: television, ice cream, and the intriguing medical gadgets that surrounded them.

From the hospital, I returned to the Dhahran airport for my flight to Lyons. I had been on the ground for only about four hours, but what I had seen had left an indelible impression. For as long as I could remember, when I'd pictured someone or something devoted to harming the United States or its citizens, I'd seen a nation or group of nations as the enemy. That instinct was doubtless a product of the times in which I'd grown up and gone out into the world. As a child in North Dakota, I had heard my uncle talk about the German enemy he had helped defeat in World War I. During my navy service in World War II, the foe was the Axis—Germany, Italy, and Japan. In the Cold War, it was the Soviet Union; in the 1970s, North Vietnam. Each was a geographically, ideologically, and politically identifiable entity. Each presented a threat that was defined by ascertainable points on the globe and understandable, if misguided, objectives.

What had happened at Khobar Towers was different in ways I had understood as an intellectual matter before my visit to Dhahran, but which I now felt viscerally, as if I had been an intended target. The enemy was not a state but a person or collection of people without an identifiable face. We had no knowledge of what they stood for or where they made their home. While we surmised that their motive derived from some extreme form of Islamic ideology and that they might be the willing tools of a rogue state, that suspicion, even if confirmed, led to no obvious conclusion as to how to anticipate or prevent such attacks in the future. Absent a demand or explanation of the act, we could only assume that its purpose was to maim and destroy, and to reap some unspecified satisfaction or advantage from the resulting fear and uncertainty.

While the vagueness of the motivations and whereabouts of the attackers vexed me as I flew westward, the bombing made something else crystal clear. No state could claim to be free of the risk of terrorism, irrespective of its dominant religious or political ideology, or its superficial tranquillity. I'd spoken countless times around the world about globalization. It had now been brought home to me forcefully, crudely, and directly that terror had also been globalized; that the nations of the world, whether we liked it or not, were bound together by faceless human enemies. Whatever the diplomatic, political, or sociological hurdles, organized society was going to have to act collectively and to exchange freely the most sensitive subject matter to avoid becoming a perpetual target. Without such cooperation, fanatics like those who had blown apart Khobar Towers would continue to plan and prepare attacks in one country, execute them in another, and flee to a third when the deed was done.

During the flight to Lyons, I telephoned Defense Secretary Bill Perry to discuss Khobar, both in detail and in its broader implications. Still harboring the belief that the Saudis were going to help us find and prosecute the perpetrators, I concentrated on communicating my concerns over the state of our security arrangements in Saudi Arabia. Within three days of the bombing, Perry appointed retired army general Wayne Downing, a paratrooper with a reputation for toughness and candor, to make an unvarnished assessment of what had happened and what we could do to avoid a repetition. Two months later, Downing issued a blistering report that laid at the feet of the top brass the failure to have accurately assessed the threat level and to have provided adequate protection.

With Downing's report in hand, Perry undertook a major analysis of what needed to be done to deal with the new threat level to our troops in Saudi Arabia. He issued a report of his own on September 15, 1996, noting more than 130 separate actions that had been taken to enhance security at Khobar Towers following a bomb attack in Riyadh the prior November. As the press quickly pointed out, however, the steps not taken at Khobar—things as simple and straightforward as shatterproofing the glass windows and barring unidentified vehicles from entering areas immediately adjacent to the apartment buildings—were the ones, in the end, that mattered. In addition, the second-guessers attacked the decision to house our troops in the heart of a populated area.

Perry addressed this latter issue head-on, directing that the principal U.S. forces in Saudi Arabia move to a remote air base and, in addition, that most family members be withdrawn from the country. Perry and I shared the conviction that while we had to take measures to prevent a repetition of the bombing and track down the perpetrators, we should not allow the incident to drive us out of the country. We were determined to avoid the kind of hasty withdrawal that had taken place after the bombing of the marine barracks in Beirut in 1983.

As to finding and bringing to justice those responsible for the Khobar Towers bombing, the early commitment of Saudi cooperation dissolved in palace intrigue and secretiveness. While I did not doubt his sincerity, I soon learned that Foreign Minister Saud's influence did not extend to investigating terrorist incidents on Saudi soil. King Fahd had been weakened by a stroke, and the royal family, traumatized by mounting internal dissent, was hesitant to share with the United States responsibility for a sensitive investigation. To this day, the Saudis have kept the FBI at arm's length, refusing to share information or to let FBI agents interrogate material witnesses. Although the Saudis claim to have the Khobar Towers bombing suspects in custody, none has been tried, and four years after the event, no one has yet been identified as a responsible party.

DEALING WITH STATE-SPONSORED TERRORISM

Part of any effective program to address terrorism must include a whatever-it-takes commitment to deal severely with those who support, as well as those who carry out, terrorist acts. The United States has repeatedly said that any state that sponsors or supports terrorism against us will pay a price for its conduct. Early in the Clinton administration, we had the opportunity to deliver on that commitment.

On Wednesday evening, June 23, 1993, I joined the president, Vice President Gore, and other senior members of the national security team in the family quarters of the White House East Wing. The location was dictated by the need for absolute secrecy. Only a handful of people in the White House knew of our meeting, and the president wanted to keep it that way. As instructed, I came without staff, as did the other principals.

We had been brought together to hear CIA and FBI briefers deliver a secret report concerning an event that had occurred two months earlier. In late April 1993, Kuwaiti officials had told us that they had foiled an Iraqi plot to kill former president Bush during a visit to Kuwait earlier that month. The Kuwaitis said they had arrested and obtained confessions from eleven Iraqi citizens who had brought a truck bomb across the border to carry out the assassination.

Our intelligence experts greeted the Kuwaiti account with skepticism. Among other questionable aspects, the report that a Toyota Land Cruiser bearing Iraqi agents and a huge bomb had brazenly been driven across the Kuwaiti border did not square with the ruthless, secretive efficiency that our experts knew to be characteristic of actions orchestrated by Iraqi intelligence. The experts also suspected that the confessions obtained by the Kuwaitis may have been coerced. Our intelligence services concluded that we needed to make our own assessment of what had occurred. On the basis of that recommendation, the president ordered a full investigation by the FBI and the CIA.

According to our briefers, CIA and FBI agents had interviewed and reinterviewed the suspects and conducted extensive forensic tests. To their surprise, their work confirmed the Kuwaitis' account of what had occurred. They concluded that Iraqi intelligence agents had indeed brought the Toyota Land Cruiser, loaded with enough explosives to blow up four square blocks, into Kuwait from Iraq, with the goal of detonating the vehicle near President Bush during a celebration of the Gulf War victory. Our investigators believed that Iraqi intelligence services, at the highest level, bore responsibility for the plan. We were told that the men in custody had provided an impressive level of detail, and that key components of their bomb matched those used in earlier bombs built by Iraqi intelligence that our own intelligence services had previously examined. It was the forensic equivalent of a DNA match.

The issue for us was not what to do with or to the individual perpetrators. Kuwait had put them on trial for capital crimes. Rather, the question was what, if anything, to do about Iraq's role in the foiled plot. Should we await the outcome of the Kuwaiti trials to assess whether the individual punishments would suffice to send an appropriate message to the Iraqi government? If we decided to retaliate directly against Iraq, should we do so unilaterally or only after we had obtained approval from the U.N. Security Council? If we took action, would we be inviting lethal attacks on Americans throughout the Middle East?

I was convinced that the United States had to respond aggressively, irrespective of the outcome of the trials of the individuals. A plot to kill a former U.S. president was an attack on our nation. I believed we could not leave punishment for such conduct entirely to another country, nor could we delegate to an international body our power to respond. I expressed that view briefly and directly to the president after the briefers had concluded their presentations. I did not expect him immediately to embrace or reject my views—that was not the Clinton style. Instead, he kept his counsel and turned to others in the room for comment. After hearing from nearly everyone on the basic questions, Clinton asked Defense Secretary Les Aspin and General Colin Powell to outline the military options. They described the ships and planes in the region that could hit Iraqi targets and the combinations of military responses that were possible. When they'd finished, the president adjourned the meeting until the next night, instructing us to reflect on what we had heard and to share this information with no one else.

When we convened the next evening, the president made it clear that he wanted to send an unmistakable, dramatic message to Iraq. Since Iraqi intelligence had launched the plot, he believed that the Baghdad headquarters of the organization should be hit. Once he'd announced his conclusion, the discussion moved to related issues—the best timing for the attack, the weapons to be used, and what the likely effect would be upon international public opinion. After listening to this interchange, the president decided that to obviate any risk to American pilots, the attack ought to be made by Tomahawk cruise missiles launched from U.S. navy ships. He also decided that the action should begin in the middle of the night in Baghdad, more than forty hours later, so as not to fall on Friday, the Muslim holy day, and so as to minimize Iraqi civilian casualties.

On June 27, at 12:22 A.M. Baghdad time, the first Tomahawk cruise missiles were fired from navy ships in the Persian Gulf and Red Sea, targeted at the Iraqi intelligence compound in Baghdad. Although their flight spanned hundreds of miles from the navy ships, twenty of the twenty-three Tomahawks hit inside the headquarters compound, and sixteen hit directly on the targeted buildings. Three missiles missed by one hundred to six hundred yards and fell into residential areas. Reports that reached us, beginning Sunday morning, said we had inflicted severe damage on the headquarters compound and had caused relatively few casualties in the civilian population. We had done what we had set out to do, and there had been no leaks.

President Clinton telephoned George Bush just before our missiles were launched to alert him to what was about to occur. Clinton told him that I would arrive shortly in Kennebunkport to brief him on the details. At the moment the first missiles hit Baghdad, I was landing at a Maine airport near Bush's home. The former president greeted me at the door in casual clothes and seemed slightly stunned by the drama and suddenness of events.

As I described the dimensions of the Iraqi plot to kill him and the details of our response, Bush's face muscles relaxed and he allowed himself a deep breath. While he did not give me a verbal message to carry back to his successor in Washington, I left with the sense that, at least for a moment, George Bush had felt a unique kinship with the man who had replaced him.

14

◆

THE MIDDLE KINGDOM

Do we scrub Beijing?"
It was March 9, 1994, and that was the question for those of us gathered in my compartment on the thirty-year-old Air Force 707 chugging from Australia toward Tokyo. This was the third leg of a trip whose itinerary read like the diplomatic equivalent of an eco-challenge contest: twenty-four hours in the air through fourteen time zones from Washington to Canberra; two days of consultations with the Australians; eleven hours in the air to Tokyo, where for two days I would press the Japanese on economic matters; five hours to Beijing for three days of tough talks with high Chinese officials; then four hours to Vladivostok to meet with the Russian foreign minister

Andrei Kozyrev on Bosnia, and finally, fourteen hours home to Washington.

The question was not whether we would all prefer to cut three days off a grueling trip. Rather, it was what price we were willing to pay for eliminating the China stop. Relations with China had become a major issue during the 1992 campaign. Governor Clinton repeatedly lambasted President Bush for coddling China's Communist dictators by refusing to use American leverage to force improvements in China's human rights record. He chastised Bush for dealing too generously with the "butchers of Beijing" and said that granting low-tariff trading privileges to China was "unconscionable."

After the election, the White House almost immediately began to draw back from candidate Clinton's sweeping campaign statements. When congressional Democrats introduced legislation to cut off China's trading privileges if it didn't alter its human rights policies, the White House successfully promoted a compromise. China's favorable trading status would continue for a year, but further renewals were subject to the condition that there be "overall significant progress" on several specific human rights items. Once the compromise was embodied in an executive order, the Democrats dropped their bill in Congress.

The central purpose of my Beijing stop was to underscore to the Chinese that under the president's policy they had only limited latitude and time to mend their human rights record. If they wanted to keep their low-tariff trading privileges, there had to be significant progress, and soon. I wanted to deliver this message to them in clear, crisp, and unambiguous terms.

On March 4, 1994, the day I left Washington, the Chinese began a crackdown on dissenters, carrying out a sweeping roundup of leading pro-democracy exponents. When questioned by reporters in Australia about the arrests, I said the Chinese were heading in the wrong direction. As I contemplated the next leg of my journey, it occurred to me that flying to Beijing from Tokyo might well be characterized the same way.

The equities of the decision were close: If I kept to my itinerary, I would likely receive a chilly reception from the Chinese and achieve nothing that the press or anyone else would characterize as progress. In addition, the start of the Chinese National Congress on the day I arrived would give China's leaders a perfect forum in which to demonstrate that they intended to stand up to America. On the other hand, if I passed up this opportunity to speak directly to the Chinese about what we expected of them, there would probably not be another chance before the decision on China's trade status had to be made in May. A last-minute cancellation of the trip would also create a storm of its own with the Chinese, a diplomatic slight that could spin out of control. By the time we landed in Tokyo, I had concluded that it would do more harm than good to cancel the visit.

THE BEIJING CHILL

The tone of my visit was quickly established. Upon deplaning on March 11, I learned that the Chinese had detained two American journalists for six hours and had picked up two more dissidents. My security detail, typically a model of stoicism and decorum, got into shoving matches with their Chinese counterparts at the airport and again at the hotel.

The following morning, my meeting with Qian Qichen, the suave, able Chinese foreign minister, was disturbingly cold and formal. Qian had skillfully guided China back from pariah status following the 1991 Tiananmen Square massacre, but on this occasion he was obviously under orders to keep me at arm's length. Our meeting went so poorly that at the end of a lunch he hosted for me I said to him, "I wish the meeting had been as good as the lunch."

The Chinese held off displaying the full extent of their ire until my hour-long afternoon session with Premier Li Peng. Winston Lord, my top aide on China, a former ambassador to China and an aide to former secretary of state Kissinger, afterward described this encounter as the most brutal diplomatic meeting he'd ever attended.

I opened, as we had planned, by explaining to the premier what China needed to do if the Clinton administration was to extend low-tariff trading status when the issue arose again. With an acerbic smile playing at the corner of his lips, Li Peng responded that China was fully prepared to lose favorable trade status, and if it did, Clinton and I could expect to be blamed for losing China.

Li went on to make it clear that China's human rights policy was none of our business, noting that the United States had plenty of human rights problems of its own that needed attention. He made the point personal by pointing out that I had investigated the beating of Rodney King in my hometown of Los Angeles. He then said that by feeding the people, the Chinese government was dealing with the most important human right. To ensure that I had not failed to appreciate the depth of their unhappiness, the Chinese abruptly canceled my meeting later in the day with President Jiang Zemin.

I frequently sent a night note to President Clinton, and that night I sent him a message saying that my hosts had been "rough, somber, sometimes bordering on the insolent." I also said that unless the atmosphere soon improved, I might cut the trip short. In fact, I was disinclined to do so, having made a personal investment in the outcome by absorbing a first round of abuse. But while I was determined to stay on, I also intended to let the Chinese know that I was unhappy with their performance. I directed my staff to decline all social invitations and to cancel the customary sight-seeing excursions that had been planned for me.

The evening hours gave me an opportunity to reflect on what underlay the rough treatment I'd received. While I knew that the Chinese harbored a paranoid fear of civil unrest, their actions seemed disproportionate to that concern. What I did not know, but learned only after I reached Beijing, was that the Chinese leadership had been incensed by a meeting two weeks before my arrival between my assistant secretary of state for human rights, John Shattuck, and a noted Chinese dissident, Wei Jingsheng. Though Shattuck's action was thoroughly defensible and, indeed, standard operating procedure for a diplomat with the human rights portfolio, it had gotten deep beneath the skin of the Chinese. Their anger was further fed by the belief that, a few months before my visit, our criticism of their human rights policies had prevented them from being designated as the host country for the 2000 Olympics. In short, I had arrived in China at a moment when a U.S. secretary of state was a convenient punching bag.

As I turned my thoughts to the day to come, I brightened a little. I saw the promise of a civil, even friendly, exchange in the morning's first scheduled event, a breakfast with local American business leaders hosted by the American Chamber of Commerce. Though it promised to be little more than a pep rally, I had to confess that a little pep and a little rallying would make for a nice change. Unfortunately, the breakfast failed to meet even my modest expectations.

After consuming their sweet rolls, representatives of American companies took the floor and blasted me for pressing the Chinese on human rights. These men were in China to further their companies' business interests, and they clearly felt my message threatened that mission. Though I understood their frustration, I was dismayed by their words. We were all, first and foremost, representatives of the most successful democracy on earth. If we abandoned the effort to promote the hallmark of democracy, the importance of individual civil rights, what would distinguish us from the undemocratic?

Following my troubling breakfast, I moved on to the rescheduled meeting with President Jiang Zemin. Though the tone of this meeting was somewhat better than that with Premier Li Peng, and his countenance more benign, there was little change in substance. Larding his dialogue with aphorisms, poetry, Confucian sayings, and riddles, Jiang successfully sidestepped any substantive exchange on the human rights issues I raised. At bottom, he was telling me that the United States should stop meddling in China's internal affairs.

As I reflected on the remarks of Jiang and Li Peng, I was reminded of the breadth of the chasm between us on human rights issues. The Chinese "internal affairs" rubric is squarely at odds with the U.N.'s Declaration of Human Rights, which binds all of its members. That each country has a different culture and different economic circumstances absolves none of them from the obligation to comply with the Declaration. Torture, arbitrary detention, and sham trials cannot be justified by incantations of sovereign rights. Whether a government respects the fundamental rights of its citizens will always have a significant influence on whether our bilateral relations reach the highest levels.

On the final day of my stay, I met again with Foreign Minister Qian and this time was able to engage with him on the heart of my message. By the end of our meeting, he had promised to release two of the dissidents who had been taken into custody before my arrival. But his condition for the release was absolute: I was to say nothing publicly about his commitment. Officially, the Chinese wanted to be free to continue denouncing my efforts, to characterize them as a failure. The American press accommodated the Chinese strategy, summing up my trip as a "diplomatic mugging."

After a brief stop in Vladivostok to confer with Russian foreign minister Andrei Kozyrev about Bosnia, I consoled myself on the long flight home with the thought that I had made a brave showing in support of the administration's policy and, by going through with the stop in China, had gotten two dissidents released. I expected the White House to issue a modest statement echoing that assessment, even though I recognized that our position on renewal of China's favorable trade status needed to be reviewed. To my surprise, however, the White House added nothing to the statement issued by the president as I left Beijing, saying that he was "disappointed" with the results of my visit. I speculated that the business community had weighed in at the White House with even stronger sentiments than I had heard at the Chamber of Commerce breakfast in Beijing. For whatever reason, the president was not about to issue a ringing endorsement of our human rights policy as to China. The press also began reporting leaks by officials in the Treasury and Commerce Departments criticizing the timing of the trip and the substance of my message.

A week after I returned from China, I appeared at the White House before nine cabinet-level officials to report on the trip and to discuss where our policy was headed. The president did not attend. I opened with Mark Twain's line about Richard Wagner's music: "It's not as bad as it sounds." Tough as the Chinese were, I said, with the possible exception of Li Peng, all had acknowledged that U.S.-China contacts were vital and should be encouraged. I then made a plea to the assembled cabinet secretaries that they and their staffs stop using the press as an intermediary for criticizing our policy, saying that disarray in the administration would only impair our effectiveness and reduce prospects of positive action by the Chinese.

When I finished, there was only silence. No one spoke in defense of continued linkage of China's trade status to its human rights progress. It was as if our policy had died in my absence or, as some at the meeting would have it, had never existed. All that remained was to arrange a decent burial.

On May 26, 1994, the president announced that China's low-tariff trading privileges would be renewed for another year. Although I agreed that the trading status should not be denied, I was determined that we not mask or sugarcoat the major change of direction reflected in the announcement. I knew that if we tried to distort or inflate China's human rights performance to justify our decision, we would undermine our credibility, not only in Beijing but around the world. In a speech at the Asia Society in New York the next day, I emphasized that our effort to use economic pressure to improve human rights had not proven effective and was at an end. While we would continue to press for human rights improvement in China, we would no longer use an economic club to force change.

TAIWAN

As I'd learned in my days with the Carter administration, the issue of greatest sensitivity to the Chinese was the status of Taiwan. During the Communist revolution in 1948, Chiang Kai-shek had fled to the island, and for two decades, the United States had pretended that his Nationalist regime was the legal government of China. President Nixon and his national security adviser, Henry Kissinger, put an end to this charade in 1972 by acknowledging that the People's Republic was China's sole legal government and that there was but one China, of which Taiwan was a part. Notwithstanding this formal reassurance, China obsessively continued to voice concern that Taiwan might seek independence.

My 1978 trip to Taiwan after President Carter had fully normalized relations with China had given me a firsthand look at just how strongly the Taiwanese felt about the issue. The violent demonstrations that had greeted me there communicated their extreme resentment of the U.S. rapprochement with the People's Republic and how much they wanted to chart an independent course. Now, fifteen years later, as President Clinton's secretary of state, I was destined to deal again with this hot-button issue.

From the outset, the Clinton administration's policy on Taiwan was identical to that of the Nixon administration and its successors: there was "one China," embracing mainland China and Taiwan. We would maintain full diplomatic relations with Beijing, the legitimate government of China, and unofficial relations with Taiwan. We also embraced the position that the ultimate status of Taiwan should be determined peacefully by China and Taiwan. In short, we planned business as usual—a balance between the realities that the People's Republic was the true government of China and that Taiwan continued to exist, indeed thrive, as a quasi-independent entity.

In early 1995, however, an unexpected, almost unreal, set of events threatened that balance and, along with it, the peace of the region. Lee Teng-hui, Taiwan's president, applied for a visa to enter the United States to attend a reunion and speak at his alma mater, Cornell University, in Ithaca, New York. His request was supported in the U.S. Senate and House of Representatives by nonbinding resolutions that passed by overwhelming majorities (with votes of

97–1 and 370–0, respectively). President Clinton was inclined to grant the visa, and I joined with Defense Secretary Bill Perry and National Security Adviser Tony Lake in a recommendation that he do so, fearing that Congress would work some mischief to the Taiwan Relations Act if we did not. In an attempt to prevent Lee's visit from being misconstrued by China, the president granted the visa on the express condition that the visit be private and nonpolitical.

The calculation we had made was that, once in America, President Lee would not say or do anything that would ruffle China's delicate sensibilities. That proved to be wrong. Instead of reminiscing about the good old days at Cornell, President Lee used his commencement speech to needle the Chinese. He bragged about the emergence of democracy on the island, proclaiming, "We are here to stay." Lee also repeatedly referred to Taiwan as the "Republic of China on Taiwan," a reference he knew to a certainty would go down badly in Beijing.

On cue, Beijing erupted. The Chinese claimed that Lee's visit signaled a fundamental shift in our "one China" policy and made it clear they would not take that change lying down. To make their displeasure concrete and immediate, they canceled scheduled meetings with U.S. officials, withdrew their ambassador, rounded up more dissidents, and, for good measure, detained an American citizen, Harry Wu, a photojournalist who had exposed grim conditions and forced labor in Chinese prisons.

Although in his Cornell appearance President Lee had gone well beyond the conditions of his visa, I regarded the PRC reaction as excessive. I felt we had to respond promptly and without a hint of apology. At the same time, I wanted to stress that our policy toward China had not fundamentally changed.

My opportunity came in a speech a few days later at the National Press Club in Washington. Noting the Chinese reaction to President Lee's visit, I explained that our policy toward Taiwan and China was the same as it had been for the past twenty years. We were not advocating or supporting either a "two Chinas" approach or "one China, one Taiwan." The status quo ante Cornell prevailed. I pointed out that this policy had produced enormous benefits for the United States, China, and Taiwan, and I stressed that all three of us had a responsibility to act so as to foster stability in the region. Delivered on a hot and humid Friday in Washington, the speech was all but ignored in the U.S. weekend press.

I was scheduled to meet with Chinese foreign minister Qian in Brunei five days later at the ASEAN Regional Forum and fully expected a diatribe from him on Lee's visit to America. To my surprise, however, Qian opened the meeting by saying he had both read my National Press Club speech and had watched a videotape replay of it. He said he was pleased by my reaffirmation of the "one China policy" and agreed with my opening suggestion that we focus on issues of common interest rather than on matters at which we were strongly at odds. Of all the speeches I delivered as secretary of state, the National Press Club presentation is the one that produced the most immediate and positive diplomatic response.

In early 1996, Taiwan was the subject of another rough patch in U.S.-China relations. Once again, the problem involved Taiwan president Lee Teng-hui. Taiwan was scheduled to hold its first direct presidential election on March 23, 1996, and Lee was the front-runner. A key part of his campaign strategy was to come just short of advocating independence for Taiwan. Predictably, this brinksmanship agitated China, both on the merits and because they still smarted from Lee's visit to Cornell.

Beijing took a series of steps, each more provocative than its predecessor, intended to undermine the Lee candidacy. First, they announced plans to conduct a massive military exercise on the China coast opposite Taiwan. Soon thereafter, they test-fired missiles that bracketed the island. The missiles that fell into the sea north of Taiwan reportedly passed over the island itself. Further, they chose to use the nuclear-capable M-9 missile—one of which flew over Taipei, Taiwan's capital. In the tense atmosphere of that moment, a miscalculation or misstep by either side could have led to an unintended war. We knew we had to do something to restore balance.

A few days later, I met with Secretary Perry at the Pentagon to discuss what we might do to lower tensions and to manifest our determination to keep the peace. Perry suggested that the president order a second navy aircraft carrier group to join one already in international waters near Taiwan, though not in the Taiwan Strait. I agreed, feeling that this powerful show of force, if accompanied by an appropriate explanation, could inhibit any escalation by Taipei or Beijing. Perry and I agreed that the right message would be to reaffirm the U.S.'s China policy and counsel Taiwan against provocations that might ignite conflict. The second carrier was dispatched and the statement made, producing loud, pro forma criticism from China for U.S. "interference," but also, in the days following, a gradual de-escalation of tension.

The results of Taiwan's election on March 23 showed that China's efforts to intimidate the Taiwanese electorate had backfired. Lee won decisively, the Taiwanese people saying that strong-arm tactics were an unacceptable tool for influencing the democratic process.

THE RING MAGNETS

While recognizing that our differences with the Chinese on the most difficult issues, human rights and Taiwan, would not soon be resolved, I saw the potential for agreement on issues with a lower profile, matters where our interests were similar. These included drug trafficking, the environment, North Korean nuclear threats, immigration, and especially, nuclear proliferation. I thought it vitally important that we keep talking to one another, to continue searching for common ground on issues of high importance.

Though some in Congress believed we should isolate and shun China as we had the Soviets during the Cold War, I saw that path as leading to nowhere but trouble. Isolating and demeaning a nation of more than a billion people could hardly be more shortsighted. At the same time, I thought it vital to recognize and define how we were different from one another—to avoid embracing the overly sanguine argument that China's impressive economic progress would soon resolve the problems that divided us. In sum, I was looking for a way to keep the dialogue open and to demonstrate that, despite our differences, the United States and China could work together.

The opening I sought came in early 1996 in the form of the arcane subject of ring magnets and the critical issue of weapons of mass destruction. We had solid evidence that a state-owned Chinese company had sold nearly $70,000 worth of ring magnets to the Pakistani organization responsible for producing the highly enriched uranium used in Pakistan's nuclear weapons program. The relatively low-tech ring magnets were an essential part of the production mechanism for such weapons.

In early 1996, we threatened to impose economic sanctions on China if the ring magnet sales to Pakistan continued. Shortly after the Taiwan election crisis subsided, I met with Foreign Minister Qian at The Hague to discuss the issue. After spending several hours discussing the facts, I made an offer to Qian that I had fashioned with our nuclear experts. The United States would withhold levying economic sanctions if China, in turn, promised to give no future assistance, including the sale of ring magnets, that would enable the construction of nuclear weapons in Pakistan or in any other country that was not subject to international safeguards.

Qian was in rare diplomatic form, jousting with me for more than two hours. In the end, he embraced my proposal but refused to agree to convene expert talks to discuss its implementation. Without such talks, the agreement could have been meaningless, and I said as much. After a series of his circumlocutions, it became clear that Qian simply lacked the authority to agree to implementation talks. We left The Hague without

With Foreign Minister Qian Qichen
in Beijing in 1996.

agreement, but a few weeks later he sent me a cable accepting the proposal in full. A benchmark for Sino-U.S. cooperative action had been established.

To try to keep the momentum going, in a May 17, 1996, speech devoted entirely to China, I proposed that we arrange regular high-level visits between Washington and Beijing. Two months later, when I met with Foreign Minister Qian at the annual ASEAN meeting in Jakarta, he endorsed the suggestion. Before the end of my term eight months later, I was able to tell the Chinese that President Clinton would soon propose the first of the exchanges. He did so, and China's President Jiang made a state visit to Washington in November 1997. In June 1998, President Clinton completed the initial cycle, making his first visit ever to China.

A FRIENDLY FAREWELL

In November 1996, I visited China for the last time as secretary of state. In contrast to my first trip two years earlier, on this occasion the Chinese went out of their way to be cordial. When I paid my farewell call on President Jiang, he even inserted a little humor in his greeting: "Happy is the man who is relieved of official duties."

The final stop on this last official trip was Shanghai, where I was scheduled to speak to students at FuDan University. I intended to use the occasion to make the case one more time that the United States and China had much more to gain from cooperating on global affairs than from arguing over differences. The proposed title of my speech was "Building a Partnership for the 21st Century," and my advance staff had created a large banner carrying the phrase that would hang behind me when I spoke.

In reviewing the speech the night before I was to deliver it, I had second thoughts about the word *partnership*. Although our relationship with China had improved, *partnership* seemed a little too cozy. I asked my staff to change the title of the speech, as well as the banner, to substitute the word *cooperation* for *partnership*.

After four years of traveling with the press, I should have known better. My last-minute, one-word change became the focus of their stories. The incident was, in

With President Jiang Zemin
on my 1996 farewell visit to Beijing.

some ways, a fitting conclusion to my four-year stewardship of U.S.-China relations. Though we had made progress, the repeated intrusion of unexpected, sometimes bizarre distractions had kept us from greater accomplishments. It has since occurred to me that this erratic pattern may be a permanent feature of U.S.-China relations—an up, down, and sideways route to healthy relations may characterize our relationship indefinitely.

However our relationship with China progresses, its management must be a front-burner matter for America's leaders for the mid-to-long-term future. The Chinese are proud and sensitive. They combine a sense of cultural superiority with political insecurity, especially when subjected to criticism on what they regard as their domestic affairs. Their hypersensitivity is always lurking just below the surface, waiting to erupt. In the United States, especially in the Congress, pressures from the far right and the far left will constantly push and pull us to isolate China, a sure way to turn an adversary into an enemy.

For the United States, the challenge is to avoid either idealizing or demonizing the Chinese and to find a way of dealing with this powerful force without illusions. So long as China retains its present form of government, perhaps the best we can hope for is stability and sporadic moments of cooperation—a relationship in which we recognize our responsibility to one another, and to the world, to remain at peace.

15

---◆---

FLASH: "IZETBEGOVIC, MILOSEVIC, AND TUDJMAN GO TO DAYTON"

FOR THE UNINITIATED, THE HEADLINE PROBA-
bly sounded like an announcement of a minor
league hockey trade. Presidents Milosevic of Serbia,
Izetbegovic of Bosnia, and Tudjman of Croatia would
meet on November 1, 1995, at an air force base in the
American heartland to talk peace. After four years of
murderous struggle for control of Bosnia, each had
concluded something was to be gained from traveling
to Dayton, Ohio.

For Franjo Tudjman, the hope was to win back
Eastern Slavonia, a slice of Croatia on the border of

Serbia that Milosevic's forces had overrun and captured in 1991. Alija Izetbegovic wanted two things:
peace and the return of Bosnian territory occupied by
the Serbs. Slobodan Milosevic, who represented both
Serbia and the Serbs living in Bosnia, wanted respect
from the international community—more particularly, he wanted the major powers to lift sanctions that
were choking the Serbian economy.

From my perspective, it had taken too long to reach
this moment. We had relied unrealistically and for
longer than was justifiable on our European allies to
resolve the problems in Bosnia. That the Balkans had
the look and feel of a Vietnam-like quagmire did not
help to stiffen spines in our government, especially
since General Colin Powell and other top Pentagon
officials had been personally involved in the Vietnam
conflict. To add to the problem, the United Nations,
which claimed to have the resolve and the capacity to
restore the peace, seemed to lack both at critical
moments. By 1995, the United States had become, by
default and by virtue of its unique superpower status,
the only hope for restoring a semblance of order and
humanity to the Balkans. Our failure to recognize earlier that no other organization or state was going to
assume that role was a lapse for which I and the rest of
the Clinton national security team shared responsibility.

Once mobilized, the American team performed
effectively. In a few short weeks in the early fall of

1995, Dick Holbrooke, the assistant secretary of state for European affairs, negotiated a cease-fire and persuaded the three Balkan presidents to come to Dayton to talk to each other. Though the men had much more in common than not—shared borders, history, and language (several variants of Serbo-Croatian)—Holbrooke accomplished no small feat. The three men frankly and openly detested one another. On prior occasions when they'd met, they did little more than exchange polemics and insults. By cajolery and not-so-subtle threats, Holbrooke somehow wheedled them into coming to Dayton, empowered to reach agreement, committed to stay as long as necessary, and most improbably, pledged to refrain from talking to the press while they were there.

We settled on Dayton's Wright-Patterson Air Force Base as the site for the peace conference after a quixotic search that ranged across opulent European palaces (the preference of Britain, France, and other European allies) and austere U.S. military bases. Wright-Patterson was ultimately selected because it was neither too close to nor too far from Washington, was off-limits to the press, and offered the bare physical necessities: a conference center, a central dining facility, and four drab barracks for visiting officers, grouped around a parking lot. With some hasty refurbishing, the barracks became a functional, if not particularly comfortable, site for what proved to be a historic meeting.

THE OBLIGATORY HISTORY

When talking about a current event involving the Balkans, the story can seldom begin with what is happening today. Revisiting history is a prerequisite for getting to the point where something contemporary can be described or discussed. The Dayton peace conference is no exception; the past is essential prologue.

Following World War II, Bosnia became one of six constituent republics of Yugoslavia. Until Marshal Tito's death in 1980, Yugoslavia was a single, multiethnic federation. Freed from Tito's absolutist, autocratic hand, the six republics began to splinter in the 1980s. Within the republic of Bosnia, Muslims, Serbs, and Croats began a bloody struggle for control.

In early 1992, the last year of the Bush administration, a narrow majority in Bosnia voted to create an independent state, while the Serb population vocally, forcefully, and unsuccessfully protested that they preferred to unite with the Republic of Serbia. War broke out in Bosnia in April 1992. The frustrated Bosnian Serbs, assisted by Yugoslav national forces under the control of Serbian president Slobodan Milosevic, began to drive Bosnian Muslims and Croats from their homes—the beginning of what the world came to know as ethnic cleansing.

Throughout 1993–94, the war raged on, with spring offensives and winter pullbacks. The Bosnian Serbs dominated most of the encounters with their superior firepower, but the Bosnian Muslims and Croats fought hard and retained control of important sectors. In 1995, the balance began to shift as the Muslims and the Croats received new weapons from friendly countries.

Prior to the convening of the conference in Dayton, the United States tried a variety of initiatives to end the war without committing U.S. ground forces—from an arms embargo to stiffer economic sanctions to a no-fly zone. None was successful. Ultimately, as is often sadly the case, it took a catastrophe to spur the major powers to risk the decisive action necessary to bring the killing to an end.

In the early summer of 1995, the Serbs overran Zepa and Srebrenica, two U.N.-declared "safe areas" in Bosnia—places where Bosnian citizens had been assured they would be out of harm's way. The slaughter of thousands of Muslim residents of these towns, widely covered by the press, galvanized world opinion and convinced the key NATO allies that the time had come to do whatever was necessary to halt the slaughter before it reached the next apparent target of the Bosnian Serbs, the safe area of Gorazde. President Clinton, deeply engaged and strongly spurred on by the vice president, insisted that we find a way to stop the killing.

On July 20, 1995, Prime Minister John Major of the United Kingdom convened an emergency meeting in London of the NATO foreign ministers, plus those of other leading countries. I attended on behalf of the

United States, along with Defense Secretary Bill Perry and Joint Chiefs Chairman John Shalikashvili. So that the meeting would not dissolve into the finger-pointing and hand-wringing that had marked similar sessions over the prior three years, we proposed that NATO make clear, absolutely and unconditionally, that it would respond with massive air strikes if the Gorazde safe area was attacked. I also proposed that, in the event of such an attack, NATO should respond without the need to seek further approval or authority from the United Nations.

As was their habit in matters relating to Bosnia, the Europeans hesitated, pointing to the risk to U.N. forces and civilians on the ground. However, with strong support from the new British foreign secretary, Malcolm Rifkind, the conference approved our proposal. U.N. Secretary General Boutros-Ghali seemed also to buy into the plan, keeping silent even in the face of a consensus that diminished the U.N.'s power to control or delay events. On paper, at least, we had turned a corner. Now an understandably skeptical world waited, yet again, for action.

Within a few days of the London conference Boutros-Ghali tried to take back what he had given up in London. He insisted that he had intended all along to preserve a U.N. veto right over NATO air strikes. On Tuesday, July 25, I telephoned him to remind him that he had sat silent as we ratified the plan in London and that backtracking now would send precisely the wrong message to the Bosnian Serbs. Boutros-Ghali responded frigidly, and I had to call him a second time before he finally stood down.

As I wrestled with Boutros-Ghali, the NATO permanent representatives, prodded by our NATO ambassador, Bob Hunter, decided that NATO should go beyond the vow to protect Gorazde with air strikes. Meeting in Brussels, they agreed that the line in the sand would be drawn around *all* U.N. safe areas in Bosnia, including Sarajevo.

In Washington, President Clinton turned to the question of how to produce a stable peace, given the NATO allies' agreement to stand up to the Bosnian Serbs. A seven-point initiative was drafted and approved under Tony Lake's direction. It called for a permanent peace based upon a 51–49 percent territorial division between a federation of Muslims and Croats on the one hand, and the Bosnian Serbs on the other. Though controlling separate territory, the two entities would coexist under a federal government that, with reconstruction aid, could begin to rebuild the country.

Lake and Undersecretary of State Peter Tarnoff traveled to the key European capitals with instructions from the president to leave no doubt as to the firmness of the U.S. commitment. By mid-August, they had mustered strong European support for the plan. The next step was to bring the warring parties to the peace table.

THE HOLBROOKE SHUTTLE

Enter Dick Holbrooke. We had served together in the Carter administration—Dick as assistant secretary for East Asian affairs and I as deputy secretary of state. Twelve years later, on a June morning in 1993, I had woken him up to tell him that the president wanted him to be ambassador to Germany. In mid-1994, needing the services of someone with both his energy and style to deal with the key issues of Bosnia and NATO's future, I asked him to return to Washington as assistant secretary of state for European affairs.

Now the question was whether Holbrooke should carry the burden of one of the most important foreign policy initiatives the administration had undertaken to date, negotiating a Bosnian peace. After giving it some thought, I concluded he was perfect for the task. The very qualities for which he was sometimes criticized—aggressiveness, impolitic interaction with adversaries, a penchant for cultivating the media— were exactly what the situation required. I could imagine no better match for the likes of Milosevic, Izetbegovic, and Tudjman, and I knew many who would have paid money from their own pockets for ringside seats.

On August 15, as the fighting continued in Bosnia, Dick began his mission with a Zagreb-Belgrade-Sarajevo shuttle, during which he laid out the peace initiative to the three warring parties. Four days after he began, the effort came to a sudden, tragic halt. As

Holbrooke and members of his team drove the treacherous Mt. Igman route to Sarajevo, one of the party's vehicles slid off the road and down the mountainside, killing three members of the negotiating team: Bob Frasure, Nelson Drew, and Joe Kruzel.

I learned of the accident while on vacation in Santa Barbara and hurried back to Washington. On August 21, Dick Holbrooke flew home with the remains of his three comrades. The next day, the president led a memorial service in the chapel at Fort Myers, Virginia. Following the ceremony, he convened an ad hoc meeting of the Bosnia team and the key national security players in a modest white cinder-block room just down the hall from the chapel. The president quietly reviewed with us the status of the peace initiative, then said simply that we now had the burden of vindicating the sacrifice of our fallen friends. When our colleagues had been laid to rest, he said, we were to resume the peace effort.

Holbrooke returned to the Balkans six days later, on August 28. Within hours, another calamity struck. The Bosnian Serbs had surrounded Sarajevo, and on that morning, a Bosnian Serb mortar shell was lobbed into a crowded Sarajevo marketplace, killing at least thirty-seven people. It was exactly the kind of attack on a safe area that the London agreement was intended to address. Two days later NATO responded with intensive bombing of Serb targets in Bosnia. We were determined to send the message that the days of pinprick response to aggression and brutality were over.

At a White House meeting on September 11, the Pentagon urged that the attacks be suspended to enable them to assess the damage and gauge the Serb reaction. I resisted, believing that such a pause would be mistaken by the Serbs as signaling weakness or fractionation of our coalition. The president agreed, and the bombing continued until September 14, when the Serbs finally agreed to lift the siege of Sarajevo.

Aided by the message our bombing campaign had conveyed and by a brutal Croat offensive that gave the Bosnian Serbs further motivation to end the hostilities, Holbrooke and his team acted quickly to bring the parties to the peace table. The extraordinary diplomatic activity of the next several weeks is recounted fully in

NATO air strike on ammunition
dump near Pale.

his fine book *To End a War.* By October 5, these efforts had produced both a cease-fire and a commitment by the principal actors to come to Wright-Patterson Air Force Base at Dayton. I flew to Dayton on November 1 to open the peace conference.

DAYTON: THE NEGOTIATION

Threats, intimidation, violence, and plum brandy. On any given occasion, Slobodan Milosevic can and will employ any of these to gain advantage over an adversary. If the adversary hesitates, flinches, or otherwise displays weakness in the face of Milosevic's weapon of choice, he invites only more of the same. Milosevic had come to power in Serbia in 1989 by playing to Serbian nationalism, initiating years of intimidation of Kosovo. A wily tactician but a dreadful strategist (Serbia has lost four wars under his leadership), he affects an air of confidence, often arrogance, that belies any realistic assessment of his situation. But his vicious tactics have served one long-term goal: he has survived.

At my first meeting with Milosevic in Dayton on the morning the conference opened, his weapon du jour was a glass of plum brandy, held before my nose. Holbrooke, who by this time was well acquainted with Milosevic's tactics, had warned me about this variant, having himself risked liver damage in the cause of Bosnian peace. Now it was my turn to step up to the Milosevic tumbler. I took the glass from his hand and, as he watched, downed a gulp of the fiery liquid. Managing to stifle the gasp that bubbled up in my throat, I could not avoid a reflexive tightening of my facial muscles. Fortunately, Milosevic seemed to think I was scowling at him, and he backed off.

Milosevic's bearing and speech on this occasion projected artificial bonhomie. Decked out in a double-breasted blue blazer, he spoke sardonically of our mutual discomfort in the bland surroundings of Wright-Patterson. He openly disdained the other members of his delegation, dropping his voice to a stage whisper and telling me to ignore them. Then he moaned about the effects of sanctions on the people and economy of Serbia, giving me the opportunity to tell him that the sanctions would stay in place until he initialed a peace agreement.

Across the parking lot, in the building housing the Bosnian leadership, I found no bonhomie, forced or otherwise. Izetbegovic was dour and apprehensive, an attitude he bore continuously through the next twenty days. He looked and acted as though he wished he were someplace, anyplace, else. An ascetic former academic, he had spent eight years in a Yugoslav jail for the crime of being an Islamic activist. He had come to Dayton with his bargaining hand strengthened by a series of military victories over the Bosnian Serbs. It was impossible, however, to find any sign of satisfaction in his face.

When Holbrooke and I called on Tudjman of Croatia, he was smug and riding high on the wave of Croat battlefield victories that had driven the Serbs out of western Croatia. A former army general and history professor, Tudjman had won the first presidential election after Croatian independence in 1990 by being the most nationalistic of all the candidates. Vain and self-righteous, he frequently aped Tito by appearing in a white military uniform that set off his carefully pompadoured silver-gray hair. For this first day of Dayton, however, he was dressed in a conservative gray business suit.

At 2:30 P.M. on November 1, the principals and their respective entourages gathered in the Wright-Patterson conference center to launch the negotiations before the world press. In a prepared statement, I reminded the presidents that this was their last, best chance for peace. Each followed with grumpy, uninspired remarks. The session concluded with reluctant handshakes all around, after which the press was ushered out and the real work begun.

We handed each president a draft peace agreement and ten draft annexes—the product of intense work and bureaucratic infighting in Washington in the days leading up to Dayton. I had planned to return to Washington immediately after the ceremony, but Milosevic and Tudjman said they wanted me to preside over their first discussion on the fate of Eastern Slavonia. After conferring with Holbrooke, I agreed.

When I entered the bungalow in which the Milosevic-Tudjman discussion was to take place, I found the two presidents sitting on sofas silently facing each other. Holbrooke and I were directed to a sofa bridging the two sides, forming a three-sofa *U*. The discussion began with consecutive translations of each leader's opening remarks. Soon, however, the two presidents began shouting over each other in Serbo-Croatian, making translation impossible. I let them proceed without interruption and simply watched their angry exchange. I inferred—and the translator subsequently confirmed—that the presidents were indulging in the well-established Balkan custom of exchanging insults over recent and ancient history. No progress was made that day, and I departed certain that the process we had set in motion would be neither easy nor short.

On the one-hour flight back to Washington I considered again the risks we had taken in bringing these three antagonists together. If the Dayton conference broke up without agreement, we might well have ensured that the parties would resume their brutal war with even greater ferocity when the Balkan winter ended. Beyond that, the credibility of both the Clinton administration and NATO hung in the precarious balance. Had it been wise to take the chance? I decided it was too early to engage in postmortem thinking. We had launched the process, and it simply had to work.

Once back in Washington I received regular, sometimes hourly reports from Dick Holbrooke on the progress of the negotiations. Unfortunately, the rest of the world did not pause in its tracks to permit me to give undivided attention to Bosnia. On Saturday, November 4, 1995, three days after the Dayton talks began, Israel's Prime Minister Yitzhak Rabin was assassinated. The next day I flew to Israel with President Clinton for the funeral and for transition meetings with Rabin's successor, Shimon Peres.

I returned to Washington early on the morning of Tuesday, November 7, and immediately convened a briefing on the state of the Dayton talks. Holbrooke reported from Dayton that the first week had been slow going. He had made some progress in strengthening Croat-Muslim ties as a counterbalance to the Bosnian Serbs, and in drafting a plan for the withdrawal of the Serbs from Eastern Slavonia. However, an attempt to get the parties to sit down with maps for a practical discussion of the division of territory in Bosnia had produced only angry exchanges of the sort I had witnessed on the first day of the talks.

By November 10, the Bosnian Croats and Muslims

had decided on a package of measures that strengthened their federation in anticipation of the moment when governing themselves would become their principal problem. While they had worked together more or less harmoniously as military allies, they had heretofore stubbornly maintained separate, redundant political institutions in Bosnia. They had now apparently decided to eliminate much of that redundancy, and I agreed to fly to Dayton to bless their accord.

When I arrived, I was greeted by Holbrooke, who told me wearily that the Croats and Muslims could not agree on how the three top positions in the federation would be filled. Tudjman insisted, reasonably enough, that a Croat must occupy one of the three. Izetbegovic was resisting because it meant he had to choose between his prime minister, Haris Silajdzic, and his foreign minister, Muhamed Sacirbey. The exclusion of either would create a rift in the Bosnian delegation. After a brief discussion, Izetbegovic bent to the inevitable, agreeing with Tudjman that a Croat had to be in the ruling troika. The two leaders then agreed to proceed with the signing ceremony.

When we took the stage before the hastily convened world press, the residual hostility between Tudjman and Izetbegovic was obvious for all to see. They stood glaring at each other as I delivered words of thin cheer to the assembled crowd. As Holbrooke and I departed Wright-Patterson's conference center, we harbored no illusions about how far this small step left us from the finish line, and how difficult reaching that line would be before one or more of the participants decided to leave Dayton.

As I prepared to return to Washington, Holbrooke asked for a private word. He said that Milosevic and Tudjman were still having trouble closing on the issue of how long the Serbs would take to withdraw from Eastern Slavonia. Milosevic demanded three years; Tudjman offered one. I suggested the parties agree that the Serbs withdraw in a year, subject to extension for another year if local authorities felt that more time was needed. We took the proposal to Milosevic, who insisted on carrying the compromise himself to Tudj-man. The two men, closeted alone, emerged saying they agreed, subject only to consultation with subordinates in the Balkans.

Two days later, November 12, the agreement on the Serb withdrawal from Eastern Slavonia was signed in Croatia. It was a major boost for the Dayton talks, but it didn't translate into immediate visible progress. As the days wore on in Dayton, the three presidents grew restless, sulky, and stubborn. The key issue of territorial divisions was made even more difficult by acrimony within the Muslim delegation. The drafting of the ground rules for a NATO implementing force (IFOR) had also become a struggle, with Russia, NATO, and the Pentagon each having distinct views.

On November 14, I stopped in Dayton en route to Osaka for the annual summit of Asia-Pacific leaders. Dick Holbrooke, usually a hard man to discourage, greeted me with a gloomy assessment. The group was not going to hold together much longer. I shuttled among the three presidents for the entire day, reminding them that they were on the verge of losing a unique chance for peace.

In anticipation of talking to Milosevic, I planned a preemptive strike: I'd brought a bottle of my favorite California chardonnay to thrust at him before his plum brandy reached me. He accepted a glass, but I could tell that he found the wine, like my person, too mild for his taste. I pressed him for a suggestion on how Sarajevo was to be controlled, but his ideas for equitable solutions were nothing of the sort. My separate meeting with Izetbegovic was so frustrating that I warned him we could not help him further if he continued to erect obstacles to every constructive idea.

I sensed that we were quickly reaching a now-or-never moment. Although Holbrooke had made great progress on the text of the lengthy peace agreement and its detailed annexes, the toughest questions—the territorial division of Bosnia and the future of Sarajevo—remained unresolved. Before departing at midnight for Japan, I told my aides to shorten my trip to three days so that I could return quickly to Dayton.

THE END GAME

Seventy-two hours later, after a round-trip to Osaka and back-to-back meetings with Asian leaders, I returned to Wright-Patterson. Before I landed on Friday night, November 17, I received a message from Holbrooke that confirmed my instinct of a few days before. The choice, he said, was either "closure or close down." After landing, I met at once with Milosevic and Izetbegovic, which only served to confirm Holbrooke's dark assessment. Then I went to bed.

The next morning, Milosevic surprised everyone with what seemed like a dealmaker. He dropped his previously nonnegotiable demand for a federalized Sarajevo with equal voices for Serbs and Muslims. He was now willing, he said, to see Sarajevo and its environs controlled by the Muslim-Croat Federation. In his characteristic style, he decided this without consulting anyone in his own delegation, certainly not the Serbs from Sarajevo, who would bear its brunt. In return for this stunning concession, the Muslims and Croats would have to cede to the Bosnian Serbs sufficient territory to bring to 49 percent the area they controlled in Bosnia, as called for in our peace initiative.

We spent much of Sunday and Sunday night poring over maps to identify the territory that could be transferred to the Bosnian Serbs. Milosevic and his colleagues made a series of suggestions, but each was greeted by the Muslims with more or less the same response: the land identified was hallowed and could not possibly be yielded to the Serb heathens. At about 4 A.M. on Monday, the Muslim contingent proposed a territorial transfer in western Bosnia to bring the

Bosnian Serbs up to 49 percent. Milosevic looked at the map, shrugged, and said yes. It looked as if we had an agreement.

Champagne corks popped and a spontaneous victory celebration was begun—lasting for all of thirty-seven minutes. It took only that long for the Croat delegation to get their hands on the new proposed map and to note that Milosevic and Izetbegovic had agreed to a transfer involving mostly Croat territory. Their reaction was brief and to the point. The Croats would not accept the division of territory. After an hour of attempting unsuccessfully to bring them around, I returned to my room, showered, and while holding my face in the hot spray for five minutes,

November 20, 1995: Reviewing maps
of Bosnia *(from left)*: Hill, author,
Holbrooke, Izetbegovic, and Milosevic.

vowed to myself that I wasn't going to lose this opportunity.

I returned to the fray after dawn, focused on persuading Tudjman to yield the territory necessary to produce a 51–49 percent division. In midafternoon, we arranged for President Clinton to call the Croat leader to press for his help. Tudjman grudgingly responded to Clinton's plea, saying he would agree to yield most of the needed land if the Muslims, in turn, would also give up a small amount of land to make up the difference. He was indifferent to the location of the land the Muslims might choose, but he plainly needed this token concession to placate his constituency. Izetbegovic, with the ball back in his court, refused to yield.

I asked to meet privately with Izetbegovic. If I couldn't convince him, I knew Dayton would likely end in failure. Before going to his suite, I called President Clinton and told him that a breakdown might be imminent. He gave me the authority to shut down the negotiations if I concluded there was no prospect of agreement, saying he knew we had gone the extra mile and that he trusted my judgment.

At about 10:30 P.M., with Holbrooke and Ambassador Chris Hill at my side, I went to see Izetbegovic. He seized the opening to recite a litany of historic grievances against the Serbs and the Croats that was by now all too familiar. Though he spoke for ten minutes, he failed even to touch on the matter at issue, the release of a small portion of Muslim territory. I neared anger. I raised my voice—an occurrence rare enough to startle my colleagues—and told Izetbegovic that we had achieved everything he'd said he wanted when he came to Dayton. I told him I couldn't imagine how the United States could possibly help him further if, as it appeared to all involved, he refused to accept what he had sought for his people.

Izetbegovic knew I was right, and he knew he had within his grasp the peace he wanted. Still he wavered. His logical and emotional sides were in conflict. After years of bitter, bloody contest with the Serbs, he couldn't quite bring himself to accept an agreement that would result in sharing power with them, even though that was the major premise of the Dayton negotiations from the outset. Standing before him, I could almost see him fighting to conquer his hatred. I told him that I wanted his answer by midnight or I would bring Dayton to an end. Then I left his suite.

Shortly before midnight, Izetbegovic sent word that he would yield the necessary territory but now wanted something new. He demanded that the strategically situated city of Brcko, in northeast Bosnia near the Croatian and Serbian borders, be placed under Muslim control. The proposal was late and addressed a matter that Milosevic had made clear was nonnegotiable. Izetbegovic knew Milosevic would never hand over Brcko, but had obviously seized on the idea as another way to avoid coming to grips with the end game. I instructed that the other parties be notified of Izetbegovic's position and, well after midnight, turned in for the first sleep in three days. I drifted off believing that the talks were on the brink of failure and bracing myself mentally for the repercussions.

I awoke early on Tuesday, November 21, prepared to announce to the press that the peace talks had adjourned without an agreement. As I discussed the details with the staff, Milosevic walked through the snow across the parking lot to our headquarters. Holbrooke and I took him into Dick's room. When the three of us were alone, Milosevic proposed that he and Tudjman sign the agreement, leaving Izetbegovic to twist in the wind. As face-saving as it might have been to salvage something, I immediately refused. I told Milosevic that we had come to Dayton to forge a tripartite agreement, and if we couldn't achieve one, we were going home. We had come to Dayton to help, not diminish, the Bosnian Muslims.

Milosevic then offered another idea. He would agree to submit to binding arbitration the question of whether the Serbs or Muslims controlled Brcko, if I would agree to serve as arbitrator. For many reasons I declined the honor, suggesting instead former State Department legal adviser Roberts Owen. Milosevic, who had developed a regard for Owen while watching him serve as Holbrooke's legal adviser during the run-up to Dayton, accepted the substitution. I then took the proposal to Izetbegovic, presenting it on a take-it-

or-leave-it basis, without elaboration or argument. Looking sorrowful and beleaguered, he said, "It is not justice, but we need peace."

This time it looked as though all three parties were on board. We were relieved and exhilarated. At the same time, we were mindful that our accomplishment would not be greeted with unalloyed joy in Washington. National Security Adviser Tony Lake had called that morning to say that while he fully supported our quest for an agreement, others in the White House did not. He said that early press bulletins reporting we had failed to forge a peace agreement had been greeted with relief by the president's domestic advisers. These advisers had read the polls showing overwhelming opposition to the dispatch of U.S. ground troops to Bosnia and had doubtlessly run models of how much such a deployment might cost.

I closeted myself with Dick Holbrooke for a sanity check—should we close the deal, notwithstanding its imperfections and the divisions of opinion at the White House? We knew we had an agreement that would be difficult and expensive to implement, could cost American lives, and might not achieve its objectives in the long term. At the same time, we had managed to convince three previously intractable parties that they might be able to live together without violence. We agreed quickly: whatever problems lay ahead, whatever missiles the naysayers might launch at what we had done, this imperfect peace had to be better than war.

SEEING FOR MYSELF

The Dayton agreement was formally executed in Paris in December 1995. Two months later, in February 1996, en route to the Middle East, I paid my first visit to Bosnia. After stopping to talk with U.S. troops in Tuzla, I flew to Sarajevo to meet with local leaders and to get a personal sense of what needed to be done to restore the largest city in Bosnia to working order.

I was not sure what to expect. As my plane flew toward Sarajevo, I recalled television pictures of the city while under siege several months earlier. With its characteristic penchant for the visually dramatic, the television news coverage featured burned-out hulks of buildings and cars, interspersed with the detritus of a society in chaos. While I knew that the people and infrastructure of Sarajevo had taken a terrible beating, I believed that the pictures I had seen could not possibly be representative of the state of the city as a whole.

I was wrong, and the extent of my error was visible

Sarajevo, circa
February 1996.

even before the wheels of my plane touched the tarmac. The Sarajevo airport, which barely ten years earlier had served as port of entry for visitors to the winter Olympics, was a scorched, barricaded shell. The jetways that had extended to permit passengers to disembark without exposure to the elements were broken and lifeless. The windows of the structure were nearly all shattered, and in their place were sandbags shielding from further damage what was left of the building.

As we drove from the gates of the airport, I saw row after row of burned-out apartment houses. In some cases, mortar fire had reduced ten-story buildings to rubble. The streets near the airport were a no-man's-land, gutted and passable only by four-wheel-drive vehicles. Because unexploded ordnance remained strewn about the streets and sidewalks, passage by any means was risky. I had not seen comparable destruction since my visit to Tokyo in September 1945.

In the car with me as we drove from the airport toward the city center was Ambassador John Menzies. Despite his matter-of-fact narrative detailing what I was seeing out the window of our armored vehicle, his tone indicated that even the sensibilities of a toughened diplomatic veteran were tested by this environment. I remained silent for most of the drive, too overwhelmed by the devastation to speak. I could not escape one question. Had we achieved peace only after peace was a meaningless abstraction to the people for whom we had acted—the people who had to live in what was left of Bosnia? I wanted to look into the faces of Bosnian people, to get some sense of whether, notwithstanding the destruction that surrounded them, the victims of the war felt some hope for their future.

We reached the heart of the city, and suddenly people were everywhere, walking in all directions. While seagoing containers that for years had shielded pedestrians from snipers remained in the streets, pockmarked by thousands of rounds of fire, the people of Sarajevo seemed to treat these former safe harbors as nothing more than annoying relics. Though it was midwinter, the temperature hovered at a springlike level. The thaw had brought children out to play, shoppers to the main commercial district, and coffee drinkers to the several squares where espresso entrepreneurs had set white or green plastic chairs and tables on the sidewalks in front of their shops. Young Sarajevans sat at these tables, engaged in the national pastime of the Balkans—smoking, drinking coffee, and arguing politics.

I asked to leave my car for a walk in the streets. My security detail was uneasy but quickly arranged for me to walk a few blocks in an older part of the city where many small shops lined either side of pedestrian malls. As I walked, crowds of smiling people gathered, shouting and waving in my direction. I visited a few stores, finding half-empty shelves but stubborn optimism among shopkeepers and customers alike. Despite complaints from Sarajevo officials that international reconstruction help was arriving too slowly, I saw evidence everywhere that people were rebuilding and reinvesting their fortunes and futures in a city whose continued existence had been in doubt only a few months before.

My day in Sarajevo was not, of course, an adequate basis on which to conclude that our actions and policies in Bosnia had been successful or wise. The experience did provide, however, a visual and visceral confirmation of what I knew to be a fundamental prerequisite for success: that the suffering these people had endured had not diminished their desire or will to restore themselves to normal lives. If they were still willing to supply the heart, I was convinced we should not shrink from providing the means.

16

◆

THE FUTURE OF NATO

W E NEEDED A SUMMIT ON THE FUTURE OF NATO and we needed it now—meaning, in diplomatic parlance, within six months. It was June of 1993, shortly after the Clinton administration had taken office, and I was attending a meeting of the NATO foreign ministers in Athens. The Cold War was over, and hallway conversations with my counterparts had convinced me that it was urgent to define a new mission for an organization whose reason for being had been to deter Soviet aggression. We needed a summit of NATO leaders to address that task.

As secretary of state, I had the power to make many decisions of significance. Committing the president's schedule was not one of them. Hence, I was on the phone from Athens to Tony Lake at the White House, pressing for a slice of the president's time in early 1994.

My argument was straightforward: the other fifteen members of NATO looked to the United States for leadership, and our immediate guidance was necessary to set NATO's course. A NATO summit would also be the perfect event to mark Clinton's first trip to Europe as president. Lake's response, which I knew to be a mirror of the negative attitudes of those surrounding him at the White House, was to question whether we were ready for a summit. I replied that six months had to be time enough to frame our positions. After several telephonic parries and thrusts, we came to terms. A NATO summit appeared on the president's calendar for January 1994. I had no problem persuading the NATO foreign ministers who were in Athens to sign on for the meeting.

NATO, the North Atlantic Treaty Organization, was created in 1949 as a bulwark against Soviet Communism. While the organization was formed to serve primarily as a military alliance, over the years it demonstrated almost equivalent value as an instrument for facilitating the spread of democracy and democratic institutions throughout Europe. By including Italy, the only defeated Axis nation among NATO's twelve original members, the alliance accelerated the democratization of that country. Similarly, the addition of Greece and Turkey in 1952, West Germany in 1955, and Spain in 1982 produced dramatic corollary benefits.

West Germany's admission contributed to the reconciliation of France and Germany and, eventually, to the formation of the European Union. The admission of Greece and Turkey prompted these adversaries to move their dispute over Cyprus from the brink of armed hostility to the mediation table. And NATO's embrace of Spain ensured that the Spanish military would remain under civilian control in the uncertain times following the death of Francisco Franco.

When I took office in 1993, no one doubted that NATO had served a critical function during the Cold War. But the question of what NATO was supposed to be and do next was ripe for decision. After reviewing NATO's achievements and the political and social environment in Europe, I was among those who concluded that the organization should be preserved, reinvigorated, and expanded. While the Communist threat had abated, we believed new threats—terrorism, the proliferation of weapons of mass destruction, genocidal violence, and instability within and between states—could and should be addressed by NATO. NATO's military and political values should, I felt, be preserved and built upon in the post–Cold War period.

I also believed that an expansion of NATO to include the fledgling democracies of Central and Eastern Europe would help to promote European integration and unification. By focusing the attention of these former Soviet satellites and republics on joining NATO, I felt that we could channel their energies toward productive goals, such as strengthening democratic and legal institutions, ensuring civilian command of the armed forces, and attending to human rights. Moreover, by requiring these countries to maintain their best behavior to demonstrate their readiness to join NATO, we could tilt them toward peaceful settlement of disputes with their neighbors.

In deciding to preserve and extend NATO, I also considered what might happen if we failed to do so. I reasoned that if we did not enlarge the alliance, we would permanently endorse the dividing line that Stalin had drawn across Europe in 1945. Countries sitting on or near that line—the Central European nations—were naturally fearful of a resurgence of Russian imperialism. To leave them in fear, I thought, would make them resentful of the West, more cautious, and reluctant to embrace democratic change.

My views were strongly opposed in elite foreign policy circles. The opposing school of thought— espoused most notably by Ambassador George Kennan, the architect of America's Cold War containment policy—held that we should do no more than was necessary to preserve NATO as it presently existed. Kennan and others believed that any effort to invigorate or expand the alliance would threaten Russia and weaken its fledgling democratic reform effort. As usual, Kennan did not mince words. He called NATO expansion "the most fateful error of American policy in the entire post–Cold War era." While having enormous respect and affection for Kennan, I thought the picture was not nearly so clear. The time was right for airing and debating our options.

THE NEW SHAPE OF NATO

The making of foreign policy seldom produces clear-cut winners and losers in the bureaucracy. More typically, decisions coming out of policy debates are compromises of strongly held views falling across a broad spectrum. In the last quarter of 1993, that was certainly the case with respect to NATO expansion.

"Whither NATO?" was a question of great interest in the relevant bureaus of the State Department. I held several lunches in September and October to permit the airing of all points of view. As these colloquies proceeded, I found little disagreement, at least within the State Department, that NATO should expand. Rather, the debate was on just how rapid that expansion should be.

One group of fast-track advocates, led by Undersecretary Lynn Davis, argued that Poland, Hungary, the Czech Republic, and Slovakia should be admitted promptly to NATO membership. They argued that NATO should seize the moment to encourage potential members to adopt immediate reforms to take advantage of the prospect of early entry. Ambassador (later Deputy Secretary) Strobe Talbott, the government's leading Russian expert, espoused another point of view. He favored a gradual, open process of expansion and, to make the pill easier for Russia to swallow, the creation of a new, special relationship between NATO and Russia. Talbott believed that cooperative endeavors between NATO and Russia, such as the joint operations in which they later engaged in Bosnia, would establish a new grounding for their post–Cold War relations. He had in mind the kind of relationship ultimately reflected in the 1997 Founding Act between NATO and Russia, which created a council to explore joint decision-making and joint action but did not impair the freedom of each to act independently.

The State Department, of course, was not the only agency in Washington with a stake in NATO's expansion. At the Pentagon, expanding NATO's membership evoked passionate resistance from both senior military and civilian officials. In addition to concern over Russia's reaction, they worried that admitting countries with outdated military equipment would dilute the alliance's effectiveness. They were also reluctant to stretch American military commitments and resources to protect an enlarged set of borders.

The Defense Department's concerns eventually found expression in a proposal for a nuanced approach to NATO expansion. General John Shalikashvili, chairman of the Joint Chiefs of Staff, advanced a concept called Partnership for Peace, intended to presage but not immediately produce an expansion of NATO. He proposed that each nation in Central and Eastern Europe, including Russia and all members of the former Warsaw Pact, be eligible to establish a separate partnership with NATO. Each of the partners would be encouraged to join in NATO training exercises and to consult with NATO on military strategy and tactics, but in the event that any partner was attacked, that country would have only the right to consult with NATO about its defense. Unlike existing NATO members, the member nations of the Partnership for Peace would not enjoy the collective commitment of NATO that an attack on one would be treated as an attack on all.

NATO expansion presented President Clinton with one of his first significant foreign policy decisions. From my earliest discussions with him about NATO, he was insistent that our goal must be to integrate and unify Europe. He saw the end of the Cold War as providing a unique opportunity to achieve that end, and NATO as a vital tool for doing so. By extending eastward the successful institutions of Western Europe, he felt we could help bring security and prosperity to the countries of the former Warsaw Pact. One of these institutions, the European Community, in his view, was moving too slowly to incorporate Central European democracies, but we had little power to accelerate the EC process. In NATO, however, the United States held a much stronger hand. This was the vehicle, he believed, that we could use to hasten European integration. Accordingly, on October 18, 1993, following a meeting of the National Security Council, the president announced that he had decided to put NATO on a course toward gradual expansion, with the Partnership for Peace serving as a first step for some nations to achieve full NATO membership.

Within hours of the president's decision, I was on my way to Europe to explain our new direction to the former Warsaw Pact members and to the Russians. Defense Secretary Les Aspin departed more or less simultaneously to brief the NATO defense ministers in Germany.

My first stop was Budapest, where I met with ministers from the so-called Visograd countries: Hungary, Poland, the Czech Republic, and Slovakia. They readily embraced the Partnership for Peace concept but were disappointed at the delay in gaining NATO membership. Clearly, however, they had no intention of standing in the way of our plan. In light of their reaction, my next appointment, a meeting with Boris Yeltsin in Moscow, took on even greater importance.

THE RUSSIAN DIMENSION

In my mind, possible Russian reactions to the Partnership for Peace ranged from wait-and-see to just-you-wait. Yeltsin might take immediate action to counter NATO expansion. It was also possible that hard-line Russian nationalists would try to use formation of the Partnership as a reason for halting reform, reversing a direction we regarded as critical to Russia's well-being.

Three weeks before I arrived, hard-line opponents of Yeltsin had attempted a coup. On Yeltsin's orders,

Russian military forces had counterattacked, relent-lessly shelling the parliament building and finally retaking it. Yeltsin had suspended the obstructionist parliament and called for new elections.

With the rebels put down and a semblance of order restored to the government, the question hanging over Yeltsin was whether the West—America in particu-lar—would back him up. Indeed, it would and did. President Clinton, concluding that the democratically elected Yeltsin was as close as we were going to get to a reformer at the helm in Russia, announced that Amer-ica would support him in his moment of peril. How-ever, how this gesture would affect Yeltsin's reaction to what I had to tell him was hardly self-evident.

On arrival in Moscow, I learned that Yeltsin had left for his hunting lodge to recuperate from health prob-lems and to unwind from the stress of the coup attempt. After a day of not knowing whether I would see him, I was hustled to a government airport where I boarded a helicopter for a forty-five-minute flight to the middle of a dense forest where Yeltsin's lodge, Zavidovo, was located. The ride gave me a final opportunity to reflect on the man who awaited me in the Russian woods.

MY INTRODUCTION TO YELTSIN

I first met Boris Yeltsin on April 2, 1993, at a summit with President Clinton in Vancouver. I'd been briefed on all of the usual grand matters—where he stood on key issues; how we intended to react officially to his positions; where he seemed inclined to compromise or hold firm. What I was not prepared for was the look and feel of the man.

When Yeltsin entered the room in Vancouver, all eyes naturally turned. In the center of a sea of dark, loose-fitting suits stood a sartorially resplendent man, cloaked in a well-tailored, light gray suit. I cannot have been the only person in the room who instantly concluded that his outfit was not a product of Russia. Yeltsin's coiffure was equally impressive. Each shiny white strand of his very full head of hair looked as though it had been individually attended to just before he walked through the door. Yeltsin bore himself with the gait of an athlete, his broad, powerful shoulders leading the way as he strode through the crowd of lesser officials.

April 2, 1993: Meeting Yeltsin.

I was still mulling over this unexpected vision when Yeltsin sat down for a working session with the president. Yeltsin withdrew from his left coat pocket a set of note cards, apparently his talking points. As he did so, I was immediately distracted by his left hand. It was not really a hand at all, but something resembling two-thirds of a hand—and the less useful two-thirds at that. Someone or something had removed everything north of a diagonal line drawn from the tip of the middle finger on the left hand to a point on the thumb below the knuckle. Yeltsin had been left with no functioning opposing thumb or forefinger, only a small slot between the two, which, on this occasion, served as a kind of collator.

As I later learned, this artless amputation was the work of Russian doctors to whom Yeltsin's parents had turned when he'd suffered a childhood accident with a hand grenade. Though the trauma of the event and the self-consciousness that had followed the surgery had doubtlessly abated for Yeltsin long before he assumed Russia's presidency, the impact of the wound lived on in a curious, indirect fashion. For those who came to deal with Boris Yeltsin in his sixth decade, the hand was something more than the physical relic of a childhood injury. It was a rough emblem of the man himself—blunt, unforgettable, and on occasion, not fully functional.

The unpredictable ups and downs of dealing with Boris Yeltsin as a statesman and negotiator had become apparent to us in Vancouver almost immediately. In our first working session he initially tried to bulldoze Clinton with his speed and command of the issues, then abandoned the effort when he realized it was having no effect on the equally well-prepared president. He then reverted to friendly bantering with "Beel," as if he had never attempted his aggressive opening gambit. At a working dinner that night, we saw still another Yeltsin: as he consumed a great deal of wine, he grew jocular, then vague, then slightly sad.

The Hunting Lodge

Seven months later, as I ascended the steps of Yeltsin's hunting lodge, I carried a vivid memory of his Vancouver performance. When the door to the lodge opened, there stood a stiff, almost robotic Yeltsin, emanating heavy alcohol fumes. His chronically bad back was evidently making him so miserable that he required "medication" to deal with it.

We moved to a room decorated with tropical plants and large stuffed birds. He was subdued and somber as he thanked me for our support in the recent coup attempt, then explained what he was doing to prepare for the December parliamentary elections. When he finished, I turned to the task that had brought me to Yeltsin's lodge—describing our plans for the Partnership for Peace. I'd begun to explain how the Partnership would lead to gradual expansion of NATO when a suddenly animated Yeltsin interrupted to say that he regarded the Partnership for Peace as a stroke of genius. My first reaction was that it just couldn't be this easy. I had expected Yeltsin to insist that our plan was a threat to Russian security, or at least to cross-examine me about its details. But that was not Yeltsin's approach, at least not on this afternoon. Instead, he instructed me to "tell Beel that I am thrilled by this brilliant stroke." The remainder of our meeting was anticlimactic.

As I flew back to Moscow, I pondered the jarringly harmonious exchange I had just had with Russia's leader. Had Kozyrev, Russia's foreign minister, deliberately failed to alert Yeltsin to the full scope of Clinton's decision, or was Yeltsin simply relieved that NATO's expansion would not be immediate? A third pretty obvious alternative also occurred to me—that perhaps Yeltsin was having what we euphemistically described in North Dakota as a "bad day."

Three months later, at the January 1994 NATO summit, President Clinton formally proposed the Partnership for Peace. In Prague, two days after the summit, to ensure that no one in Moscow or elsewhere would misread our intentions, the president said that it was not a question of whether, but when and how NATO would enlarge. Soon after the announcement, countries in Central Europe and the former Soviet Union began petitioning to join the Partnership. Strobe Talbott kept the Russians fully posted on developments and, to our relief, found that Moscow continued to respond with relative sanguineness. It occurred to me that Yeltsin's performance at the hunting lodge might have been less spontaneous or uncontrolled than it appeared. As I soon discovered, however, the other shoe was yet to drop.

In late November 1994, Kozyrev telephoned to ask that we convene a special session of foreign ministers at NATO's December meeting so he could formally record Russia's joining the Partnership for Peace. Though other nations had taken this step without formal fanfare, Russia's accession was obviously a major event. Accordingly, I agreed to ask for a special session to be scheduled for the afternoon of December 1, 1994.

Anticipating a historic moment, the foreign ministers of all the NATO countries appeared at NATO headquarters outside Brussels on the appointed afternoon. When the critical moment arrived, however, Kozyrev announced that Russia was not ready to commit itself. He neither apologized for nor explained the sudden reversal. I was flabbergasted and embarrassed. We had put our prestige on the line in convening the session, and now, before the assembled foreign ministers of Europe, Russia was putting a thumb in our eye.

I improvised what, for me, was a passionate case for reconsideration. The foreign ministers of the United Kingdom, Germany, and Italy chimed in. When the four of us had spoken our piece, I turned to Kozyrev for a response. He sat immobile, looked straight ahead, and remained silent. There was nothing left for anyone to say; we adjourned the meeting.

As the NATO ministers were dispersing, Kozyrev drew me aside to say quietly that minutes before we'd convened, he had received a telephone call from Yeltsin's chief of staff in Moscow. He was told that the hard-line advisers to the president had convinced Yeltsin that the Partnership for Peace was a Trojan horse for NATO enlargement. Yeltsin had decided, at least for the present, that what he had characterized to me as Bill Clinton's "brilliant stroke" was really a dangerous thrust aimed at Russia's borders.

A few days later I flew to Budapest to join President Clinton at the annual Conference on Security and Cooperation, an event that drew all European heads of government, including Boris Yeltsin. The White House schedulers, always trying to shave time off the president's stay on foreign soil, had arranged for him to fly overnight from Washington and arrive just before the opening of the conference, leaving no opportunity to meet in advance with Yeltsin or any of the other heads of state.

Shortly after the meeting began, Clinton made a powerful statement about the need for European unity and NATO's peaceful intentions in helping to advance that goal. When Yeltsin spoke, his face was red and angry. He launched into a belligerent, theatrical tirade in which he spoke of a cold peace descending upon Europe. When he had finished, everyone in the room knew that on this particular day Boris Yeltsin did not regard the expansion of NATO as a good idea.

Yeltsin's public rebuke of the Partnership for Peace

was unquestionably a shock. But the Russian reaction, we quickly concluded, was driven more by a sense that America and its allies had failed to accord Russia the respect it deserved than by a fear that the move would make for a less secure Russian state. We had seen this same reaction—described by Strobe Talbott as the Rodney Dangerfield syndrome—in other contacts with the Russians on matters small and large. As we had with those prior flare-ups, we resolved to handle the dustup over the Partnership for Peace by putting the issue on hold.

Several weeks later, we decided the time was right to resume the diplomatic battle. We launched an effort, led by Secretary Perry and Talbott, to draw the Russians back to accepting and participating in the Partnership for Peace. We emphasized to the Russian hierarchy that while the decision to expand NATO was irreversible, it would be a slow and gradual process. We also said that we intended to open a dialogue with Russia in hopes of forging a special relationship between it and NATO. By May 1995, when President Clinton visited Moscow for the fiftieth anniversary of V-E Day, the groundwork had been laid. In a one-on-one meeting, the president convinced Yeltsin to agree to Russian participation in the Partnership. On May 31, in Brussels, Kozyrev quietly signed a document formalizing the decision.

SEARCH FOR A LEADER

Though NATO members had agreed with relatively little bloodshed that NATO should expand, deciding who would serve as the organization's civilian chief executive—the secretary general—proved much more fractious and messy. The post of secretary general has always been filled by a European, while the top military post, supreme allied commander, has historically gone to an American four-star general. Because the secretary general manages relations with the civilian leaders of the member nations, the position is of proprietary interest to NATO's European members.

When the Clinton administration assumed office in 1993, Manfred Wörner of Germany was secretary general. After Wörner lost a heroic battle to stomach cancer in August 1994, he was replaced, without controversy, by Willy Claes, the former foreign minister of Belgium. Claes served effectively for a year, but was forced to resign in October 1995 when he became the target of bribery allegations in his home country.

The vacancy in the secretary general's post came at a sensitive moment for NATO, not simply because the organization's future was under active discussion, but because its immediate present was also in hot dispute. The question of the moment was whether NATO should take an active role in implementing a peace agreement in Bosnia, a sobering challenge. Taking on this task would require the alliance to act on turf outside the territory of its member countries, an unprecedented act for the alliance. If NATO did so, the results of every action we took would be exposed for the world to see. Success would mean that NATO's vitality was tacitly reestablished. If we failed, many would cite the result as evidence that NATO was no longer equipped to handle difficult European security issues. The outcome might well turn on the ability and character of the next European civilian to hold the post of secretary general.

Perhaps to foreclose the announcement of competitors, Britain and France quickly and publicly announced that their candidate was Ruud Lubbers, prime minister of the Netherlands from 1982 to 1994. When Germany announced it would also support Lubbers, the Dutch were ready to break out the champagne.

To seek U.S. support for their candidate, the Europeans sent Lubbers to Washington for interviews with our national security team. We thought well of Lubbers's performance as Dutch prime minister and approached his candidacy with an open mind. Though my meeting with him went pleasantly enough, when I had some time to reflect at the end of a crowded day, I felt uneasy. Lubbers had seemed wan and unfocused. An hour after we'd talked, I had difficulty remembering any subject on which he had taken a firm position. As I knew I was a better listener than a talker, this was more than slightly disturbing. I began to wonder whether, in the face of a challenge, he was the sort of person who would let events roll over him rather than seize the initiative.

I telephoned Bill Perry, who was to see Lubbers the next day, and told him of my concerns. The next afternoon I received a call from Perry, who said his reaction to Lubbers mirrored my own. We agreed to hold our fire until Tony Lake had met the candidate. When Tony weighed in with the same concerns, we concluded that Lubbers simply did not have the requisite force for the job. We conveyed our unanimous lack of enthusiasm to the president, who, after considering the likely fallout in Europe, agreed not to approve Lubbers. Since a unanimous vote of members is required to select a new secretary general, the president's decision doomed the candidacy.

As we expected, all hell broke loose when the Dutch learned of our intended veto. They angrily withdrew Lubbers's name before a formal vote could be taken, and their foreign minister, Hans van Mierlo, called to tell me he was deeply offended that we would turn down a former prime minister of his country. To make matters worse, Queen Beatrix of the Netherlands arrived in Washington on a state visit a few days later and complained bitterly to President Clinton about what she regarded as a snub. All the president could do in response was change the subject. While he never asked us to revisit the decision, he left none of us in doubt that the timing of this fracas displeased him.

The Europeans next suggested Uffe Ellemann-Jensen, the former foreign minister of Denmark. We interviewed him in Washington and decided we could support him. However, the French said they would veto him, in large part because he did not speak French well enough to suit them. The objection was not entirely unexpected, since the French believe that Paris is the center of the universe and that French is the universal language. If one does not have a fluent command of French, one is, at least in French eyes, not entirely civilized. Still, it seemed a preposterous basis on which to deny a capable man a job he was well suited to perform.

I had my own brush with the gall in Gallic in 1996, when my term as secretary was coming to a close. As I was departing from a meeting in Paris, the French foreign minister, Hervé de Charette, knowing that I neither spoke nor read French, gave me as a birthday present a collection of paperback novels—in French. He did so in full view of the press, ensuring that stories documenting the event internationally would underscore his elegantly contemptuous gesture. I kept my counsel in the face of this slight, leaving the French to ponder whether I had even understood their minister's *sale coup*.

After Ellemann-Jensen failed his French exam, I floated the name of Javier Solana, the Spanish foreign minister. I'd recently spent time with him in Madrid and came away impressed. He seemed to know what he thought, why he thought it, and how to persuade others to join in his views. He also had the perfect personality for the fellow at the front of the store: articulate, empathic, and a good listener.

Trained as a theoretical physicist, Solana had been a visiting professor at the University of California and understood and appreciated the United States. While he passed all of the lesser tests for the job of secretary general—diplomatic experience, personality, tough-mindedness—we held our breath while awaiting word on whether he passed the ultimate test: command of the French language. To our relief, the French pronounced his skills adequate—or however one pronounces adequate in French. The white smoke rose figuratively above NATO headquarters. Javier Solana was the man.

A VISION FOR EUROPE

As 1996 dawned, I felt as if I could exhale for the first time in months. We had finally put in place a new direction for NATO and a new leader to keep the organization on course. Reflecting on 1995, I wanted to make clear that the decision to move NATO into new territory, literally and figuratively, was the manifestation of an American policy directed to drawing Central and Eastern Europe into a unified European system. It was time, I thought, for a clear expression of that vision.

As the place to make the statement, I chose Prague, a former Soviet captive capital whose new commitment to democracy was emphatic. The choice of site underscored that we did not intend to deal with the former Soviet bloc as de facto extensions of their former master. NATO would enlarge, and states such as the Czech Republic would be strong candidates for inclusion.

My March 20, 1996, speech in Prague called for reuniting Europe, with NATO expansion playing a pivotal role. I responded to Russian arguments that Central European countries ought not become involved in a Western institution such as NATO, suggesting that the same objection had been voiced by Stalin to deny the benefits of the Marshall Plan to what became Russia's satellites. I urged the extension of Western institutions into Central and Eastern Europe and indicated that the first wave of NATO expansion, then on track for 1997, would not be the last.

I knew my remarks would be well received in Prague and like-minded Central European capitals, but that Moscow would likely be a different story. I did not have to wait long to be proven right. On the night after my speech I met for dinner in Moscow with Yevgeny Primakov, who had become foreign minister in late 1995 after Yeltsin had sacked Kozyrev. Primakov, who had begun his career as a journalist and had served as a Middle East expert for Soviet leaders from Brezhnev to Yeltsin, had earned the mistrust of many U.S. officials by his meddlesome dealings with Saddam Hussein of Iraq in the days preceding the Persian Gulf War. Two months earlier in Helsinki I had met him for the first time and had found him

informed, confident, and pragmatic. I was not prepared for his reaction to my Prague remarks.

We were still on the soup course when Primakov
launched his attack, replete with raised voice and bit-
ing sarcasm. He claimed I had gone beyond official
U.S. policy in describing the U.S. commitment to
NATO expansion. I responded that I was not freelanc-
ing, that my remarks represented the president's position as well as my own. I tried to lower the volume of
our exchange by taking him through the speech point
by point, but he blustered and filibustered, claiming
we were treating Russia with contempt.

Initially I was dumbfounded by the vociferousness
of Primakov's display. Then I recalled that the Moscow
morning papers had reported that Yeltsin had criticized him for being too accommodating during an
interchange with NATO secretary general Solana. Primakov, I concluded, had decided he would not make
the same mistake twice. Though he calmed somewhat
as our meeting progressed, we parted with a chilly
handshake.

I was scheduled to meet the next day with Yeltsin
and, again, had no idea what to expect. We met in a
strikingly beautiful, high-ceilinged room in the Krem-
lin, decorated in bright yellow tones. During our hour
together, he complemented the decor by displaying
for my benefit every color of congenial in the rainbow,
a refreshing change from the previous day's meeting
with Primakov. Though we touched on a variety of
diplomatic subjects, Yeltsin's principal interest was

whether President Clinton continued to be his friend. He obviously wanted to confirm that the United States was not hedging its bets on the Russian presidential election. When I told him our president remained squarely in his corner, he tilted his head and briefly smiled, as though he had heard a few bars of pleasant music.

The acronym NATO crossed neither Yeltsin's lips nor those of our translators until we were both on our feet and heading for the door. Only then did Yeltsin remark that I was wise not to raise the subject. In response, I said I felt I didn't need to raise the subject, as Primakov and I had had a full and frank exchange about NATO the evening before. Then, to be absolutely sure that Yeltsin firmly grasped our intentions, I told him that the expansion of NATO and integration of Europe were official U.S. foreign policy objectives. I waited for his reply, but he just looked at me, grimaced, then turned and walked slowly away.

17

$\diamond$

YESTERDAY A WAR,
TODAY A COUNTRY

ISOLATED FROM ALL CONTEXT, THE INCH-LONG
shard held before me would have evoked no particular reaction. It had the look of a small piece of drift-
wood or rock—nothing likely to trigger memories,
passions, or even interest. But I was standing in the
U.S. Army's Central Identification Laboratory at
Hickam Air Force Base, Hawaii, the only U.S. military facility in the world dedicated exclusively to the
search for and identification of the remains of servicemen and women killed or missing in action. And
being held forward for my inspection on March 5,
1994, was not wood or rock, but a piece of human
bone.

The forensic experts surrounding me were charged

with determining whether this fragment of a life was from an American serviceman who had gone missing during the Vietnam War between 1959 and 1975. The experts and their predecessors had done this job with intensity and dedication, day in and day out, for more than two decades—a job whose principal reward, ironically, was the ability to confirm the worst.

Many who have lost loved ones or friends find the comfort of closure in seeing, even touching, their mortal remains. I do not number myself among this group. I could never piece through how the sight or touch of death in its literal form could produce anything other than upset for the living.

The first funeral I attended, at age sixteen, was my father's, and it undoubtedly fixed my attitude on this subject. I hated everything about the event, most memorably my uncle's walking me up to the casket and urging me to "take a last look at your dad." I kept my eyes tightly shut, preferring to recall him as he was in life. He was gone, I knew that, and I was consoled by the picture of him I carried in my head, an image wholly at odds with that of the lifeless vessel that lay in the casket.

As the years passed, I came to realize that wakes and viewings, public mourning and burial rites, are important to many people. For more than twenty years, the American public and its government have spoken with a single voice: the remains of our men and women who served in Vietnam must be found and returned. There can be no real peace, no rapprochement, no normalization of relations, until we are satisfied that we as a nation have fulfilled this last, sad duty. The name of the military unit in charge of the search says it all: Joint Task Force—Full Accounting.

America's obsessive insistence on the repatriation of the remains of its servicemen and women was not born with the Vietnam War. But in the case of Vietnam—the longest war we ever fought and the only one we ever lost—the symbolism of the act, the salvaging of American honor by the unshakable insistence on leaving no stone unturned in locating our dead, is especially powerful. Three million Americans fought in Vietnam between 1959 and 1975, and 58,000 of them perished there. Those who returned without physical wounds carried and still carry psychic scars from what they saw and heard, and from a feeling that their country, two decades after the fact, remains somehow embarrassed or ashamed of the mission on which they were dispatched.

Vietnam also left a scar on our political and diplomatic psyche that mirrors the terrible loss of human life it produced. It denied Lyndon Johnson his second term in the White House and, in turn, probably cost Vice President Hubert Humphrey his chance for the presidency. An entire college generation—Bill Clinton's, in fact—was traumatized when National Guardsmen shot and killed four unarmed students during an antiwar demonstration in May 1970 at Kent State in Ohio.

Since 1975, each new American military challenge

has been evaluated by the media, the public, and presumptively, America's leaders against the question "Could it be another Vietnam?" When the Gulf War ended victoriously for us, President George Bush exulted, "By God, we kicked the Vietnam syndrome once and for all." As it happened, however, the specter of committing our blood, resources, and national dignity to a military cause in which we might not prevail continued to be asserted by opponents of every subsequent American military excursion.

I was too old to serve in Vietnam or to have felt a part of the generation of young people whose lives were disrupted, if not threatened, by the war. My life, nevertheless, was drawn into the issue. As deputy U.S. attorney general, I was often called upon to mediate or devise strategies to help contain the violence of draft protests. As President Johnson's law enforcement representative at the 1968 Democratic convention in Chicago, I watched the police riot against anti–Vietnam War demonstrators and pondered whether federal troops might have to be deployed to bring the disorder under control. Even in 1977, when I returned to Washington as Cyrus Vance's deputy secretary of state, Vietnam remained such a vital topic that in preparation for his confirmation hearings, Vance asked for my counsel on what position he should take in his testimony. (The war was a "mistake," he ultimately testified.)

When the Clinton administration took office in 1993, Vietnam in the minds of most Americans was still a war, not a country. The word evoked for most a memory of anguish, whether directly experienced or inherited. Our official contacts with Vietnam reflected this continuing trauma. We had had neither an embassy nor normal diplomatic relations with Hanoi since withdrawing from South Vietnam in 1975.

With the war almost two decades behind us, I believed that the time had come to reestablish a working relationship with Vietnam, to recast the word in the American consciousness as a place rather than a nightmare. I directed my staff to pursue a calibrated approach to accomplishing that goal. Depending on the extent of Hanoi's cooperation in the search for the remains of our servicemen and women, we would first support loans to Vietnam by international financial institutions; next, we would lift the bilateral trade embargo; then, open a liaison office in Hanoi; and finally, establish full diplomatic relations.

I knew from the outset that the "third rail" for anyone proposing to move the United States closer to Vietnam was failing to make absolutely clear that any positive change in the relationship had to be accompanied by intensified cooperation from the Vietnamese in locating the remains of our unaccounted-for servicemen and women. In 1993, about sixteen hundred Americans were still in that category. Many, perhaps most, were pilots or other members of air crews who had crashed in inaccessible mountainous terrain or jungles. Locating their remains required operations akin to complex archaeological digs. What we wanted from the Vietnamese as a quid pro quo for establishing normal relations was assurance that U.S. search teams would have the complete cooperation of local Vietnamese authorities, as well as help in the physically and psychologically difficult work of unearthing remains.

Even with an earnest dedication by the Vietnamese to assisting us in solving the remaining cases, I anticipated passionate, vocal resistance to normalizing relations from some quarters in the United States. As I expected, the principal opposition to our proposal came from veterans and organized POW/MIA support groups. Although a greater percentage of our dead had been recovered from Vietnam than from the battlefields of World War II and Korea, the opposition groups were adamant that everything possible had to be done to locate and return the remains of those who had not yet been accounted for. From their standpoint, no cost/benefit analysis, either as to dollars or diplomatic impact, was relevant.

My 1994 visit to the Central Identification Laboratory in Honolulu was a key part of our plan to move toward improved relations with Vietnam. I felt that the images and stories depicting the U.S. secretary of state involved in the technical details of resolving missing-person cases would help confirm to America and the world that this activity was important and would not cease. Between 1993 and 1995, the president sent several missions to Vietnam to ensure that every feasible step was being taken to obtain information on POWs and MIAs. In Washington, Tony Lake and Assistant Secretary of State Winston Lord met frequently with the MIA/POW support groups to describe our efforts and hear their views.

By the summer of 1995, President Clinton was satisfied that we were getting full cooperation from the Vietnamese in the search for remains and concluded that the time to restore full diplomatic relations was approaching. The various missions that he had sent to the country had returned with uniformly glowing reports of Vietnamese assistance. The domestic political landscape also favored the opening of a new chapter in U.S.-Vietnam relations. Democratic senators John Kerry and Bob Kerrey, both of whom had served and been seriously wounded in the war, supported the president's initiatives. Republican senator John McCain, as well as Democratic congressman Douglas B. (Pete) Peterson, both of whom had been shot down and imprisoned in North Vietnam during the war, spoke in favor of resuming full diplomatic relations. McCain, a conservative, was particularly helpful in finding ways to assess and deal with potential opposition from his fellow Republicans. He made it clear he wanted to help put the war finally behind America.

Despite growing support for restoring full diplomatic relations, the president's decision to proceed required both personal and political courage. In the 1992 campaign for the presidency, his opponents focused on his protests against the Vietnam War while a student, and the controversy later over his never being drafted. Then, within weeks of his inauguration, he ignited an emotional battle with the nation's military leaders and Main Street America by proposing an end to the ban on military service by gays. Though, by 1995, Clinton had managed to quell much of the furor, his standing with the military establishment remained in doubt, particularly within the Beltway. As a result, the betting by insiders was that the pragmatic Clinton would postpone any announcement of closer ties to Vietnam until after the 1996 election.

However, on July 11, 1995, the president announced the restoration of full diplomatic relations with Vietnam, "an act that required some courage," according to Senator McCain. In his statement, the president spoke positively of Vietnam's growing cooperation in the search for unaccounted-for American servicemen and women, noting that twenty-nine families had recently received remains of their loved ones, for whom they could provide, at last, a proper burial. He also announced that he would send me to Vietnam the next month to give formal effect to his decision.

Almost immediately, the American Legion denounced the president's action, and Senator Bob Dole, the majority leader, threatened to withhold funding for an embassy in Hanoi. In response, Senator Kerrey said Dole was "wallowing in the past," publicly confirming his own support for the president's decision and for my planned visit.

HANOI, 1995

Even before I landed at Hanoi's airport on August 5, 1995, images from our decades-past conflict confronted me. My plane descended slowly over a ring of mountains that, during the war, had been known as Thud Ridge. The name, I suspected, was intended to mimic the sound of North Vietnamese antiaircraft guns placed on these mountains to shoot down American planes before they could reach Hanoi. As I gazed below, the peaceful rolling hills seemed the antithesis of a place where so many American airmen had met violent deaths.

In planning my visit, I wanted to emphasize from the outset that the issue of finding and repatriating remains still had first priority on the American agenda. Accordingly, we decided to devote the first day of the visit to that issue. As the only secretary of state ever to visit Hanoi and the highest-ranking U.S. official to set foot in Vietnam since National Security Adviser Henry Kissinger in 1973, I didn't know if I would be received as an unwelcome reminder of the destruction wrought by America on the country, or as a symbol of reconciliation. Whatever the initial reaction, our plan would not vary. The first images of this visit to be transmitted back to America would portray our continued focus on the recovery and identification of remains.

Landing at the Hanoi airport, I descended the steps of my plane into wilting heat. I then stood at attention

Aluminum containers hold human remains to be transported to Hawaii for analysis.

as an honor guard of American soldiers placed four aluminum cases containing what were believed to be the remains of four American servicemen on a nearby transport aircraft for their journey to the forensic laboratory in Honolulu. The contents of the cases were the product of months of search efforts by teams of dedicated Americans and Vietnamese.

The bumpy ride into town over partially unpaved streets provided my first glimpse of the startling contrasts of Hanoi circa 1995. We drove down tree-lined boulevards graced with stately French-style villas abutting new mini-mall-type shops. Placid, lovely Hoan Kiem Lake, one of eleven in the Hanoi area, was ringed by a street crammed with hundreds of people riding motor scooters, rickshaws, and bicycles, all seeming to be headed in conflicting directions. Reaching our hotel, the Metropole, we found a beautiful turn-of-the-century structure that had been faithfully restored to French colonial splendor. The wide corridors, louvered doors, and ceiling fans created a wonderful, albeit fleeting, sense of nineteenth-century languor. The spell was quickly broken by the sounds of motor scooter horns and street vendors hawking compact disc players on the streets outside.

At a welcoming lunch hosted by Vietnam's foreign minister, Nguyen Manh Cam, I said that before we spoke of any other topics I wanted his firm assurance that the Vietnamese government would do all within its power to help resolve the outstanding POW/MIA cases. Cam plainly anticipated my message. He responded with a recital of recent Vietnamese efforts to help and committed his country's assistance until all remains had been located and returned to us.

When I indicated that I was satisfied by his response, Cam then described the top item on his agenda: a trade agreement that would provide low-tariff treatment for Vietnamese goods entering the United States. He sounded as if he thought that such an accord could be easily and quickly concluded. In the face of his too sanguine expectations, I decided to send Joan Spero, the undersecretary for economic affairs, who had accompanied me on the trip, to visit her Vietnamese counterpart to explain just how complicated the negotiation of a trade agreement was likely to be. Ultimately, it took until 2000 for Vietnam to meet our traditional requirements for such a pact.

THE RANCH

After my meeting with Cam, I moved on to the "Ranch," a collection of temporary buildings on the outskirts of Hanoi that, since 1992, has served as U.S. headquarters for the effort to find the remains of American servicemen and women. The facility serves five search teams, each headed by a U.S. lieutenant colonel and each composed of 120 American army personnel, 20 Vietnamese officials, and 600 local laborers. Some of these teams had been responsible for finding and transporting back to Hanoi the remnants of human life contained in the four metal cases I had dispatched to Hawaii upon my arrival in Vietnam.

In a briefing by U.S. military officers assigned to the Ranch, I learned that the teams sift clues from a variety of sources to pinpoint the location of remains. These sources include documents obtained from the Vietnamese, American battle reports, and statements from Vietnamese villagers that are passed along to officials in the Vietnamese government. Given a credible lead, a team from the Ranch will travel to the farthest reaches of the country to investigate and, if warranted, to excavate. The process is slow, grueling, and often disappointing. In the eight years since the Ranch opened, the possible remains of 307 American servicemen and women have been sent on to Hawaii for examination. Despite the frustrating task, morale at the Ranch is high and the Americans selected for the mission prize their assignment.

The American servicemen who briefed me at the Ranch were eager to relate stories of how Vietnamese civilians had helped them. I learned that one multi-national team had hacked through dense jungle growth for five days to recover remains at the site of a downed aircraft on the Vietnam-Cambodia border. Another team searched for weeks before locating Vietnamese villagers who led them to the remains of a helicopter crash in a heavily wooded mountainous area. These tales were of singular importance to us in assessing the sincerity of the Vietnamese commitment to help the recovery effort, and they also proved valuable when, after we returned home, we had to convince congressional skeptics of the wisdom of our initiative.

Americans and Vietnamese work
side by side to unearth remains.

Nearly every American with whom I spoke at the Ranch attached special importance to the active involvement of so many Vietnamese in searching for remains. Like me, our soldiers were surprised to find selfless, uncomplaining cooperation in such a task from citizens of a country that had lost 3 million people in a war with America. When asked to explain the Vietnamese willingness to assist the United States, they typically responded that the Vietnamese had come to terms with what had happened to them and had decided that lingering resentment was a luxury they could not afford. For them, tomorrow had become much more important than yesterday.

At the conclusion of my first day in Vietnam, I gathered my staff to assess our mission. After reviewing the events of the day, we agreed that the Vietnamese officials understood that the continued search for the remains of our servicemen and women was a matter of great importance to America. We concluded that it was appropriate to proceed to the ceremonies and discussions that would mark the opening of the new chapter in U.S.-Vietnam diplomatic relations.

RETURNING TO NORMAL

The next day began with the raising of the U.S. flag over the office building that would serve as our embassy. As my car approached the site, we slowed, then crawled, through a crowd of hundreds of smiling, cheering Vietnamese. As best I could ascertain, these people had not been assembled for the purpose of making an impressive showing. To my eye, they seemed to be men and women of varying ages and means who had come to witness what they regarded as a genuinely momentous event for their country.

As I stood watching the American flag move slowly up the flagstaff in front of the new embassy, I thought back to pictures I had seen from the predawn hours of April 30, 1975, when America's last ambassador to Vietnam, Graham Martin, had hurried to board a helicopter on the roof of the U.S. embassy in Saigon as our flag was quickly lowered and folded. That scene of humiliation and defeat was flashed around the world and seared into the consciousness of every American over the age of ten. Even now, twenty years

August 3, 1995: Raising the flag over the
new American embassy in Hanoi.

later, the image remained vivid and painful for me. It took a nudge to my ribs from an aide, urging me forward to deliver my prepared remarks, to bring me back to the moment.

I stepped to the lectern to speak, but found myself still shaken by my memories. Fortunately, this audience was not apt to be critical of my delivery. I focused on the crowd, cleared my throat, then noted that this moment marked the end of a decade of war followed by two decades of estrangement. We had lost a third of a century to tragedy and mistrust. The time had come to lay the unhappy past to rest and to dedicate ourselves to a future of productive cooperation. The Vietnamese officials present clapped with elation, but the Americans on hand seemed subdued and pensive, as I was.

Immediately after the ceremony, I went to a meeting with the dominant figure in the country, Communist Party leader Do Muoi, and later in the day I met with Prime Minister Vo Van Kiet. Both men were veterans of the U.S.-Vietnam conflict, and both meetings followed approximately the same script. They welcomed me, endorsed my mission, and like Foreign Minister Cam the day before, promised complete cooperation in locating and returning the remains of our servicemen and women. While I knew these war-hardened leaders were not about to announce spontaneously the abandonment of Communism in favor of democracy, I was pleasantly surprised by the absence of ideological polemics in our interchanges. They had apparently chosen to avoid even pro forma confrontation in hopes of winning early agreement on matters that would accelerate the modernization of the Vietnamese economy.

The afternoon of our second day gave me more opportunities to talk directly with Vietnamese civilians as I visited the Temple of Literature and other local shrines. Each of these conversations seemed to reveal a passion for things American, Western, or high-tech. A member of the Vietnamese military told me that nighttime English classes were filled to overflowing across the country, while French instructors couldn't lure new students even with the promise of free croissants and espresso. As I rode and walked through the streets, evidence of business being done or begun was everywhere, from closet-sized offices crammed with computers and fax machines, to crowds of people armed with cell phones, jostling one another for standing or walking room. The engines of Vietnam's future—members of the three-fifths of the country's population under age twenty-five—were everywhere.

Late in the afternoon I went to Hanoi's Institute for International Relations to talk with about two hundred young students. Although earphones for translation were available, nearly the entire audience listened to my remarks without assistance. Knowing that Vietnam's economic future was their key interest, I wove a message about economic progress, using threads emphasizing the importance of democratic reform. I stressed that sustained economic development was more likely in places where courts provided due process, where newspapers were free to expose corruption, and where businesspeople could make decisions with free access to information—conditions notably lacking in Vietnam.

I could not read with any assurance the reactions to my message, but noted a number of heads nodding in agreement when I said that each member of the audience ought to have the right to shape his or her own destiny, as well as that of his or her country. The young of Vietnam were not accustomed to hearing this kind of message from government figures, and I half expected to be interrupted in midparagraph by school officials and ushered from the room. But, again, there was no confrontation. Whether motivated by politeness or economic self-interest, the Vietnamese allowed me to say my entire piece.

As I contemplated how I would characterize my experience in Vietnam to the president and the Congress, the headline was undoubtedly the absence of any apparent animosity toward the United States or me. To be sure, I had seen pointed governmental effort to keep the war in the public consciousness, such as the preservation in a popular pond of a downed U.S. B-52 bomber. However, our party, particularly those among us such as Lieutenant General Dan Christman, the Joint Chief's representative on my delegation, who had fought in the war, had received the warmest possible welcome. I had no doubt that the Vietnamese had and would continue to harbor unexpressed hostility toward the foreign power that had besieged their country. Still, they clearly wanted to turn the page.

Of the welter of images and conversations that I carried with me from my two days in Vietnam, none affected me more than a strange, sweet gesture from an elderly policeman who stood guard outside a Vietnamese temple. As we left the building, the policeman, wearing a worn military-style uniform, straightened his back and snapped a sharp salute to General Christman, who was walking beside me. The general returned his salute, and with ramrod posture, the policeman maintained his salute as we climbed into our car and closed the doors. Then, as our motorcade began to move, the old man bent over slightly, his right hand still at his forehead, brought his left hand to his lips, and blew us a kiss.

Before I turned in for the night, one task remained. I wanted to call each of the four members of Congress whose support had been critical to the trip, to describe to them as best I could what we had done and how the Vietnamese had responded. Of the four calls, I remember most clearly the one to Senator John McCain. When he came on the line, I told him the Vietnamese had promised their best efforts to find and return the remains of America's missing airmen. I also described the greeting I had received and said that, thanks in large part to him, we were on the cusp of a new era in U.S.-Vietnamese relations.

The lengthy silence on the line made me think that we'd been disconnected or that McCain was experiencing regret. Then, his clear, precise voice came shooting across the line again with only three words: "It was time."

Afterword

FOR FOUR YEARS, I'D BEEN A REGULAR VISITOR to the White House, usually once a day, sometimes more. Whatever the purpose, whatever entrance I used, I always approached with a little awe, for the building is the living, breathing embodiment of America's history. As the gates to the grounds opened to allow my passage, I would inevitably put down my briefing papers, stare out the window, and remind myself, yet again, that I was really the secretary of state.

On November 7, 1996, my 1,386th day as secretary, I was immersed in memories as I headed to what I thought of as my "swearing out" as the sixty-third secretary of state, a ceremony the White House had organized to announce my decision to return to private life.

I'd felt for some time that if the voters gave President Clinton a second term, he should have a new secretary of state. I'd developed a long mental list of pros and cons about staying or going, but in the end it came down to instinct. Mine told me that four years was long enough in the ring. I didn't want to interrupt the president's campaign to tell him of my decision, but I did want to deliver it personally and as soon as possible after his campaign was over. So we arranged to meet on election day at the Excelsior Hotel in Little Rock.

The 20-story, 417-room Excelsior dwarfs the other buildings in downtown Little Rock. I had stayed there during the presidential transition in 1992 and remembered that it constantly echoed the sounds of Arkansas conventioneers. Because the president had designated the hotel as his election-night headquarters, when I arrived at midday on November 5, 1996, it was teeming with Secret Service and other serious-looking types.

By the time we met at 4 P.M., the president's long-anticipated victory was assured. Only the winning margin, and whether the Democrats would wrest back control of Congress, remained in doubt. I had never seen Bill Clinton more relaxed or looking better, notwithstanding that he had just completed a brutally demanding, months-long marathon. He was the picture of a winner. He was also a far more confident figure than the young governor I had met four years earlier. Having taken the measure of other domestic and world leaders, he knew to a certainty, as he had probably sensed all his life, that he could be the best in his class. This was a special moment—Bill Clinton suspended between yesterday and tomorrow—and he was savoring it.

We talked for nearly two hours, a little about the past, a lot about the future. When I told him I wanted to return to California, he responded generously by recounting what we had done together, ending by saying he accepted my decision. Because I was leaving for the Middle East the next weekend, I asked him to announce my decision promptly so that my trip would not be dogged with will-he-won't-he press speculation. He agreed, leading us two days later to the ceremony in the marbled-floored Cross Hall, one of the most beautiful rooms in the residential wing of the White House.

When I walked in with the president, I was surprised to find assembled, despite the short notice, nearly all of my senior colleagues from the State Department, as well as many from the White House and other official places. The president approached the lectern with a smile on his face. I sensed what was coming. Bill Clinton has a terrific sense of humor that the public rarely sees because he tends to reveal it only at relaxed, personal moments. When he does unleash his wit, he typically brings down the house. I braced myself.

"Yesterday at the wonderful welcome home that Hillary and Al and Tipper and I had at the White House, I saw a remarkable sight—Warren Christopher wearing a T-shirt." Laughter. "He did have it on underneath his Savile Row suit. Nonetheless, it was there. This is the same Warren Christopher, I would remind you all, who made *People* magazine's best-dressed list; the only man ever to eat presidential M&M's with a knife and fork."

He had me. My boss had successfully skewered me, and by day's end most of the world would know it. When the chuckling died down, I braced for the really tough material, the hyperbole. I'd been around Washington long enough to know that comments made on occasions such as this tested the envelope of reality. I wasn't wrong, but in spite of my habitual discomfort in the face of excessively nice words about me, on this occasion I was moved.

The president reviewed my distant as well as my recent past, summarizing generously many of the events and opportunities described in the chapters of this book. He praised me for the good things that had marked my public life and, even more graciously, did not mention the less good ones. He delivered his comments with the timbre and accent he normally reserves for person-to-person communication, ending with, "From the bottom of my heart, I thank him for his service to the nation and his unique friendship to the president."

Then he gave me a bear hug. Though I'm not a hugging kind of person, when the president of the United States is the hugger, you can't just stand there. So I hugged him back.

When we released each other, I moved to the lectern and delivered a brief thanks and farewell. When I fin-

ished, the crowd rose to its collective feet, as it must on such occasions, and delivered prolonged applause. As I looked around the room, the reality of what had just occurred came home with force. I was out of a job, maybe the best job I'd ever had in my life.

Fortunately, I had been there before. I'd known when I took the job that this moment had to come, and I knew how it would feel when it did. I was losing something that, in truth, was not mine to lose. My charge had been to serve as steward, not proprietor, of an extraordinary public trust. The question was not whether that asset had to be returned, only when. My sense of loss gave way quickly, as I knew it would, to something else—a thought I have carried with me for most of my life: that public service is a transient gift that America bestows generously . . . and sometimes unexpectedly.

Acknowledgments*

T HIS MEMOIR IS A SELECTION OF EVENTS FROM my public life that I believe might be of interest to followers of history, foreign affairs, and human nature. Although in theory an account of one's personal experiences shouldn't require assistance from others, in fact I needed and received much help, and I take these few words to express deep appreciation to some of those who rose to the occasion.

Mark Steinberg, my friend and law partner, was

---

*Note : The Department of State has reviewed the manuscript for this book to ensure that its contents do not compromise national security. This review should not be construed as concurrence with the text. The opinions and characterizations expressed herein are those of the author and do not necessarily represent official positions of the U.S. government.

deeply involved in every aspect of this book. He encouraged me to believe that readers might be interested in my reminiscences, and then he urged me to develop a text driven by events. He pushed me to record not just the basic facts, but to remember how I felt and what I did and said.

Mark critiqued the draft of every chapter, and fortunately our rapport is such that he felt able to send several back, saying, "Start over." Then usually followed a conference, often over lunch, in which we discussed themes and approaches. Only after I'd done another draft would he begin to bring out his imaginative editing pen, sometimes providing the music to amplify my words. He was quick to chide me if I began to wander off into policy debates and was also invaluable in helping me select the photos and resolve myriad organizational problems. The book would not have been written without his constant support. My thanks also go to his secretary, Sue White, who, among other virtues, was able to translate Mark's inscrutable handwriting.

Lisa Drew's warmth and wit overcame my trepidation at dealing with a New York publisher. She edited the chapters, one by one, urging me to dig deeper into my memory and saying enough good things to keep me writing. Her quick responses to my letters and calls made me think I was her only author. She also opened the door to the highly capable staff at Scribner. I am also grateful to the publisher, Susan Moldow, and the editor in chief, Nan Graham, for their support.

My friend and former colleague Deputy Secretary of State Strobe Talbott somehow found time—often on the homeward leg of an overseas trip—to read and make detailed comments on nearly every chapter. As the author of six successful books, he provided wise counsel and generous encouragement. Former undersecretary of state Peter Tarnoff, who served with me in both the Carter and Clinton administrations, read almost the entire manuscript and served up the kind of insights that only someone with comprehensive knowledge of foreign policy can provide.

Derek Chollet, a young political scientist of immense promise, provided energetic research assistance, serving as my liaison with the State Department, which graciously permitted me to examine documents from my time in office. Derek contacted the Johnson and Carter presidential libraries on my behalf, and I am grateful to their staffs for their forthcoming responses. I am indebted to Margaret Grafeld and her staff for smoothly carrying the manuscript through the State Department's customary review process. My gratitude also goes to Liz Lineberry, who was my executive secretary from 1993 to 1997; Liz kept my daily schedules with a care and fidelity that I fully appreciated only during the writing of this book.

O'Melveny & Myers, the law firm with which I have been happily connected on and off for half a century, provided many kinds of essential support for which I am deeply grateful. My partner Rick Ross deftly handled contractual and literary-property issues. Kathy Osborne, my executive assistant, managed my scores of contacts about the book with grace and efficiency, all the while juggling my schedule to keep time free for research and writing. Our librarian, Pat Smith, always responded to my requests promptly and cheerfully—and found what I was seeking and more. At O'Melveny, the person most regularly involved daily was Kerin Holmes, my secretary. She not only processed every word of the text several times, but also organized the files, maintained the chapter log, helped with research questions, and kept a vigilant eye out for mistakes and ways to improve the text. My thanks also go to Nancy Parker, an O'Melveny secretary who assisted in preparing the manuscript.

Because I kept no diaries and had few contemporaneous notes, I owe a special debt to the authors of the books and articles in the bibliography, without whose texts I would have been unable to report accurately on the order and context of many events touched on. I am also indebted to daily publications such as the *New York Times,* the *Washington Post,* and the *Los Angeles Times,* as well as weekly newsmagazines such as *Time* and *Newsweek,* whose pages I consulted on contemporary events.

Finally, I am grateful to my family. My wife, Marie, read drafts of every chapter and provided good advice, support, and love in generous quantities, as she has during all forty-four years of our marriage. My sisters, Jean Iverson and Lois Riopelle, provided help on biographical details. My children—Lynn Collins, my daughter from a prior marriage; Scott; Thomas; and Kristen Henderson—gave me loving reassurance that this book would have at least some readers.

Despite all of this help, my memory remains the source for much of the book. If events have been unconsciously enlarged or diminished, or if other inadvertent errors have crept in, I alone am responsible.

August 1, 2000

Bibliography

Acheson, Dean. *Present at the Creation: My Years in the State Department.* New York: W. W. Norton & Company, 1969.

Ball, George W. *The Past Has Another Pattern.* New York: W. W. Norton, 1982.

Bell, Griffin B., with Ronald J. Ostrow. *Taking Care of the Law.* New York: William Morrow and Company, 1982.

Bill, James A. *George Ball: Behind the Scenes in U.S. Foreign Policy.* New Haven and London: Yale University Press, 1997.

Blackman, Ann. *Seasons of Her Life.* New York: Scribner, 1998.

Brinkley, Douglas. *The Unfinished Presidency.* New York: Viking Press, 1998.

Brook, A. F., II. "When Ignorance of the Law Became an Excuse: Lambert & Its Progeny." *American Journal of Criminal Law* 279 (winter 1992).

Brzezinski, Zbigniew. *Power and Principle: Memoirs of the National Security Adviser, 1977–1981.* New York: Farrar, Straus & Giroux, 1983.

Califano, Joseph A., Jr. *The Triumph and Tragedy of Lyndon Johnson: The White House Years.* New York: Simon & Schuster, 1991.

Cannon, Louis. *Official Negligence.* New York: Random House, 1997.

———. *Reagan.* New York: Putnam, 1982.

Carter, Ashton, John M. Deutch, and Philip D. Zelikow. *Catastrophic Terrorism: Elements of a National Policy.* Vol. 1, no. 6. A Report of Visions of Governance for the Twenty-first Century, a project of the John F. Kennedy School of Government, Harvard University. California: Board of Trustees of Leland Stanford Junior University and Board of Trustees of Harvard University, October 1998.

Carter, Jimmy. *Keeping Faith.* New York: Bantam Books, 1982.

Christopher, Saunders, Sick, Carswell, Davis, Hoffman, and Owen. *American Hostages in Iran: The Conduct of a Crisis.* New Haven and London: A Council on Foreign Relations Book, Yale University Press, 1985.

Congressional Record, July 23, 1968, 318–60.

Countryman, Vern. *Douglas of the Supreme Court.* Garden City, N.Y.: Doubleday, 1959.

Dallek, Robert. *Flawed Giant: Lyndon Johnson and His Times, 1961–1973.* New York: Oxford University Press, 1998.

Douglas, William O. *An Almanac of Liberty.* New York: Doubleday, 1954.

Goldman, Peter, Thomas DeFink, Mark Miller, Andrew Murr, and Tom Mathews. *Quest for the Presidency 1992.* A Newsweek Book, Texas A&M University Press, 1994.

Goldman, Peter, and Tony Fuller. *The Quest for the Presidency 1984.* New York: A Newsweek Book, Bantam Books, 1985.

Gormley, Kenneth. *Archibald Cox: Conscience of a Nation.* Reading, Mass.: Addison-Wesley, 1997.

Holbrooke, Richard. *To End a War.* New York: Random House, 1998.

Mann, James. *About Face: A History of America's Curious Relationship with China, from Nixon to Clinton.* New York: Alfred A. Knopf, 1999.

Maraniss, David. *First in His Class: A Biography of Bill Clinton.* New York: Simon & Schuster, 1995.

McNamara, Robert S. *In Retrospect: The Tragedy and Lessons of Vietnam.* New York: Times Books, Random House, 1995.

Murphy, Bruce Allen. *Fortas: The Rise and Ruin of a Supreme Court Justice.* New York: William Morrow and Company, 1998.

National Advisory Commission on Civil Disorders Report, March 1, 1968. Washington, D.C.: U.S. Government Printing Office, 1968, O–291-729.

Packer, Herbert L. *Mens Rea and the Supreme Court.* The Supreme Court Review, 107, University of Chicago Press, 1962.

Peres, Shimon. *Battling for Peace.* New York: Random House, 1995.

Peterson, Peter G. *Gray Dawn: How the Coming Age Wave Will Transform America—and the World.* New York: Times Books, Random House, 1999.

Rabinovich, Itamar. *The Brink of Peace: The Israeli-Syrian Negotiations.* Princeton: N.J.: Princeton University Press, 1998.

———. *Waging Peace.* New York: Farrar, Straus & Giroux, 1999.

Rapaport, Roger. *California Dreaming: The Political Odyssey of Pat and Jerry Brown.* Berkeley, Calif.: Nolo Press, 1982.

Report by the Governor's Commission on the Los Angeles Riots. *Violence in the City—an End or a Beginning?* December 2, 1965.

Report by the Special Adviser to the Board of Police Commissioners on the Civil Disorder in Los Angeles. *The City in Crisis.* October 21, 1992.

Savir, Uri. *The Process: 1,100 Days That Changed the Middle East.* New York: Random House, 1998.

Sick, Gary. *October Surprise.* New York: Random House, 1991.

Stephanopoulos, George. *All Too Human.* Boston: Little, Brown, 1999.

Talbott, Strobe. *Endgame: The Inside Story of SALT II.* New York: Harper & Row, 1979.

Vance, Cyrus. *Hard Choices: Critical Years in America's Foreign Policy.* New York: Simon & Schuster, 1983.

White, Theodore H. *America in Search of Itself: The Making of the President, 1956–1980.* New York: Harper & Row, 1982.

———. *The Making of the President.* New York: Atheneum, 1973.

Witcover, Jules. *Crapshoot: Rolling the Dice on the Vice Presidency—from Adams and Jefferson to Truman and Quayle.* New York: Crown Publishers, 1992.

———. *The Year the Dream Died: Revisiting 1968 in America.* New York: Warner Books, 1997.

World Almanac and Book of Facts, 1997. Mahwah, N.J.: World Almanac Books, 1996.

Photo Credits

Index

Page number in italics refer to illustrations.